THEATER EAST AND WEST

Theater East and West

PERSPECTIVES TOWARD A TOTAL THEATER

by

LEONARD CABELL PRONKO

UNIVERSITY OF CALIFORNIA PRESS

BERKELEY, LOS ANGELES, LONDON

UNIVERSITY OF CALIFORNIA PRESS
BERKELEY AND LOS ANGELES, CALIFORNIA

UNIVERSITY OF CALIFORNIA PRESS, LTD.
LONDON, ENGLAND

© 1967 BY THE REGENTS OF THE UNIVERSITY OF CALIFORNIA
FIRST PAPERBACK EDITION, 1974
ISBN: 0-520-02622-5
LIBRARY OF CONGRESS CATALOG CARD NUMBER: 67-22176
DESIGNED BY DAVID PAULY
PRINTED IN THE UNITED STATES OF AMERICA

FOR *Takao Tomono*

Preface to
the Paperbound Edition

"Yeeeooowww! Instant Kabuki!" shouted the title over a review of two kabuki performances presented at the American College Theater Festival in Washington's Kennedy Center in April, 1973. The presentations, on consecutive days, were by a student group from Pomona College and the Kabuki Apprentices of the National Theater of Japan. The fact that two such groups were appearing in the Festival at all was an indication of the growing number of Asian-inspired productions in the United States, and the increasing interest of other theatre people in these productions. The reviewer in the *Washington Post* went on to say that "for one who has been exposed only to the authentic article, Kabuki-in-English is a breakthrough."

Across the country, in Los Angeles, Dan Sullivan, reviewing an English-language production in the *Los Angeles Times,* called it "a reminder that the world of Kabuki isn't nearly as forbidding as the language barrier makes it seem." Time and again, for performances of Chinese opera, Kabuki, and other oriental forms which, more and more, are being studied and performed with varying degrees of skill and authenticity, particularly in the colleges and universities of this country, reviewers and spectators have described their pleasure and joy at the discovery of a totally new world revealing "the larger possibilities of theater," or their surprise at the accessibility of a form which in a foreign language had seemed forbidding and difficult.

Perhaps we are on the eve of a boom in Asian theater productions, and it is to be expected that this should begin in educational institutions, which are not under the same economic pressures as most professional theaters. In a recent survey carried out by Professor Andrew Tsubaki, of the International

Theatre Studies Center at the University of Kansas, it is revealed that in the past ten years or so there have been thirty-seven full-length Asian theatre productions in U. S. schools. The majority of these have probably been in the most recent years of the decade. While ten years ago one was hard pressed to locate an Asian production in any given year, the year 1972–73 witnessed the production of Kabuki plays in English in no less than four American schools: *Narukami* at the University of Hawaii, *Kanjinchō* at the University of Kansas and at the University of Wisconsin, and the double bill of *Gohiiki Kanjinchō* and *Fishing for a Wife* at Pomona College. In addition to these, Shozo Sato, at the University of Illinois in Champaign, toured his production of *Narukami*.

It would be tedious to detail all the developments in Asian-American theatre relations since this book was first published in 1967. Much of the exciting activity in this field is covered in the *Asian Theatre Bulletin,* published by the American Theatre Association, and since the spring of 1971, when it became independent of the African Theatre Program, under the capable editorship of Samuel Leiter of Brooklyn College. New books, articles and dissertations, foreign artists on tour, American productions, news of theatre meetings, symposia, reports from abroad and news of the activities of members are all included in the brief but well-packed issues of this stimulating and encouraging publication. Professor Leiter is also the author of a number of illuminating articles, including "Four Interviews with Kabuki Actors," (*Educational Theatre Journal,* December, 1966) and an account of the IASTA production of *Kanjinchō* (Theatre Crafts, September–October, 1968).

The brief Afterword to the first edition of the present volume outlines a few of the manifestations which came to my attention between the time the manuscript went to the publisher and its publication. In this Preface I would like to update several points which have changed since I wrote *Theater East and West,* note some of the major advances since 1967, and indicate a few of the problems and dangers which may lie ahead, if, indeed, they are not upon us already.

In Chapter VI I alluded hopefully to the Chinese opera house and Kabuki theater which were planned for San Francisco. The first has never materialized, although a step in the right direction has been taken with the founding of the Chinese Culture Center, under the directorship of Dr. William Ding Yee Wu. The Kabuki Theater Restaurant came and went leaving no trace at all on the cultural life of San Francisco, much less on the country at large. Thanks to a policy of attempting to satisfy all the people all the time, it managed to satisfy no one any of the time. Instead of aiming at a serious theatrical audience by presenting authentic kabuki productions with artists from Japan, the Kabuki Theater Restaurant imported all-girl dance reviews, hoping to bring in spectators by the hundreds, and padded the program with authentic Kabuki selections. The man-out-on-the-town was bored by Kabuki, and the theatre buff put to sleep by the reviews, if he went at all. The true possibilities of an American Kabuki Theater Restaurant remain to be explored.

While waiting for the total feast available only in a theater which is at the same time a restaurant, the American theater has gone ahead exploring the other feasts possible without kitchen facilities, or with only limited ones. The Cafe La Mama, like a few other New York-based groups, has experimented with oriental techniques, most notably in plays of Yeats and in the delightful staging of *Demon,* an adaptation of the Noh play, *The Damask Drum.* A dramatic and imaginative staging of *Titus Andronicus* in Central Park, under the aegis of Joseph Papp, revealed a strong influence of Chinese opera.

The same play, in a college setting, was brilliantly transposed to a Japanese setting by director Henry Horwege of Bakersfield College, and performed in a bigger than life Kabuki style well adapted to the violence and heroics of that melodrama. *Macbeth,* rewritten, underwent the same transformation in an East coast school. And here at Pomona College a short play, *Oedipus at Phokis,* was written by a student in the Noh form, with music in a sparse modern idiom recalling that of Noh, and choreographed in a style blending modern dance with Bharata Natyam and Kabuki dance. More than one reviewer commented on the successful transposition. "It proves kabuki to be a form bound by elaborate conventions but marvellously malleable within them," declared Sylvie Drake in the *Los Angeles Times*.

While professionals and students shared their exploratory discoveries, the Japanese themselves were also exploring. Kara Jurō and his Situation Theater incorporate Kabuki techniques into their avant-garde productions, while Tadashi Suzuki, director of the Waseda Little Theater, calls his productions modern Kabuki. Even the conservative world of Noh has seen the imaginative experiments of Kanze Hisao and Kanze Hideo. United States audiences were able to see the production of "The Man from the East" by Stomu Yamash'ta's Red Buddha Theater on tour in this country in 1973 after highly acclaimed performances in France and England. "The Man from the East" is an entertaining blend of some traditional stories and techniques with modern theatrical styles, but it struck this viewer as being more a review than a perfectly integrated presentation.

Appearances of authentic classical troupes from Japan, the Republic of China, India, Indonesia and other countries of Southeast Asia, have shown that there is a large and responsive audience for these performers in this country. Even the austere Noh has made two visits to the U.S. since 1967. Such visits have given theater people of the West a better opportunity to observe at close hand the finest traditional artists of Asia. But the very fact that theater people must usually wait for such visits underlines one of the major difficulties for this kind of cultural cross-fertilization: most actors and directors are either so desperately busy, or so desperately poor, that they cannot conceivably take off a year or two to study at the feet of the great masters in Asia. A partial solution might be for us to import these masters to teach us here, but this is impractical for a number of reasons. Most importantly, the finest actors and teachers are impossibly busy in their own countries. But care must be exercised to bring over only actors and master teachers of the highest competence, for second rate actors lack both the experience and the heart necessary to impart the secrets of the traditional arts.

Should the master teachers of oriental theater, or those of us who have had the good fortune to study with them, attempt an authentic reconstruction of the original plays? Should we attempt to adapt them to the capabilities of our own students? Or should we simply use the oriental techniques as a means to develop better actors in the western tradition? These are fretful questions. It should be obvious to the reader of this book that I do not ascribe to the last of these views, although I agree that oriental techniques may profitably be used in training western actors. Indeed, today Tai chi is widely used in theater courses which otherwise make no pretense of exploring Asian modes in their performances.

There is certainly room for authentic performances (or rather, as authentic as we can become in English with actors who have trained for months rather than decades), as there is for transposed presentations. But what I think is irrefragable is the importance of insisting upon a discipline based upon authentic modes, only allowing departures and transpositions once that discipline has been learned. I have treated this question, and related ones, in "Oriental Theatre for the West: Problems of Authenticity and Communication," (*Educational Theatre Journal,* October, 1968).

For the student who is able to spend a year or two, and who is able to gain some mastery of an oriental language, the possibility exists of studying with a private teacher or in one of the schools in Asia. It is not impossible, for example, to get into the Chinese opera schools in Taipei. In Japan, foreigners have already entered the training schools of Noh, Kyōgen and Japanese dance, even appearing occasionally onstage. Even Kabuki, the training for which was traditionally transmitted within families, has recently opened itself to the outside: in 1970 the National Theatre of Japan began its Kabuki Training Program. It is the first carefully planned training program aimed at bringing young men outside the Kabuki world into the Kabuki family system, and was developed, at least in part, to replenish the diminishing supply of young Kabuki actors on the lower echelons.

I found myself in Japan during the year that the program was begun, and was fortunate enough to be admitted to it for fifteen months. I was the only foreigner among ten young men who, in the space of three years, have shown that with talent, dedication, and good teachers, they could in that time master much of what was traditionally imparted in ten or fifteen years. I have discussed this training program in some detail in my article, "Learning Kabuki," (*Educational Theatre Journal,* December, 1971). The second group of students is now being trained, and among them there is another foreigner: a young Australian woman. While the program is intended, of course, for young Japanese who will become professionals, the director, Mr. Sasaki Einosuke, is most kindly disposed toward foreigners, and is making an effort to institute another training program chiefly for foreigners. At this point, however, only a limited participation can be envisaged, in order not to deflect the program from its primary goal.

The appearance of the Kabuki Apprentices of the National Theatre (the graduates of the original training program) at the American College Theater Festival in 1973 may well mark the beginning of a kind of graduation tour of the students to the United States. Those who observed the performances and demonstrations at the Festival were impressed by their skill, seriousness, professionalism and the dazzling brilliance of much of their work—all acquired within the space of three years by young men who, in many cases, had never even seen Kabuki before they entered the training program. The benefits for us, as well as the conclusions to be drawn by the traditional worlds of the East are obvious.

Less dazzling, professional and skillful, no doubt, but equally serious has been the work of young American student actors over the past few years, in their efforts to evoke for their audiences the bigger than life, highly refined world of

Asian theater. Professor Tsubaki's survey shows that Kabuki is far and away the most popular form for performance by students, with at least half of the 37 full length productions being in the Kabuki form. Many of these productions were made up of two plays. A total of fifteen different plays are listed in the survey many of them having been performed a number of times. I mentioned above two performances of *Kanjinchō* in 1972–73. James Brandon, while at Michigan State University, did the first U. S. *Kanjinchō* in 1963, as he did the first American *Sukeroku* in a splendid production at the University of Hawaii in 1970. During the past year he directed *Narukami,* the play most frequently performed in English-language Asian productions. It has been presented at the Institute for the Advanced Study of Theatre Arts in New York, by Shozo Sato in Illinois and on tour, by Brandon, and by myself in three different productions.

There have been several Chinese opera productions, notably those by A. C. Scott at Wisconsin, and the handsome *Black Dragon Residence* directed by Daniel S. P. Yang at the University of Hawaii and taken to the Kennedy Center as part of the American College Theater Festival in 1972.

It is not possible to mention all the Asian productions of the past few years, but it seems only just to recognize the work carried on from year to year in this field at the University of Hawaii, formerly under the direction of Earle Ernst, and at present supervised by James Brandon. Nor can one overlook the dedication to Japanese arts, and among theatrical arts, to Kabuki, by Professor Sato in Champaign, Illinois.

The Department of Theater Arts at Pomona College has sponsored seven different Kabuki productions since 1965. The experience gained through these productions, as well as the insights afforded me by fifteen months of study at the National Theater of Japan and a number of summers spent studying with private teachers, have, of course, brought about certain changes in my outlook on oriental theater and its relationship to the West. My fundamental position, however, remains the same, as does my admiration and enthusiasm for the artists of

Asia and the exciting forms in which they work. Some of my more recent perceptions, particularly those related to Kabuki, are dealt with briefly in "What's Wrong with Kabuki?" (*Japan Quarterly,* Summer, 1971), and at greater length in "Kabuki Today and Tomorrow," (*Comparative Drama,* Summer, 1972).

In 1967 I lamented the lack of a new translation of that perennial Kabuki favorite, *Chūshingura.* This lacuna has now been filled by Donald Keene's fine translation (Columbia University Press, 1971). Professor Keene is also responsible for two other enlightening volumes of recent vintage: *Nō: The Classic Theatre of Japan* (Kodansha, 1966), and *Twenty Plays of the Nō Theatre* (Columbia University Press, 1970). Masakatsu Gunji's impressive volume, *Kabuki* (Kodansha, 1969), is another invaluable contribution. Less impressive for their texts, but dazzlingly illustrated, are the series on the Performing Arts of Japan, published by Weatherhill in Tokyo.

An outstanding addition to the critical studies of Japanese theatre as a whole is Peter D. Arnott's *The Theatres of Japan* (St. Martin's Press, 1969), in which the distinguished scholar of Greek theater, who is also a well known puppeteer, analyzes Japanese theater in a sensitive and original way.

A. C. Scott's *The Theatre in Asia* (Weidenfeld and Nicholson, 1972) presents an excellent historical survey of the vast field, with an overview on "The Framework of Asian Theatre." Robert Rickner's brilliant *Theatre as Ritual: Artaud's Theatre of Cruelty and the Balinese Barong,* as yet unpublished, is the finest work I know dealing with Artaud, and magnificently illuminates many aspects of Balinese theatre. James R. Brandon's splendid *Theatre in Southeast Asia* (Harvard University Press, 1967) discusses in great detail the extremely varied theaters ranging from Burma through Indonesia and up into the Philippines. The prolific Professor Brandon is also the author of *On Thrones of Gold: Three Javanese Shadow Plays* (Harvard University Press, 1970) and an anthology of *Traditional Asian Plays* (Hill and Wang,

1972), and promises an anthology of important Kabuki plays in the near future.

John D. Mitchell, president of the Institute for Advanced Studies in the Theatre Arts, has recently edited translations of three Peking operas of the new revolutionary theatre, *The Red Pear Garden* (Godine, 1973).

Vera R. Irwin's *Four Classical Asian Plays* includes works from India, China and Japan, among them Miss Miyoko Watanabe's translation of *Narukami,* which has been used a number of times in performances in this country.

These are but some of the numerous books on Asian theater which have appeared recently. For a more thorough account of those dealing with Japan, the reader might consult my *Guide to Japanese Drama* (G. K. Hall, 1973).

If volume and quality of publications and performances are any indication, western theater may just have burst into its Meiji era. As more audiences become aware of the exciting theatricality and subtle nuances of oriental theatrical forms, perhaps we can look forward to the day when we will all sit down to the feast which is suggested in these pages.

Preface

This book is intended for the intelligent lover of theater as well as for the theater specialist. I hope that it will open up new perspectives for the reader and make him aware of the many unexplored theatrical forms of the East which have been described extensively by scholars, theater historians, and Orientalists, but remain an almost totally blank spot in the field of experience of the professional theater people of the West. Since I am dealing with the theatrical, rather than the literary, aspects of the forms, I make no effort at completeness in either historical or descriptive approaches. The reader is referred to some of the excellent volumes mentioned in the bibliography for a more thorough discussion of those parts of Oriental theater. A certain amount of repetition is necessary, and I hope those readers already familiar with one or another of the forms I discuss will forgive the summary descriptions I have given, for other readers, less familiar with the terrain, will find them helpful, and perhaps even too sketchy.

I am indebted to the Guggenheim Foundation for its generosity, without which the research for this project could not have been carried out, at least not so completely and effectively. A study of theater requires familiarity with the theater in presentation; the Guggenheim Foundation made possible a prolonged stay in Asia, particularly in Japan, and a final sojourn in France where I was able to bring together certain strands of the research I had done elsewhere.

I am equally indebted to the many kind theater people around the world who enriched my inquiry by allowing me to talk with them, to watch them in rehearsal and backstage, and on occasion sharpened my comprehension and appreciation by long conversations. I should particularly like to express my thanks to Onoe Baiko and Bando Mitsugoro of Tokyo's Kabu-ki-za. Mr. S. Masubuchi, at the same theater, was a world of help to me, aiding me to meet actors and visit them backstage, arranging tickets for me, and obtaining many of the photographs that illustrate this volume. Two specialists in the Japanese theater gave me their time and knowledge most generously, Professor Masakatsu Gunji of Waseda University and Professor Benito Ortolani of Sophia University.

In Taiwan, Professor M. K. Li of the College of Chinese Culture was most helpful in arranging for me to attend performances of Peking opera, and to visit the two training schools of Chinese opera in Taiwan, the Foo Hsing and the Air Force School.

The actors, directors, writers, and scholars in Paris who were of assistance are too numerous to mention, but I should like here to acknowledge the valuable help given me by Jean-Louis Barrault, Jean Dasté, Gabriel Cousin, Georges Neveux, Professor Robert Ruhlmann, Professor René Sieffert, Lucien Arnaud, André Veinstein, and Mlle Christout, of the Bibliothèque de l'Arsenal.

Dr. John D. Mitchell, founder and president of the Institute for Advanced Studies in Theater Arts, in New York, has been a constant source of information and encouragement. It is a pleasure to record my gratitude here, and my admiration for the work he is doing to further theatrical growth in the West.

Ruby Cohn gave me the benefit of her keen criticism and editorial eye during various stages of the manuscript, and for her help I am deeply grateful. A grant from Pomona College helped in the typing of the final manuscript.

L. C. P.

Pomona College
Claremont, California

Contents

Illustrations

(Following page 106)

Rangda attacks the prince in the Balinese Rangda drama
The Rangda play
The conclusion of the Rangda play
The *ketjak* or monkey dance
General Chang-fai in *The Beautiful Bait* as presented by the
  Foo Hsing of Taiwan
The Beautiful Bait, presented by the Foo Hsing
An Edo theater about 1802
Onoe Baiko as the monster in *Momiji-gari* (*The Maple-
  Viewing*)
Onoe Shōroku as Tadanobu in *Yoshitsune Sembonzakura*
  (*Yoshitsune's Thousand Cherry Trees*)
Onoe Shōroku as the defeated General Tomomori in *Yoshi-
  tsune Sembonzakura*
Onoe Baiko in two scenes from a dance play, *Kagamijishi*
  (*Lion Mirror*)
Nakamura Senjaku as he appears in real life (inset) and as
  transformed into the beautiful Shizuka in *Yoshitsune Sem-
  bonzakura*
Nakamura Utaemon in the role of the courtesan Agemaki in
  Sukeroku
Nakamura Utaemon as the *oiran* Yatsuhashi in *Kagotsurube
  Terakoya*
Benten the Thief at the University of Hawaii, directed by
  Earle Ernst
The Monstrous Spider at Pomona College
Benten the Thief, Act II, at Pomona College
The production of *Narukami* by the Institute for Advanced
  Studies in Theater Arts
Jean Dasté's production of Gabriel Cousin's *Drame du Fu-
  kuryumaru*

xx

Introduction

A Theater of Feast

> And you seriously ask us to admit that we
> prefer a dull and mechanical theatre such
> as we have today to one where all the
> gayest, freshest theatrical art flourishes?
> It is preposterous!
>
> E. G. CRAIG

The traveler who has feasted on the theaters of Japan, China, and Bali cannot repress the feeling, when he returns to the West, that the actors are exceedingly loquacious and singularly incapable of doing anything other than talking. Our hypertrophied rational faculties have led us in the past three hundred years, and particularly since the industrial revolution and the late nineteenth-century age of science, to a theater that is most often as small as life itself, a theater that requires careful listening and intelligent understanding. We sit in plush seats, fatigued after two or three hours of dialogue interspersed with a bit of movement, then disperse to discuss the "issues" of the play, if it was a drama of any "significance." Our serious theater is so sociology-psychology-philosophy centered that it begins to acquire (as Ionesco claims Brecht might wish) all the charm of a night-school course. Instead of a feast for all the senses and for the mind as well, we are given the intellectual scraps from the top of the table of theatrical history. As Genet has said, for us everything happens in the *visible* world.

The theater this book deals with treats at least to some degree the invisible world, and it treats that invisible world (as well as multiple facets of the visible, palpable, audible one) in a total way that makes of it a feast—a feast the audience enjoys on most occasions, not for a trifling two or

I

three hours, but for five, six, seven hours and occasionally for the whole night through. It is a theater of the inner eye and of the outer eye at the same time. Like our great theaters of the past, it is both realistic and theatricalized, both illusionistic and presentational. It possesses at once reality and style, whereas we most often seem to embrace one or the other. One reason for this polyvalence is the stress laid upon spectacle, often to the detriment of words; we are accustomed to the converse, and anything else strikes us as heretical, since for us theater is above all dramatic *literature*. Working with images—that is to say, with a purely theatrical poetry which exists in space and time rather than in any abstract sense on the printed page—the Oriental theater can appeal, in different ways and to varying degrees, to that part of the human makeup which is refractory to intellectual and conscious stimulation. Obviously, no generalization will hold true for all the theaters under discussion. Kabuki, for example, often uses dialogue extensively, while Balinese dance drama in many instances uses no speech at all.

Parallels are no doubt as invidious as comparisons, but it is tempting to imagine the story of a class-B horror film of the supernatural, performed by some Bernhardt who would also be a Pavlova, choreographed by Petitpas or Massine, with music of, say, Stravinsky, and costumes by Bakst. If such a mixture could achieve harmony, and if the supernatural element were somehow connected with our religious life, it might evoke in us a feeling similar to that experienced by the peasants of Bali as they witness the fearful Rangda and Barong play, or the more sophisticated reactions of the Japanese as they view one of the Kabuki demon plays. The whole world of the supernatural, denied us by our intellectual proclivities, is summed up in these tremendous spectacles, and experienced in a very real way by the observer, who is more a participant than we usually manage to be in the theater. The dimension lacking in our horror films is here supplied by traditional religious and national themes, and a style imposed upon the whole which is capable of raising the meanest occurrence (a father scolding his child, for instance, in a Balinese Djanger) to the level of art.

Such a theater of magic and hallucination both engulfs the watcher and keeps its distance—for it is highly stylized, a conscious work of art. It is at once subjective and objective. While it depicts our personal dreams and aspirations, our nightmarish fears and feverish hopes, evokes our childhood heroes and demons, sweeps us up in what Artaud called its great "indraughts of metaphysical air," it does so with a profound sense of formal perfection.

Bred on the small world of television and domestic comedy in films, we have lost touch with the vital, full-blooded total experience of great ages of theater. We are cowardly, pampered, small-minded; too timid, too lazy, too unadventurous to give ourselves from head to guts to a theatrical performance of five or six hours. What we like to think of as the healthy, complete, vigorous theatrical experience of the Greeks or the Elizabethans is beyond us. Perhaps there is more than a grain of truth in Artaud's violent contention that our theater today is a "theater of idiots, madmen, inverts, grammarians, grocers, antipoets and positivists, i.e., Occidentals." [1]

Prisoners of the self, we seem unable, at any significant level of artistic endeavor, to break loose from the moorings that bind us to our everyday existence, incapable of liberating the spirit that might allow us to enter other spheres, investigate other levels of experience. Caliban stalks the boards, and Ariel has flown. Or rather, no, not even Caliban—he is far too heroic for us, too imaginative and monstrous for most of us to swallow. Prospero, with his familiars, has disappeared, leaving the stage to the purely human, as though reality were made up of nothing but Mirandas, Trinculos, and Stephanos.

Most of the rich feasts of theater in our century are indebted to men whose vision embraced both Trinculo and Prospero, Caliban and Ariel, visible and invisible forms of reality; to men who attempted to renew their vision through a contact with classical forms of theater, including those of the East. Directors like Reinhardt, Copeau, Dullin, and Barrault

3

turned not only to Greece, the *commedia dell'arte*, and Shakespeare for inspiration, but sought new air and new techniques in the theaters of Asia. Among dramatists, Claudel, Brecht, and Genet reflect significantly an acquaintance with Oriental theater forms.

Alan Pryce-Jones, writing in *Theater Arts* (Oct., 1963) about "The Plays That Never Get Written," suggests that, "if Brecht could take a hint or two from Noh drama, so, with greater logic, could one of our native dramatists. Or from the Chinese, the Indian, the early moralities." A hint, yes, but a well-informed hint. To employ a technique without understanding it is to defeat its purpose. The so-called invisible men on stage in certain popular American "Chinese" plays, or the black-clad invisibles used by Tennessee Williams in *The Milk Train Doesn't Stop Here Anymore*, all of whom draw attention to themselves, quickly degenerate into the cuteness of false theatricality. Such distortion is widespread, for there is confusion and misunderstanding regarding Oriental theater, even by those who are theater specialists. Or rather, there is no misunderstanding, for there is no understanding at all, but total ignorance. People who might discourse for fifteen minutes on the significance of the Morris dance as a predecessor to drama, or the role of the interludes in Elizabethan theater, are incapable of distinguishing between Noh and Kabuki, to say nothing of the finer differences between genres so utterly dissimilar as Kabuki and Chinese opera.

But the ignorance is not ours alone. The abyss that separates Kathakali, for example, from Noh, or Peking opera from Kabuki, is as deep as that which distinguishes a Balinese dance drama from *Oedipus*. And the Orientals, whom we disobligingly lump together, are as ignorant of one another's drama as we are of theirs. This ignorance was brought forcibly to my attention soon after an international theater meeting in Tokyo. The delegates were entertained by a presentation of several scenes from a Kabuki history play at the Kabuki-za. A month later I encountered the delegate from China and asked her how she had enjoyed the performance. Her reaction was that of any foreigner totally unacquainted with the traditions of Kabuki—surprise, wonder, confusion: "It was so different, I didn't know what to think!"

Such ignorance is deeply ingrained and venerable, but today at last we have reached a point where intimate cultural rapports are not only possible and desirable, but absolutely necessary. Writing in 1952, Joshua Logan claimed that Kabuki "throws open a door and gives us a clear view of the Japanese people, customs and art." [2] He looked forward to the day when the Kabuki theater would come to the United States (which it did in 1961), and expressed the belief that such a visit would be "a great contribution to world understanding." But beyond that undeniably desirable goal, in a purely theatrical and artistic sense such an encounter between East and West can offer immense riches to us, just as the awakening to Western theater has already brought certain benefits to the Orient.

The happy blending of style and content revealed by the theaters of Asia (and I mean content in the sense of overall action with its implications unverbalized and even incapable of verbalization) deserves our study and meditation, for the Oriental theater has a number of lessons to offer the West. I do not mean a vague lesson of the "Oriental spirit," but specific lessons in technique and approaches to particular theatrical problems. Most of us are cowardly—or perhaps simply lazy—and say that it is all very well to understand the spirit of the East, but we must beware of imitating the techniques of Eastern playwrights. On the contrary, the Asian theater can offer us a rich repertory of techniques on which we may draw, seeking out Occidental parallels to Oriental classical forms. Not imitation, but re-creation.

Such a confrontation might result in a renaissance like the one brought about by the rediscovery of another literature in western Europe three or four hundred years ago. Oriental literature and theater might well be the fertilizing element we need to bring forth fruit as rich as that produced by the cross-fertilization of sixteenth- and seventeenth-century western Europe with classical antiquity.

5

At any rate, such theatrical dialogue of East and West would allow us to see our own theater in a wider perspective, to understand which elements are essential and which are pure provincialism. A number of interesting questions might arise regarding freedom and discipline in the theatrical art, the functions of the various parts of a play, and even the possibility of *writing* a play. That such an encounter is bound to take place sooner or later seems quite clear. As I begin writing, a glance at current periodicals reveals that the Comédie-Française has revived Voltaire's *L'Orphelin de la Chine,* one of the first European plays to take as its point of departure an Oriental drama; plans are announced for the Kabuki-za to tour Europe; an issue of the *Tulane Drama Review* carries several articles about the Polish Laboratory theater including a number of illustrations that show actors using training techniques of Indian Kathakali, Chinese and Japanese classical theaters, and Japanese wrestling. The Orient is very much in the air, and has been for some years now. But this is not enough. We need a thorough knowledge of specific techniques and of how they may be applied to already existing plays, or give rise to new works. A number of excellent studies of Asian theaters already exist, and I do not intend simply to repeat those works in diluted form. The chapters that follow do not attempt a historical study of Oriental theater, nor even a full description of the genres involved. They essay rather to evoke and describe the spirit and the techniques of performances in order to suggest what impact these theaters have already exercised on the more adventurous dramatists, directors, and theoreticians of the West, and, more important, to show what fresh approaches are available to Western theater through a better understanding of the great theaters of the East.

I Antonin Artaud and the Balinese Dream

A theater, in a word, which is not an
operation of sorcery, is not.

A. Artaud

One of the major impacts of the Orient on the West has been
an indirect one, through the writings of that fiery prophet of
the theater, Antonin Artaud. His collection of essays, written
between 1931 and 1937 and published as *The Theater and Its
Double,* has been called by Jean-Louis Barrault "far and away
the most important thing that has been written about the
theater in the twentieth century." Through his contacts with
Dullin, Barrault, Vilar, and the young generation of directors
and playwrights, Artaud has exercised an incalculable influence
on the direction the theater has taken in France—and probably in other countries as well—for the past twenty or thirty
years.

He forms, moreover, an excellent wedge with which to penetrate into the realm that in the theater separates the East from
the West, for his criticisms strike at the very roots of the
problem, centering as they do upon two divergent ways of
envisioning the theater: one psychological, peripheral, ameta-
physical, intellectual; the other religious, integral, metaphysical, sensuous. The opening sentence of his essay, "On the
Balinese Theater," is not merely an introduction, it is a résumé,
a definition, and a program calling for a return to metaphysics,
tradition, and total theater: "The spectacle of the Balinese
theater, which draws upon dance, song, pantomime—and a
little of the theater as we understand it in the Occident—
restores the theater, by means of ceremonies of indubitable age

7

and well-tried efficacity, to its original destiny which it presents as a combination of all these elements fused together in a perspective of hallucination and fear." [1] Through a spectacle employing all the means at the disposal of the theater, governed by a respect for the quasi-religious, ceremonial roots of drama, the Balinese theater, Artaud claims, presents an overwhelming stage experience, which might be called "Metaphysics-in-Action."

This lengthy essay, the first quarter of which appeared as a review in the *Nouvelle Revue Française* soon after Artaud had seen the Balinese dancers at the Colonial Exposition of 1931 in Paris, is, along with two shorter essays, "Oriental and Occidental Theater" and "Metaphysics and the Mise en Scène," the chief testimony for Artaud's Balinese dream. But there are constant references to Bali and to other Asian drama throughout the articles in *The Theater and Its Double*, and the concepts that Artaud associates with Balinese dance and drama inform the general aesthetics of the theater he espoused.

The man of thirty-five who, in the summer of 1931, sat in the Pendopo (Theater) of the Dutch Pavilion at the Colonial Exposition was no neophyte in the arts and manners of the East. Years of perhaps scattered reading, a propensity for the mystical and the magical, a commitment to the inner life as supreme, a fanatical conviction that the West was a "bleached tomb," a place where "dogs" and "rotting reason" were rapidly strangling the spirit—all this, coupled with the fact that Antonin Artaud was a frustrated actor and a frustrated director, prepared him for the experience that was to be the focal point of his important role as the greatest "metaphysician of the theater" in the twentieth century.

Some years before the 1931 moment of revelation, Artaud was a declared Orientomane. In 1922, while a member of Dullin's troupe at the Atelier, Artaud witnessed what was probably his first performance of the theater of the Far East: in Marseille, before a reconstruction of some temples of Angkor, a Cambodian troupe presented a program of dance drama. By this time, however, Artaud had already explored the field with some thoroughness, and was convinced that the path to rebirth and renewal in the theater lay to the East. "The techniques and masks of the Chinese and Balinese theaters obsessed him very early," claims one of his biographers. "Having read a great deal about them, and remembering not a little, he spoke of them constantly." [2]

In 1922 Artaud wrote to a friend, enthusiastically describing the work of Dullin: "The decors are even more stylized and symbolic than at the Vieux-Colombier. His ideal is the Japanese actor who performs without properties." [3] And Dullin himself, many years later, evoked for Roger Blin, Artaud's youthful enthusiasm for the Oriental theater:

> While I was attracted by the techniques of Oriental theater, he already was going much further than I in that direction, and from a practical point of view it sometimes became dangerous. When, for example, in Pirandello's *Pleasure of Honesty* he was playing the role of a businessman, he came on stage one evening with a facial makeup inspired by the little masks which serve as models for Chinese actors; a symbolic makeup which was just slightly out of place in a modern play. [4]

In 1924 Artaud became acquainted with Breton, Aragon, Desnos, and Vitrac, the embryo of the surrealist movement, and with them he became active in that revolution. The third issue of their review, *La Révolution surréaliste,* was under his direction, and most of the articles in this number, "a hosannah in honor of the Orient and its values," [5] were written by Artaud himself, although signed by other members of the group. [6] The "Letter to the Schools of Buddha" and the "Address to the Dalai Lama" stress both the negative and the positive aspects that the surrealists were to find in the East: on the one hand a savage, destructive force which repudiated the positivism, logic, and materialism they considered typical of the Occidental way of life, and on the other an invitation to spirituality, to unity, to an inner life, and to an art that would reflect that inner life. The surrealists admired the East of both Buddha and Attila. "We are your very faithful servants, Oh Great Lama!" Artaud cries. "Give us, send us, your illumination, in a

9

language our contaminated European minds can understand, and if necessary, change our Spirit, make for us a Spirit that is turned toward those perfect heights where the Spirit of Man no longer suffers." [7] And he calls upon the Buddha to "come pull down our houses."

Artaud's allegiance to the East was stronger than his allegiance to the surrealists, and it was inevitable that so strong-minded an individualist should leave the group—or be expelled. He fustigates them energetically a few years later for their political affiliations, their efforts to bring about a social revolution, their commitment to the physical, whereas, according to Artaud, the great revolution must be a revolution of the spirit, a metamorphosis of what he called the soul. The point is, I believe, important because it underlines the kind of revolution he hoped for in the theater. Physical changes in the theater, like those in the life of a man, can arise only from a radical change of the inner conditions. "For me," Artaud claimed, "surrealism was never anything more than a new kind of magic. Imagination, dreams, all that intense liberation of the subconscious whose purpose is to bring to the surface of the soul that which it usually keeps hidden, must necessarily bring about profound transformations in the scale of appearances, in the semantic value and symbolism of what is created." [8]

All his life Artaud was preoccupied with finding what he described as a magical culture. It was for this purpose that in 1936 he voyaged to Mexico, where he lived among the Tarahumara Indians, taking peyote, witnessing their ritual dances, and attempting to lose his sense of self in an identity with the rugged mountainous landscape which corresponded so well with his own inner anguish. One can only regret that Artaud did not have the opportunity to discover the magical culture of Bali which, with its relative complexity, its completely integrated culture centered on religion, might have satisfied him more profoundly than the simple, if impressive, culture he found among the Tarahumaras.

Bali presents an anomaly in today's world: a civilization that has lived for several hundred years in touch with other entirely different civilizations and yet has managed to preserve its purity. Because of an astounding resiliency, the Balinese can accept influences from the outside and assimilate them to such a degree that they become part of native Balinese culture. The capacity to assimilate—and yet remain pure—is no doubt due largely to the unity of Balinese life, given it by its religion. Nowhere else does one feel that all aspects of living are so centered on a people's religious life. In Bali it is utterly impossible to separate religious life from profane; everything one does, whether it is work or play, whether it gives pain or pleasure, is related to the gods and indeed performed for the gods. To dance in Bali is to dance for the gods: to delight them, to show them one's joy at being a Balinese, at having been given the lovely island as a home—or, in times of disease or disaster, to seek the beneficence of the gods.

The Balinese dancer is not a professional in the sense that Western dancers are professional. He is not (or only in rare instances) devoted exclusively to the dance, for he most often works in the fields, or in the village; and when some tourist purchases a daytime performance of his village's dance, he must give up his work for that period of time without remuneration. The money the tourist may pay to the village for the performance will go into the temple treasury to pay for new costumes for the dancers, for new instruments for the gamelan (gong orchestra), or for the upkeep of old equipment. One of the most astounding metamorphoses in all the world of theater takes place when the tense, wide-eyed, heroic warrior who has been dancing the Baris walks out of the playing area and, without removing makeup since he has worn none, becomes a laughing schoolboy or a shy peasant. The Balinese performer is a professional, however, in a sense in which many Western actors are not. He has spent years of discipline and training to learn his technique, sometimes in the use of vocal cords, but more often in a complete mastery of the whole body, a total control of each muscle in legs, arms, torso, head, and face.

In Bali perhaps more than in any known culture, dance is central and organic to the life of the community. One should really say dance *and* drama, for in Bali one embraces the other and they are not distinguished generically. Performances, rather than being classified according to predominance of words or of choreographed movement, are categorized by the type of story they reflect. Any celebration of importance is accompanied by dance drama. Indeed a celebration is not even necessary, and few are the evenings when the visitor to Bali cannot find some form of dance or drama to watch. Curiously enough, in a country where dance is so prevalent, there is no social dancing.

The dance in Bali is highly specialized, and is the only dance drama, so far as I know, which preserves for us a form of theater so close to ritual that no performance is possible without certain religious ceremonies first, yet at the same time Bali "theater" is far enough removed from ritual that it is looked upon as a performance, as exhibition or entertainment. Dance drama considered as exhibition is typical of relatively advanced stages of civilization, while ritualistic and magical dances seem more typical of primitive levels of culture. The art of theater in Bali can be caught at precisely that moment when religious ceremony emerges from its purely ritualistic origins and becomes the beginnings of what we know as theater.

A detailed description of Balinese dance and drama would be out of place here, particularly when Beryl de Zoete's admirable study, *Dance and Drama in Bali,* and Miguel Covarrubias' lively introduction, *Island of Bali,* survey the subject so well. These particular works possess another value for us; published in 1937 and 1938, they reflect the state of dance in Bali about the time that Artaud saw the dancers at the Colonial Exposition. Despite its flexibility the Balinese dance has not changed radically since then. "The great and ineradicable charm of the Balinese is that their tradition is at once so sure and so flexible," [9] says Miss de Zoete. Side by side with the strong traditional elements one finds a love of novelty and experimentation, which leads to an incredible variety from village to village, as well as from year to year within the same village. Dances come and go, new forms growing out of old ones; foreign influences (the Malayan opera, for example) leave their mark on the content or the costume of the dance without giving the Balinese any feeling of incongruity.

The Balinese performer, like the creators of the dances and dramas themselves, is in a sense anonymous. There are no stars (a rare exception is the world-renowned Mario, creator of the Kebyar), and when the dancer takes the stage—which in Bali is anywhere—he becomes possessed by his part. Although occasionally he may dance for hours without realizing what specific character he is portraying (since the stories are sometimes decided upon only after the performance has begun), the dancer always serves as a vehicle for the dance; he never expresses himself. After having watched certain patently magical or ritualistic dances, one will be told that a god or a demon was dancing in the performer, who was entirely possessed. There are, indeed, little girls who, without ever having received dance training, perform the most complicated dances while in a state of trance, sometimes standing on the shoulders of male attendants.

Needless to say, Artaud was acutely sensitive to this state of trance, possession, or other-mindedness of the Balinese dancers, and some of his most impressive passages are descriptions of moments during which the performer seemed to provide a liaison with some mysterious higher force:

> Here we are suddenly in deep metaphysical anguish, and the rigid aspect of the body in trance, stiffened by the tide of cosmic forces which besiege it, is admirably expressed by that frenetic dance of rigidities and angles, in which one suddenly feels the mind begin to plummet downwards.
>
> As if waves of matter were tumbling over each other, dashing their crests into the deep and flying from all sides of the horizon to be enclosed in one minute portion of tremor and trance—to cover over the void of fear.[10]

Such a submerged state of being is immensely important in understanding Artaud's reaction to the Balinese dance, and no doubt goes far in explaining the magical spell it exercises.

Through the dancer, who has become a kind of medium at the same time he is an artist, we the audience are put into contact, however dimly, with some experience beyond that of our everyday physical world. We are somehow brought into touch with what Artaud would call an absolute. And this, precisely, is the function of the theater—not to deal with the petty adulteries of our contemporaries or the sociological, psychological, and political preoccupations of the day. The theater for Artaud must aim at something deeper, more universal, more ultimately meaningful than the world of knaves and fools. What he envisions is a kind of cosmic tragedy in which the great themes of creation, becoming, chaos, and destruction are revealed.

In our present degenerate state, Artaud feels this purpose can be accomplished only through the organs; the attack on us must be a physical one, using the senses. In the Balinese theater one has the impression that before becoming reduced to logical language, to the formulas readily apprehended, these cosmic themes have found their way into the very bodies of the dancers, and become through them what Artaud calls thoughts in a pure state. The gestures of the dancers, their costumes, facial expressions, headdresses, all serve as a kind of symbol. And like a symbol they must be vague, only pointing the way to some absolute, or secret reality. To say that Mallarmé's swan is the poet is to destroy the symbol, just as to say that Orpheus is the poet is to annihilate the myth. The truth of myth and symbol must necessarily be ambiguous, polyvalent.

Artaud makes the same observation of the theater. That the intelligence cannot grasp these secret levels does not matter: ". . . it would diminish them, and that has neither interest nor sense. What is important is that, by positive means, the sensitivity be put in a state of deepened and keener perception, and this is the very object of the magic and the rites of which the theater is only a reflection." [11] It is not surprising that the Balinese theater appeared to Artaud as the answer to all the ills of Occidental drama, for Bali dance drama lies precisely at that bifurcation where magic and ritual can find their reflection in the theater.

A corollary of such ambiguity is that language as a means of intellectual communication has little function in the drama. And indeed, if we agree that the purpose of drama should approach that of poetry as envisioned by the major Symbolist poets, one cannot help reflecting that the Symbolists' search for the Absolute led to the rejection of words. For poetry such rejection is fatal. The theater, however, has other resources, and it was one of Artaud's major goals to remind us that the theater is above all a physical space to be filled. This fact, which we seemed long since to have forgotten, had a salutary effect when recalled in the thirties.

In his more fanatical moments Artaud inveighs against the uselessness of language. He is willing, however, to admit that words do have their function in the theatrical performance; but that function, he insists, must be redefined, because we have lost our ability to conceive of theater in terms divorced from literature. Language, rather than serving as a vehicle for thought, for the conveying of ideas, must be wrenched from its "normal" function and forced to express something new; that is,

> to reveal its possibilities for producing physical shock; to divide and distribute it actively in space; to deal with intonations in an absolutely concrete manner, restoring their power to shatter as well as really to manifest something; to turn against language and its basely utilitarian, one could say alimentary, sources, against its trapped-beast origins; and finally, to consider language as a form of *Incantation*.[12]

Through such language, which takes on a new kind of presence, and through the movements of the actors, we create a "natural poetry," a "poetry in space," which must be the true sensuous poetry of the theater. Such a use of language cannot, of course, deal coherently with ideas. But Artaud does not wish for clear, coherent ideas in the theater, because clear ideas, "in the theater as elsewhere, are dead finished ideas." [13] We should strive rather for a dynamic, constantly changing

15

work of art, from whose depths a meaning is always just about to materialize. This electric current, quivering always between being and nothingness, points to a world of Absolutes, the invisible world of cosmic forces which should be the real preoccupation of theater. Like religious ritual, the drama should be that meeting point where human and nonhuman, meaning and chaos, finite and infinite, come together.

Such a metaphysical dimension is suggested on many levels in the Balinese dance: the stories themselves drawn from the great Hindu religious books, the *Ramayana* and the *Mahabharata*, or from ancient Balinese legends; ceremonial or ritual elements; the state of trance already referred to; themes of cosmic struggle embodied in the Barong and Rangda dances; the constantly changing facial expressions of the performers, their fluttering movements, and even their costumes which, Artaud feels, relate them in some strange way to the rest of nature and even to something beyond it: "They are like huge insects full of lines and segments drawn to connect them with an unknown natural perspective of which they seem nothing more than a kind of detached geometry." [14] Perhaps the most dramatic of all these cosmic devices, if we may call them that, are the monsters who appear in many forms of Balinese dance and drama. We in the West seem to have lost our sensitivity to these embodiments of cosmic forces. We might be tempted to laugh, Artaud claims, but instead we tremble before the spectacle of the Balinese demons, for they effectively bring back to the theater "a little of that great metaphysical fear which is at the base of all ancient theater." [15]

The music that accompanies much of Balinese dance and drama itself plays a large role in inducing a state of sensitivity to invisible forces. The music of the gamelan, largely composed of gonglike instruments, now tinkling and beguiling, now a whirlwind of violence, sucks us into its incredibly complex patterns, exercising a hypnotic power and inducing at times in both performer and listener a trancelike state. So intimate is the relationship between performer and musicians that in certain dances it is the dancer who dictates the pace of the gamelan, and gives the impression that his very movements bring about the muted metallic beats of the gongs or the sharp thuds of the drums. Artaud, with his usual lyricism and fervor, describes it this way: "These metaphysicians of natural disorder who in dancing restore to us every atom of sound and every fragmentary perception as if these were now about to rejoin their own generating principles, are able to wed movement and sound so perfectly that it seems the dancers have hollow bones to make these noises of resonant drums and woodblocks with their hollow wooden limbs." [16]

The universe suggested by the dance drama, like the world inhabited by the Balinese villager, is a magical one, for the metaphysical and supernatural are fundamental in Balinese society and religion. The natural and the supernatural are not two separate worlds, but different facets of the familiar, everyday world. From babyhood the Balinese is accustomed, by the magically powerful shadow plays, dance dramas, and trance dances, to see the symbolic representation as a reality in itself. And by the same token he learns to see the multiple forms of reality as symbols, although he might not have the sophistication to verbalize this attitude. Night after night, for hours on end, the Balinese sits enthralled before the spectacle of a world in which gods and demigods, demons, witches, and heroes encounter princes, prime ministers, lower mortals, and clowns and animals. In times of stress he may witness trance dances in which the gods themselves come down from Mount Agung to walk upon the earth. Certainly in his everyday life the Balinese constantly comes upon magic, incantation, ritual. A young student from Ubud once confided that he disliked a certain woman because she was a *leyak*—a demon who feeds on human flesh. He was convinced that she was because one night he had seen her, walking down the road, suddenly turn into a rabbit.

If the supernatural is a familiar landscape for the Balinese, the same may be said of his experience at the theater, for the theater is anywhere. Most often it is before a temple wall, but it may just as well be a clearing on the road or a pavilion

especially constructed for communal meetings. Like the Elizabethan—or the Chinese or Japanese—the Balinese feels a real
intimacy with the performance, and can view it from any of
three, or even four, sides. But the classical theaters of England, China, and Japan have gone some distance beyond their
ritual beginnings, and in them therefore a greater feeling of
distinction between actor and viewer has developed. In Bali,
children and adults crowd about the "stage," squatting, sitting,
standing for hours on end.

On one side of the stage area is the gamelan, of which there
are many varieties, determined by the kind of story or the style
of dance drama to be enacted. In this central staging there is
no use of settings, and never any visible indication of a change
of scenes. Instead, the location is suggested through dialogue,
gesture, or facial expression. Properties are few, including
occasionally a curtain through which the dancers enter, a few
umbrellas, banners, lances, and fans. There is no makeup aside
from powder and beauty marks (used by men as well as
women), the clown's whiteface, and masks for certain genres.
Facial expression, suggestive use of body line, degree of intensity, strength, or gentleness, are sufficient to transform an old
man into a young warrior or into a beautiful princess.

The characters in Balinese dance drama are, like those of
the *commedia dell 'arte,* stock characters. The women's roles
include the gentle princess or queen, the demon, secondary
feminine leads (sometimes rather masculine in their style: the
rival, the stepmother), and the *tjondong* or female attendant.
All these roles may, at times, be played by men. The male
roles—generally as kings, princes, lovers, demons—belong to
one of two categories, *aloes* or refined style, *krasa* or rough
style. Major male characters usually have two attendants: the
penasar, a kind of master of ceremonies or minister who also
serves as interpreter, either speaking for the chief character or
reflecting his language in the local Balinese idiom; and the
kartala, or clown, whose movements and dialogue are largely
improvised. These two attendants are favorites of the crowd,

and often are allowed to run away with the play, developing the comic interludes at great length.

The use of gesture and movement in Balinese dance is a complex science, closely regulated by tradition. Only in a very few instances are the *mudras,* a kind of sign language deriving from Indian dance, used. In general the gestures serve to evoke feelings, attitudes, moods; they never stand for specific words as they do in countries closer to India.

There are many kinds of dance and drama in Bali, and many variations of each ranging from extremely simple, primitive trance dances to the highly complex dance dramas. I propose now to describe performances of five of the most impressive numbers I was able to see during a visit to Bali in 1964. Of these, the Legong and the Baris were witnessed by Artaud at the Colonial Exposition of 1931, and I had the good fortune to see them performed by the same group—the Peliatan game-lan—which Artaud had seen at the Exposition. At least one member of the Exposition group is still playing in the gamelan. The other dances I shall describe, the Ketjak, the Sanghyang Djaran, and the Barong play, although apparently not wit-nessed as such by Artaud, contributed elements to the program he saw and will help illuminate his reactions.

The most abstract and ethereal of all Balinese dances, the Legong, is no doubt largely responsible for the erroneous idea, so widespread in the West, that all Balinese dancers are young girls. Girls of all ages perform certain dances in Bali, but in the Legong only prenubile girls may perform. There are no doubt religious reasons, relating to the purity of the premen-strual period, but there are equally important aesthetic rea-sons. In a country of delicate women, only the loveliest and most delicate of children are chosen for the difficult Legong performances. They enjoy a certain distinction in their commu-nity and also give it a degree of prestige by their skill.

Wearing high pyramid-shaped crowns of gilt leather or beaten gold, finely pierced and worked and laced with fresh flowers, their bodies tightly encased in heavy silks, stiff brocades of gold and bright magenta, three girls enact the tale of the King of Lasem who, having abducted the daughter of his enemy, attempts to woo her; she rebuffs him and he sets off to war against her father, encountering a bird of ill omen on the way with whom he fights. Perhaps "enact" is too strong a word, for the story of the King of Lasem is only suggested in the most tenuous way. In order to understand what is happening, one must have been acquainted beforehand with the events, for the Legong is so far removed from narrative that it is almost pure dance. The first dancer enters with her fingers widespread, bent back toward the wrist and ceaselessly quivering, and her body in that curious asymmetrical position so typical of Balinese movement. She is usually a bit older than the other two girls. She is the *tjondong,* a lady-in-waiting to the princess. After she has danced an introductory piece, the princess enters; she is danced by the two young girls, and this double apparition is upsetting to no one. At certain moments one of the girls represents the King, who attempts to woo the other. Later, one of the dancers enters, wearing wings over her arms—this is the most clearly "representational" part of the dance. Using a fan as a sword, the King defends himself against the bird, and later, in battle, against the princess' brother.

Legongs vary from village to village; they may be played in their entirety or the dancers may simply perform certain sections of them. The essence of the Legong in any form, however, is its immateriality, its mysterious vagueness, its mingling of ethereal lightness and charm with the suddenly vigorous parts in which, distantly, dreamily, abstractly, the young girls—eight or ten years old—evoke the love of the King, his going forth to war, and his fight.

Similar to the Legong in its stylization is the Baris, a ceremonial war dance. Unlike the Legong, however, it is an extremely virile dance, most often performed by a boy or by groups of men. Today it is generally seen in its solo form, as a highly abstract dance without narrative content, accompanied by wildly throbbing gamelan music. The angular, swift, nervous movements of the dancer and his wide-open eyes, darting constantly from side to side, evoke the tension of the warrior as he approaches his enemy, carefully guarding himself on all sides, tremulous with apprehension.

If the Legong and the Baris are highly refined forms of dance, the Ketjak seems to revert to a more primitive type. The famous monkey dance, which all tourists in Bali witness, is performed at night by a large group of young men circling a blazing candelabra. Their bare brown bodies, clad only in a loin cloth, glisten in the light as they sit closely interlocked, now still, now moving forward and raising their quivering hands in the air, now lying back in the lap of the person behind them, all the while chanting or chittering "chak-a-chak-a-chak," the sound swelling into the dark night about their circle of light. Occasionally half of the circle rises like a wall, as the other half falls back. Rhythmically, magically, the young men chant while slowly a reciter, or a dancer or two, rises from their midst or enters from outside the circle. By the flickering flame, under an occasional rain of sparks, the dancers and the reciter evoke the story of the *Ramayana,* which describes how the demon king of Lanka steals the bride of Rama; in order to recapture her, Rama engages the aid of the monkey god and his army.

Again, as in the Legong, the uninitiated would be completely unaware that a story in being enacted. The part of the tale evoked varies with the village and the year. A few young girls doing a Legong recall the ravished bride and her attendant; a young man with flowers in his hair represents, perhaps, Rama, whose clownlike attendant wears a grotesquely humorous mask. The story is unimportant, for the drama contained in most Balinese dance is entirely unlike that in traditional Western drama. The Balinese spectator could not be less interested in the story as such. Since all the tales are familiar, any part of a story can stand for the whole, and it seems to be of small importance to the spectator at what point the story begins or ends. For the Balinese, drama is *action,* movement; they are absorbed, Beryl de Zoete points out, "in the rhythm, in a general not a particular action." Drama, she adds, "is only conveyed through the heightened rhythm of dance, never at the flat pitch of actuality." [17]

The Ketjak arose from the trance-dance accompaniment, and it keeps today all the eerie, magical hallucinatory aura that one associates with possession and trance. After seeing the Ketjak, I witnessed the Sanghyang Djaran or horse trance dance in the same village. The same young men in their loin cloths chanted the accompaniment, but this time, instead of circling a candelabra, they were seated in two groups at either end of the performing area. In the middle was a fire, just beginning to burn down as we arrived. A villager stirred it up, and when the embers were glowing brightly he scattered them into a flat area 3 or 4 feet in circumference. The village priest then entered wearing about his waist a strange kind of hobby-horse, which had a small head lost in a white mane and a high tail rising some 6 feet in the air behind him. When he had fallen into trance the priest began to trot back and forth through the glowing embers, kicking the coals with his bare feet. As the Ketjak chorus chanted on one side he would trot toward it, then would be called back through the fire by the chorus at the other side. Here was a purely ritualistic performance intended to store up the good influence of the gods; it could be classified only loosely as a dance for there seemed to be no pattern, no choreography or stylized movements. Had the trance lasted too long it would have become tedious, for the artistic means were not sufficient to exercise their magic upon the nonbeliever. But we were impressed at the end of the performance when the priest fell over stiff on the ground, and the village headman invited us to examine him closely if we wished. There were no traces of charcoal or burns on his feet; it was explained to us that a god had come down to dance in the priest, and it was the deity who had kicked through the bright embers.

At the antipodes to the primitive, purely ritualistic Sanghyang Djaran is the complex Barong play, the Tjalonarang, which, like all things in Bali, exists in a multitude of forms. But in all its forms, far removed though it may be from pure ritual, religious and magical elements are still very much in evidence.

The Barong play uses all the forms of Balinese dance and drama: refined, rough, and masked dances; clownish interludes; spoken and sung dialogues; and gamelan accompaniment. The most popular version of the play shows episodes of the struggle between the eleventh-century Javanese king Erlangga and the hideous widow-witch Rangda, an evil woman of great supernatural power who in Balinese drama becomes the embodiment of all that is nefarious, deadly, disastrous. Pure dance interludes and moments of slapstick comic relief alternate with tense scenes in which the witch and her followers rob graves, devour dead babies, prepare to bring ill fortune to all of Bali, and are finally challenged by a prince. The climax of the play occurs when the Barong, a beneficent monster on the side of man—but a monster nonetheless— attempts to kill Rangda. When the Barong appears to be getting the worst of the battle his assistants, a group of young men from the village who are particularly disposed to trance, rush to his aid. With their krises they attack the monstrous old witch, but her magic cloth protects her from them. Frustrated, they fall into trance, turning their krises upon themselves, and attempt to penetrate their own chests. The good power of the Barong, however, prevents them from injuring themselves— and, if any of them should run amok, there are plenty of assistants standing by to seize their krises, and a priest to bring them out of trance with holy water and flowers. To witness this performance is to enter a world where our rational everyday bearings no longer seem to possess any reality. One is drawn, almost despite oneself, into the magic of the great cosmic struggle being played out, and is lured into the dim world of the unconscious and what lies beyond as suggested in the fierce trance dances.

Interestingly enough, there is no resolution to this drama. One does not feel that the Barong conquers Rangda or that Rangda herself is victorious. If Rangda were vanquished in the play, the spirit of Rangda in the village witches might be angered and bring evil to the community. The world of evil must be flattered and placated. But there is a healthy balance in the Balinese world; so long as sufficient white-magic strength is stored up for the community, illness and disaster can be held in abeyance.

The magical world of the Balinese, in which man stands midway between the invisible netherworld of demons and the invisible upperworld of gods and in constant contact with both, so effectively embodied in this particular play, could scarely fail to appeal to Artaud. The program, which he saw in the Dutch Pavilion of the Colonial Exposition, gave him a generous sampling of the various aspects of Balinese dance drama. It consisted of nine numbers of which two (the first and the fifth) were apparently instrumental: (1) Gong; (2) Gong Dance; (3) Kebyar; (4) Djanger; (5) Lasem; (6) Legong; (7) Baris; (8) Rakshasa; (9) Barong.[18]

Poetry of the theater—a concrete active presence, a poetry in space—is sometimes seen as sound reflected visibly. Such poetry, Artaud believes, can "fascinate and ensnare the organs" and "put the spirit physically on the track of something else." The gong dance, apparently a Kebyar, is a magnificent example of such visible poetry. It is usually performed by a young man sitting in the midst of the gamelan. He rarely, if ever, rises to his feet, moving himself about on folded legs which he manipulates like supple springs. This dance shows a close association between dancer and music; indeed, the movements of the dancer are most often an exhibition of the music, a projection of every subtlety of its rhythm and melody through the dancer's constantly varied, controlled gestures and facial expressions. In Artaud's words, it shows how a sound "has its equivalent in a gesture and, instead of serving as a decoration, an accompaniment of a thought, causes its movement, directs it, destroys it, or changes it completely." [19]

Beryl de Zoete's description of the Kebyar is so vivid that it deserves to be quoted at length. The passionate frenzy of the dance historian's description suggests that Artaud was not unusual in his appreciation of the Balinese performers. The major difference, it will be noted, is that Miss de Zoete, more objective than the French poet, does not see (or at any rate does not describe) a metaphysical dimension in the pure gestures of the dance. But she does find such a dimension in the encounter of Rangda and the Barong, as well as in other manifestations of Balinese dance.

> The *Kebyar* dancer sits with bowed head, fan in hand, in the middle of the square formed by the gamelan. . . . The drummer gives the signal, there is a clashing chord, and immediately the dancer springs to life, tense and erect, his fan wildly fluttering. His eyes dart rapid glances from right to left, upwards, downwards; his neck quivers in an incredibly swift yet precise movement from side to side. His whole body is in constant, tremulous response to the music. Frenzied accents and lyric sweetness interchange; he will sweep forward like a whirlwind, then freeze in a gesture, as if filled to rigidity with the beating sound. His eyes narrow as if he would defend himself against the crashing accents, by closing every inlet.
>
> But in *Kebyar* everything is fleeting. Suddenly he comes dazzlingly to life, and lives brilliantly in the air, every fibre of his body, eyes, fingers, neck, wrists, hips, responding to the music with a subtle inner orchestration. Dropping his fan, he weaves the texture of the music into visibility with marvellous fingers and lovely curves of arm and wrist.[20]

Such a performance, reflecting a hundred emotions, suggesting fear and terror one moment, simpering sweetness the next, then shifting to suspicion, scorn, wonder, amusement, draws the spectator, almost unawares, into a series of emotions that he experiences himself. At the same time he admires the immense skill, the training, the ancient traditions (although the Kebyar itself is a modern form) which permit the performer to achieve what one is tempted to call a whole universe of emotion with such restrained economy, to create a visible poetry whose meaning is embodied in the performance itself.

The part of the program which impressed Artaud most was no doubt the final numbers, beginning with the striking war dance, the Baris, which, according to the program notes, leads into the Rakshasa and Barong dances. He remarks upon the theatrical sumptuousness with which the Balinese have been able to clothe the inner struggle of the hero: a fight between him and a world of phantoms which unleashes all the forces of cosmic fear and chaos waiting behind the mask of order we try to impose upon life.

The description of the final dance in the program shows that it is a variant of the Barong dance described earlier, although here the Barong is a personification of the black demonic forces, resembling Rangda more than the beneficent Barong.

Arjuna [the hero of the *Bharata Yuddha,* the Javanese poem based upon the battle in the *Mahabharata*] retires from civil life in order to obtain, by penitence, the right to use a miraculous weapon which will allow him to conquer his enemies. Shiva wishes to test him and sends heavenly nymphs to sway him from his goal. After the failure of this first temptation, Shiva sends Suprabha, the most beautiful of the nymphs, but not even she can seduce Arjuna. Shiva then decides that he is worthy of using the miraculous weapon. The demons oppose with all their strength Arjuna's ascension to a pure spiritual life, and send to combat him:

Rakshasa (a demon). He cannot find Arjuna, so he is changed into a legendary animal called a:

Barong, which, as king of the forest, provokes Arjuna to combat.

Arjuna wins and kills the *Barong.*

The Balinese "sense of the plastic requirements of the stage is equaled only by their knowledge of physical fear and the means of unleashing it," Artaud claims. And he reminds us of the terrifying demon with which Arjuna struggles. The Western theater, tied to its everyday preoccupations, has forgotten the theatricality of monsters, the pure dramatic thrill derived from the simple view of what is monstrous. In a recent performance of *Six Characters in Search of an Author,* as Mme Pace stepped through the beaded curtains of her shop, the audience as a single being caught its breath for a long moment: the creature we beheld was an immense actress of some three or four hundred pounds, an incredible monster of flesh who seemed the visible embodiment of the evil threatening the characters. How much more profoundly might we be seized by such a sight, and wounded by it, if the monster had some real connection with our deepest preoccupations? The Eastern theaters can still afford us this significant thrill, and the Balinese revel in the monsters, the demons, and the witches drawn from their numerous pantheon. The most imposing are no doubt the Barong and Rangda. Artaud saw the Barong in one of its multiple forms in the performance described above. At a Balinese gala given in September of the same year he must have seen the Rangda play, similar in many ways to the Tjalonarang dance drama (see pp. 22–24), as well as a Sanghyang (trance) and a Topeng (masked play).

Rangda, the widow-witch, the haunter of graveyards, is undoubtedly the most terrifying of Balinese monsters. She has a grotesque white mask with gilded nose and brow, huge protruding eyes, two large white tusks rising from her mouth and any number of sharp, gleaming teeth through which falls a long, wide, red tongue covered with mirrors and other decorations. Her hair, of white feathery goat fur, falls in great profusion about her head and to her feet. On her hands she wears gloves with hairy fingers and long fingernails. From her front dangle long pendulous breasts and the sausage-like intestines of the dead she has consumed. She carries a magical white cloth which renders her invisible and protects her against her enemies.

Her opponent in the Tjalonarang play, the beneficent Barong (who is, however, only one of many forms this monster assumes) is an immense creature manipulated by two men inside, one forming the rear and the other the front part. The latter manipulates the clacking jaws of Barong's small scarlet head which, despite its broad gold leather decorations and its bright protruding eyes and black beard, seems lost in the midst of the mane and too small for Barong's vast body. The tail rises 6 or 8 feet in the air, from its extremity dangling a bell that tinkles with every step as, slightly silly, the Barong prances about the clearing in a good-humored way. (When religion is not separated from life it can afford to keep its sense of humor, and man can laugh with, or at, his gods and demons.)

Through these frightening, sometimes amusing, always expressive and imposing mythical beasts and monsters, very meaningful and alive to the spectator, the dance drama strikes at a level below consciousness, and at the same time causes a physical reaction not only in the trance, which often follows the appearance of Rangda, but also in the thrill of fear, which grips the onlooker, and in the breathtaking power with which such unreal yet real visions take hold of us. The senses are involved; the human being is transformed, no longer able to leave the performance the same smug individual he was when he arrived.

A vocabulary of the senses, used to draw forth a spiritual or subconscious response, points to a unity of the worlds of sense and spirit, a primal state of undifferentiated being to which poetry since the nineteenth century has been attempting to return. As a matter of fact, Artaud uses one of the key words of this movement, Baudelaire's *correspondance,* which refers to the spiritual unity between physical manifestations and their "ideal" or "absolute" reality as well as to the unity existing between the various experiences of the senses. Artaud gives precise examples of this phenomenon:

> And the most imperious *correspondances* spread perpetually from sight to sound, from intellect to sensibility, from the gesture of a character to the evocation of the movements of a plant through the scream of an instrument. The sighs of wind instruments prolong the vibrations of vocal cords with a sense of such oneness that you do not know whether it is the voice itself that is continuing or the identity which has absorbed the voice from the beginning. A rippling of joints, the musical angle made by the arm with the forearm, a foot falling, a knee bending, fingers that seem to be loose from the hand, it is all like a perpetual play of mirrors in which human limbs seem resonant with echoes, harmonies in which the notes of the orchestra, the whispers of wind instruments evoke the idea of a monstrous aviary in which the actors themselves would be the fluttering wings.[21]

Such a "metaphysics of gesture," like much modern poetry, is not intended to present ideas in a clear, predigested form. Nor are we expected to derive an intellectual pleasure from a working out of the subtle meanings of the drama. Here in the

Balinese drama, as Artaud would have it, we witness a pure drama, undergo an experience in which the many languages peculiar to theater, including the human hieroglyphs, create a poetry in space and set up vibrations on all levels. This drama is not to be talked about, to be read, or to be described; it is a drama to be known in the only way that real drama can be known: in performance.

In other words, the purpose of theater is to express objectively certain secret truths—objectively, because these truths are conveyed to us in images on the stage, and aside from the spectacle itself the truth is not evident. When the dancers stop dancing, when the gamelan ceases its deluge of sound, the drama has disappeared, unlike the drama we know in the West which, according to some at any rate, still exists in the text when it is not performed. Artaud would claim that a written text is not a drama until it is performed on a stage and thus finds its visible, full-blown dimensions. And even then most of Occidental theater is not drama for Artaud because it is concerned with problems that ought not to be the concern of the theater. The theater was not made to resolve the social and psychological conflicts of contemporary man, he claims, and indeed, if primitive theater is a valid indication of the function of drama, Artaud is right. Returning to sources, he would seek out the drama's magico-religious beginnings, attempt to find once again the "spirit of fable" which we have lost.

Even so simple a dance as the Djanger witnessed by Artaud, which the program notes describe as representing the "remonstrances of a father to his daughter who has flouted tradition," strikes him only as a pretext. Calling it a "symbolic sketch," he points out that the conflict is not one of sentiments but of spiritual states, which are ossified into gestures and thus rendered objective. The result is that we experience the drama directly, without intellectualization between us and the experience. The drama becomes an "exorcism to make our spirits flow." [22]

Such a preoccupation with an invisible, inner reality is typical of Artaud and was, we noted, one of the obsessions he shared with the surrealists. His search in poetry, in drama, in life itself, was for the still, throbbing center of existence. It was in this search that he explored yoga, studied alchemy and tarot cards, and voyaged to Mexico. It is this center that drama must reveal. In order to do so, drama must speak the many theatrical languages that appeal to the senses, rejecting largely the language of words with its appeal to the intellect. A further corollary is, of course, the rejection of the author and the supremacy of the *metteur en scène*. Ideally, Artaud believes, the creator of the entire theatrical experience is the director, who not only stages the performance but is responsible for the text—or, rather, the scenario—as well. The relegation of text, words, literature to an unimportant part in the theatrical experience, with the consequent rejection of the author, is no doubt, in Western eyes at any rate, Artaud's major heresy. But Artaud belongs to the generation that, all too aware of the mediocrity of the theater of its day, attempted a revolution, a return to the sources, whether through the language-as-incantation of Giraudoux, the visual poetry of the theater of Cocteau, or the total use of theatrical resources advocated by men like Gaston Baty and Max Reinhardt. We are only beginning to taste the fruits of this revolution today, or perhaps we are still in the very midst of it. The extremity of a position like Artaud's can help to establish a healthy balance in a culture where the text is god, where the purely theatrical resources are relegated to a secondary place.

What is undeniable is the significant influence Artaud has exercised over today's theater in the work of directors like Barrault and of playwrights as different as Ionesco, Adamov, Genet, and Weiss. It is impossible to read *The Theater and Its Double* without being struck time and again by the fertility of Artaud's ideas on the importance of the decor and props as living objects in the play, the concretization of language, the visual splendor of the monstrous and gigantic, and the profound effect of a "cruelty" that would wrench us out of our placidity.

Artaud's encounter with the Balinese theater was a *coup de foudre,* for in it he found embodied all his dreams of what the theater should be. The astounding thing is that he should have understood it so well, for despite his preparation in the religions and arts of the East, Artaud could not have had any intimate knowledge of Bali and Balinese dance before his contact with the troupe at the Colonial Exposition of 1931, since no studies of that art had yet been published in French. And yet he was extremely sensitive to the spirit of Bali; he managed through a brief encounter to grasp the essentials of its dance and drama, and their firm integration within the life of the Balinese. He is the most genial and creative of interpreters of Bali for the West; if he misunderstands an occasional detail, he makes ample repair in freshness and brilliance.

It might be objected that Artaud sees more in the Balinese dance than does the average Balinese. The role of the critic, the poet, the genius has always been to see what the average observer is incapable of seeing, or unaware that he is seeing. It was Artaud's genius to verbalize through his magical prose, which carries within it so much of that dazzling spirit of the dance and the gamelan, what others had perhaps often felt but had never been able to express.

When one looks at Artaud's own theatrical creations—his scenarios and the text of his play *The Cenci*—one is struck by the fact that his own works do not resemble in any way the techniques we associate with the Balinese dance. Artaud was not so mad as to believe that a manifestation of a foreign temperament, which had slowly developed its own traditions over the centuries, could be transplanted part and parcel into our Western culture. To place Rangda or the Barong in the context of a Western play, to attempt to use the same fluttering movements of the fingers or the darting eyes of the Legong or the Baris, would most certainly be to take a blind alley. Our problem, rather, is to find the equivalents of those manifestations for our own theater. A monstrous Mme Pace in *Six Characters* and Mother Peep in Ionesco's *Killer* are perhaps examples, or on a more sumptuous level, the fantastic

31

dream creations of Genet's General, Bishop, and Judge in *The Balcony* or the monstrous, hieratic whore Warda in *The Screens*. Many possibilities exist for exploration in this realm, and they may well lead us to the rediscovery of a part of ourselves to which our rationally oriented theater has blinded us.

The relationship between Bali and the West is different from that between the Occident and the other countries whose drama we shall treat. China and Japan, however different they may be from Europe and America, have achieved highly complex civilizations, and during the centuries have moved away from their primitive, indigenous spirits, opening themselves slowly to outside influences. They are no longer completely integrated cultures like Bali, but their national life, like ours, has been fragmented into various facets. Does this mean that we cannot use the spirit and techniques of Bali because they are too foreign to our way of thinking, to our kind of organized, fragmented society? On the contrary, a better understanding of the Balinese theater may help to lead us back to a drama of our own, more central to our experience of life. Bali embodies, as no modern country in the West can, the "idea of a theater" evoked by Francis Fergusson, the idea that the theater is central to a country's life and well-being. Our understanding of such an idea might help us to work toward a theater that, dealing less with the accidents of the particular moment and appealing to the histrionic sensibility as well as to the pre-logical faculties, might be a unifying force in our life pointing to the secret sources of being and to the mysterious origins of the "human condition."

If we are able to use specific techniques developed by the Balinese, so much the better, for they may help us to develop a theater that will speak through all the senses to the total man. We might relearn the effectiveness of the eyes, the lips, the limbs used in a nonrealistic way, the possibility of combining high stylization and masks with utter realism. In Bali the Topeng or masked dance can create characters as alive as any seen in Western theater: through stylized movement a young man, wearing an old-age mask which seems now laughing, now sober, dazzlingly evokes an old man in most naturalistic details, blowing his nose, scratching his arms, and picking lice from his body.

In order to bring about Artaud's double renewal of theme as well as technique in the theater, we must arrive at a new understanding of the theater, at a new attitude of mind. After all, Artaud is not preoccupied with the quaint and peripheral aspects of the Balinese drama, except insofar as they relate to its essence. He is seeking a true spiritual renewal, not merely a decorative fringe.

II Servitude and Grandeur of the Chinese Opera

If art is, as I believe, a challenge; if it
is an epic effort to create, in the face of
'stepmother nature,' a universe which is
human and only human, comprehensible
to man alone—then, what we have before
our eyes here is its supreme accomplishment. Everything here is created—re-
created.

VERCORS

[The Chinese actors] have just proved
that they can do whatever they wish, and
lead the theater to its most exalted
formula, to its perfection.

J. COCTEAU

When the Peking opera appeared at the Paris Théâtre des
Nations in 1955 the reviewers drew upon such superlatives
as "stupefying perfection" and "the finest spectacle in the
world," comparing the performance with those marking the
great ages of classical theater in the West, or evoking the
brilliant revelations of the Diaghilev Ballets Russes in 1909.
Such an attitude toward this exotic form of theater was relatively new, and could be traced at least in part to the broadening attitudes brought about by Artaud's remarks concerning
Oriental theater and the Balinese drama in particular.

The Balinese dance drama had had the good fortune to be
discovered at a relatively late date, and then interpreted with
understanding by a writer of genius. But Chinese opera was
not so fortunate. This dazzling genre, which Faubion Bowers
considers "one of the most perfect forms of theater anywhere

in the world," has had a history of singular miscomprehension and misinterpretation in the West. Europe first became aware of Chinese drama through the large volume by Father J. B. du Halde, *Description of the Chinese Empire and of Chinese Tartary,* published at The Hague in 1736. The play it contained, translated by Father de Prémare, was to inspire two major figures of eighteenth-century letters, Voltaire and Metastasio.

The Orphan of the House of Tchao was written during the first great period of Chinese dramatic literature, the Yuan dynasty (1277–1368). With its strict requirements, the Yuan drama fixed the formula of Chinese drama for the next five or six hundred years, and in it we find many of the characteristics associated with the Peking opera today: stylized symbolic movement and gesture, musical accompaniment, sung portions, lengthy and complicated stories with a moral implied. A notice preceding the text of Father de Prémare's translation advises us that it is an exact rendering, and warns us that we will be surprised by the songs mixed with the dialogue. Prémare adds that "among the Chinese, song exists to express some great movement of the soul, like joy, sorrow, anger, or despair." In his text, however, the Jesuit scholar simply notes that a character "sings" or that "he now recites some verse," but he fails to translate either the songs or the verse. These lacunae gave rise to certain errors in Voltaire's understanding of the genre. Perhaps it is too much to expect a Frenchman of the eighteenth century to admit that any other country had achieved a civilization equal to that of France. The smug, self-satisfied attitudes adopted by Voltaire and other Europeans in the eighteenth century are typical of Western attitudes toward the Oriental theater until a relatively recent period.

In a later edition of Father de Prémare's translation, edited in "Peking" (actually Paris) by a M. Desflottes in 1755, the editor warns his reader: "You will be shocked no doubt by the extravagance that dominates the play; our rules are not at all observed. . . . The Chinese paint Nature in all her colors, but they do not cover it with that polish of art which adds to its beauty." In conclusion he says, "Nature alone, devoid of any assistance from art, is their only guide."

It is piquant to find in the writings of an eighteenth-century European the very criticisms that the Oriental theater might well make of our own theater today. One suspects that M. Desflottes had not witnessed many performances of Chinese theater, for his conclusions are radically contradicted by his contemporary, La Loubère. I quote the latter at length, for his is one of the few eighteenth-century descriptions we have which stresses the production rather than the text of a Chinese play. It underlines a feeling for style, convention, and artificiality:

> All their [the actors'] words are monosyllables, and I have never heard them pronounce a single one without a new effot from the chest: one would think they were being butchered. . . . One of the actors who played the part of a Judge walked in such grave fashion that he would first place his heel on the ground, then slowly pass to the sole, and finally to the toes, and as he put his sole to the ground he began to raise his heel, and when the toes were touching, the sole had already risen. On the other hand, a different actor, walking about like a maniac, would shoot out his arms and legs in many directions exaggeratedly, and in menacing fashion, but much more overdone than the action of our braggarts or Matamores: he was a General of the Army. . . . The theater had a cloth hanging at the back and nothing at the sides, like the theaters of our traveling circuses.[1]

If we can believe these words of La Loubère, the eighteenth-century theatrical production exhibited many similarities to those of today: the high sharp voice used by many actors, the very precise way of walking and moving determined by rank and character type, the simple decor contrasting sharply with the highly decorated costumes that La Loubère mentions elsewhere. The brilliant costumes of Chinese theater are justly famous, and aroused the admiration of the West as early as the first years of the sixteenth century, when Magellan reported having seen a pantomime performed "with extraordinary luxury of costumes."

Unfortunately, the text of a play is often a poor representation of the performance itself, particularly when we are dealing with a work so foreign to a familiar tradition. When Prémare notes "they sing," the Western reader can only imagine the singing that he knows. Such dependence upon familiar parallels partly explains the first European play based upon a Chinese work. It must have been very much like a *Mikado* for the eighteenth century, although the intent was no doubt more serious than that of W. S. Gilbert. In 1741 William Hatchett published a play with the following lengthy title and subtitles: *The Chinese Orphan, An Historical Tragedy Altered from a Specimen of the Chinese Tragedy in du Halde's History of China. Interspersed with Songs, after the Chinese Manner*. Hatchett's work is actually an English neoclassic play, observing the unity of time (the original takes place over some twenty-five years), and written in blank verse. The songs "after the Chinese manner" have a strangely Handelian ring.

Voltaire's *L'Orphelin de la Chine* (1755) is no more faithful to the original, nor was it intended to be. The European authors of the Age of Enlightenment turned to the exotic in their search for plots and characters of interest. But it was not their intention to introduce their public to anything resembling the "barbaric" theater of the Orient, for they all agreed that the Chinese, who had advanced so far in other respects, were still in their infancy as far as drama was concerned. The Chinese were not the only such primitives, for France's European neighbors were not entirely civilized in their dramatic taste either: "One can only compare *The Orphan of Tchao*," Voltaire tells us, "with English and Spanish tragedies of the seventeenth century, which still please audiences beyond the Pyrenees and across the Channel. The action of the Chinese play lasts twenty-five years, as in the monstrous farces of Shakespeare and Lope de Vega, which they call tragedies; they are a piling up of incredible events." [2]

The Chinese author succeeded in giving his play both interest and clarity, we are told, but aside from these two qualities it lacks everything: unity of time and action, development of

37

sentiments, portrayal of manners, eloquence, reason, passion. Since Voltaire could know the text only through the partial translation of Father de Prémare, he was bound to feel that the play lacked passion and eloquence, for the missionary had simply omitted the lyrical passages, verse and song which, as La Loubère had explained, existed to express the "movements of the soul."

The production of *L'Orphelin de la Chine* at the Comédie-Française took at least one step in the direction of authenticity, for Mlle Clairon in the role of Idamé no longer wore the hoopskirts that actresses used for all roles, but a Chinese garment instead. When the play opened—it had a run of sixteen performances—Voltaire expressed some misgivings. In a letter to the Marquis d'Argental (Sept. 17, 1755) he writes that "all should have been new and daring, nothing should have smacked of these miserable French proprieties, and these civilities of a nation ignorant and mad enough to want people to think in Peking as they do in Paris."

Since Aristotle and Horace had discovered the immutable laws of the theater and Boileau had codified them for the modern civilized man, it no doubt seemed useless to spend time studying the dramatic forms and conventions of less enlightened peoples. Surely, as Voltaire was the first to admit, a knowledge of the Chinese plays could deepen our understanding of the country and its people as no travel books could. But the interest of Voltaire, and of most of his contemporaries, was extradramatic; it was made up of curiosity, humanitarianism, and a taste for the exotic which became more and more pronounced during the eighteenth century, whether in literature, in painting, or in bibelots. With Romanticism came a search for authenticity in Chinese drama, and even then it was chiefly the scholars who pursued that search. Until 1829, Europeans could read only three imperfectly translated Chinese plays: that of Father de Prémare and two dramas translated into English by John Francis Davis, *An Heir in His Old Age* (1817) and *The Sorrows of Han* (1829).

The 1830's and 1840's saw a number of scholarly works

and translations, led by those of Stanislas Julien. His *Tale of the Chalk Circle* (1832) was to enjoy a prodigious success more than a century later when the genius of Brecht adapted the old Chinese parable to the modern stage. Julien followed *The Chalk Circle* by a correct and complete translation of *The Orphan of the House of Tchao,* omitting only certain indecencies. In 1838 M. Bazin Aîné published a volume of four Chinese plays with an extremely interesting introduction, pointing out the value of study in exotic theaters, either as a picture of foreign manners or as a tableau of historical events. The theatrical values of the play or of its presentation are of little concern, although critics begin to note similarities in production techniques with those of the Shakespearian stage, a comparison mentioned by nine out of ten writers dealing with the subject in the next century.

Bazin Aîné stresses what he calls the moral ends of the Chinese theater which, he claims, should carry the beholder to the pinnacle of virtue. He believes that the theater moves the Chinese to be ethical not only through moral stories but also through a strong appeal to the emotions; even the most ignorant, Aîné points out, weep and groan during the sad scenes. In his introduction to the *Tale of the Lute,* translated in 1841, Aîné calls it "the finest dramatic monument of the Chinese," and adds that, although some find its forty-two tableaux too long, it *is* very edifying. "Whoever could read the *Tale of the Lute* without weeping copious tears," he concludes, "is a man who has never loved his father or his mother." [3]

Today, what seems most striking in a Chinese play is above all the stylization, the symbolism, the imaginativeness of the staging, the movements, the makeup, the music. The early nineteenth-century scholars breathe scarcely a word on these subjects. Occasionally we are told that a man carrying a whip symbolizes a rider, that certain parts of the performance are sung, that all the actors are men, that the costumes are exceedingly rich. Otherwise the contemporaries of Scribe, Hugo, and Pixérécourt tend to see in Chinese theater only what they have been accustomed to see in Western plays. No one conceives of presenting an Oriental drama in the style of the Orient or of using any of their techniques in a Western production. We must wait for the twentieth century to find such startling ideas, and for the genius of dramatists like Brecht and Genet.

The differences between European and Chinese drama were summed up by Brunetière in one of his less enlightened moments, for his knowledge of the genre was only secondhand:

> Between our theater and the Chinese theater the only real difference I find . . . is the difference between the mumbling of a baby and the words of a grown man. The Chinese theater is of course the creation of a very ancient civilization, and as such, a civilization that is very advanced in many ways, but on many points it has remained in its infancy; or if you prefer, it was immobilized very early into rigid forms from which it has not succeeded in freeing itself.[4]

This statement forms part of Brunetière's review of a book entitled *The Chinese Theater* by General Tcheng-Ki-tong, published in French in 1886. The General's work, dealing in vague generalities, common places, and clichés, teaches us more about the ignorance of a Europeanized Chinese than it does about the theater. Stressing moral ends, and even suggesting that Chinese theater is veristic, Tcheng-Ki-tong fails to touch on such essentials as makeup, costume, gesture, symbols, stylization. It is not surprising that Brunetière gleaned so negative a view of the Chinese drama.

Even nineteenth-century Europeans with firsthand experience of Chinese theater seem to have approached it with a closed mind. A particularly irritating example is that of a certain M. de Bourboulon, who was in China apparently in some naval or military capacity. His conviction that all Chinese were totally devoid of artistic feeling was only strengthened by a visit to the theater. The singers, he tells us, "use a voice piercing beyond description. The effect of this shrill melody recalls the meowing of a cat whose larynx was particularly badly organized." After his study of the theater he concludes: "I shall continue more than ever to formulate the same aphorism: The Chinese have no artistic concept."[5]

40

Ironically, this nonappreciation of Chinese theater was paralleled by Parisian appreciation of Oriental art. Théophile Gautier wrote pseudo-Chinese poems and tales; one of Sardou's heroes (in *Pattes de mouche,* 1860) went around the world carrying a Chinese fan and a parasol. Hugo, a collector of Oriental art, attempted to write a "Chinese" poem. Perhaps the most astonishing person of all these Orientomanes was Théophile Gautier's daughter, Judith. Without ever having traveled, this remarkable lady wrote a travel book about the Orient. Without ever having witnessed an Oriental play, she wrote pseudo-Chinese and Japanese dramas. But her knowledge of Oriental, particularly of Chinese, culture was quite solid, for from an early age she had studied Chinese. Her father, taking pity on a Chinese residing in Paris who had been thrown into jail, secured his release and employed him as tutor to his daughter. So closely was the tutor connected with the household that he came to be known as "le Chinois de Théophile Gautier."

In 1863, after four years of study, Judith Gautier published a volume of translations of ancient and modern Chinese poems and, five years later, an original "Chinese" novel. Her greatest theatrical success was a "Japanese tragedy," produced at the Odéon in 1880, *The Vendor of Smiles.* It was followed by equally quaint Japanese and Chinese dramas with such names as *The Daughter of Heaven, The Geisha and the Knight, Princess of Love,* and *The Heavenly Tunic.* The plays of Judith Gautier are the best among many dozens of plays and operettas depicting the charming, quaint behavior of picturesque, doll-like creatures with names like Forest Well, Veiled Light, Little Fir Tree, Golden Lotus, and so on. These plays are replete with such titillating absurdities as a struggle between the Tartar and the Chinese emperors in 1900, a kiss given the Empress of China by the Emperor, a Japanese lantern bearer who speaks of swallow's nest soup as a great delicacy.

By the end of the first decade of the twentieth century, provincial attitudes had begun to disappear. Travelers, scholars, and theater people admitted that Chinese actors could play with subtlety and charm and that the drama of the Orient could not be judged by criteria of the Occident. A very tasteful adaptation and presentation of a Yuan dynasty drama in 1910 is symptomic both of the changing attitudes and of the distance still to be covered. M. Louis Laloy's *Sorrow in the Palace of Han* shows the hand of a scholar well acquainted with the Chinese theater, who yet did not dare present a play without adapting it to French taste: "In order to present such a work on the French stage, it has been necessary to rework it radically, for on the one hand Chinese drama abounds in sung portions, and on the other it does without decors. It has been necessary to develop the dialogue, to diminish the musical part, reduced here to the resources of poetry, and above all to tighten the style." [6] In other words, one might conclude, it has been necessary to make a Chinese play a thoroughly French product. On the other hand, Laloy was eager to avoid the fictitious China of paper lanterns, mandarin robes, long finger-nails, and mincing steps, not so successfully avoided in *The Yellow Jacket,* which was enjoying great popularity in the United States about the same time. This praiseworthy aim resulted in a play that was a faithful representation of a *human* China, even if the play itself is a betrayal of Chinese dramaturgy.

In one of the most sympathetic studies of Chinese drama, Camille Poupeye stresses that the usual Chinese spectacle we see in the West has little in common with the Chinese dramatic spirit. Even the plays that are taken directly from Chinese literature, like *Sorrow in the Palace of Han, The Yellow Jacket,* or *The Chalk Circle,* are, he tells us, "as distant from the original production as an American musical comedy is from a Wagnerian opera." [7] He ascribes this to the liberties that the adapters take with the text. It seems to me that a more serious cause lies in the ignorance of Western producers and in the inadequate training of our actors, who are unaccustomed to using their bodies and voices in a nonnaturalistic way.

The year 1924 witnessed Klabund's adaptation of *The*

Chalk Circle, which was to inspire Brecht's masterpiece. From that date until the present we see an ever-broadening understanding of China and other Oriental countries and of their arts and literature. Much credit is due to people like Prémare and Judith Gautier, who prepared the way in works that may strike us today as incomplete, quaint, or biased. Equally important were the rapidly developing cosmopolitanism of the twentieth century and the technological developments which permitted wider and more frequent travel, thereby increasing contacts and understanding of foreign cultures. Scholars like Tchou-Kia-kien and Iacovleff,[8] enlightened diplomats like Claudel and Soulié de Morant, who wrote works dealing with Chinese culture, exercised a certain influence as well. But it was above all the visits of Mei-Lan-fang to America and Russia, and later voyages of troupes from China and Taiwan, which have made the rest of the world conscious of the artistry of the Chinese actor and suggested the possibility of using this artistry, or the texts themselves, in some more fruitful way.

The fame of Mei-Lan-fang, one of the greatest of all Oriental artists, was already widespread in the twenties, and his tour of the United States in 1930 was a personal triumph which opened rich vistas to the theatrical world of the West. The Russians, already familiar with certain Chinese techniques, which theatricalist directors like Vakhtangov and Meyerhold had used in experimental productions, were likewise fascinated by the Chinese actor when he toured their country in 1935; Mei-Lan-fang made a lasting impression on such figures as Eisenstein and Brecht, who met him at this time.

The visits of the Peking opera to Europe in 1955, 1958, and 1964 were a new revelation of the fascinating possibilities suggested by another world of theater. Before discussing four modern productions "abstracted" from Chinese opera I would like to mention several particularly interesting techniques associated with it, relating them to the Peking opera productions in Paris and their critical reception, for these productions led to several artistic creations by major figures of the contemporary French theater world.

43

By Chinese opera one usually means Peking opera, the *ching hsi* that evolved roughly a hundred years ago, combining various styles of performance and kinds of music. In its broad outline it was fixed in the Yuan dynasty (1277–1368), but has assumed its particular form only quite recently. Although the various parts of a performance are well integrated, we can for convenience divide them into the visual and the aural. Westerners unaccustomed to Chinese music are unlikely to appreciate the latter. Indeed, few critics fail to mention the cacophony and din raised by the orchestra against which the shrill whining voices of the singers rise.

The visual impact of the performance draws power from a startling contrast between the bright and gorgeous costumes of the actors and a bare stage on which a few pieces of furniture stand as symbols. In painted-face roles, the characters' visages are covered with fantastic geometric patterns in a dazzling range of colors. The patterns and the colors have a symbolic meaning: the connoisseur recognizes treachery by the amount of white on the actor's face, loyalty by the amount of red, piety by yellow, supernatural qualities by gold.

The highly stylized, carefully controlled movements of legs, arms, and sleeves carry specific meanings. The same is true of the position of the head, the movements of the eyes and mouth. Every movement of any part of the body reveals character, situation, and some specific action, usually in symbolic terms. The best-known example is that of horseback riding, symbolized by the actor's carrying a whip. When he dismounts, he hands the whip to his servant. In another example, from *The Autumn River,* a young girl crosses a river to join her lover; there is no boat and no river, but the rhythm of the crossing is perfectly mimed.

Like other Oriental actors, the Chinese is a dancer and often a singer as well as a speaking actor. The simplicity of means, centering the entire performance in the actor and his body as instrument, is one of the great lessons of Chinese opera. The appeal to the creative faculty of each observer, permitted to imagine his own mountain (a chair) or doorway (an invisible sill stepped over by the actor), reminds us of the Shakespearian stage. Indeed, the construction of the Chinese theater and the hubbub that often goes on during the performance (chatting, drinking tea, eating) are surprisingly similar to Elizabethan conditions.

As in the Shakespearian theater, the lighting of Chinese opera does not change to indicate night. Instead, the actors reveal the degree of darkness through their movements. One of the plays performed in 1955 was entitled *The Three Encounters;* it depicted a night meeting at an inn during which officers from enemy armies attempted to steal a letter. The fight was portrayed through a brilliant display of acrobatics. The acrobats shone again in the battle scenes of *Trouble in the Heavenly Kingdom,* and their virtuosity—exhibited in great leaps, back turns, flips, leaping in and out from among a maze of whirling bodies and banners—aroused great enthusiasm among the spectators. Indeed, one of the aspects of Chinese opera which has attracted most attention in the West is the skill of the acrobats. Kenneth Tynan warns us against taking a shortsighted view of theatrical acrobatics: "You may object that nothing very profound takes place; but I cannot call superficial an art that explores, with entranced and exquisite love, the very wellsprings of physical movement, speaking the language of the body so ardently that a flexed arm becomes a simile and a simple somersault a metaphor." [9]

M. Georges Lerminier, a leading Paris critic, was overwhelmed by the performance of Chinese acrobats, but in 1955 he hesitated to admit that such athletic prowess belonged in the theater. When the troupe returned in 1958, however, he was most enthusiastic: "The fight of the heavenly warriors and the warriors of the water, and the single combat of the woman rebel and the heavenly general are . . . Shakespearian. For three years I have been thinking of what a Western director might do with the battles in *Julius Caesar, King John,* or *Richard III,* calling on the acrobats from the Medrano Circus." [10]

Jean-Louis Barrault apparently shared this enthusiasm, for

in his subsequent production of *Julius Caesar* he employed athletes from the Ecole de Joinville in the battle scenes, which were completely stylized. It was, perhaps, not so much an imitation of Chinese opera battles as a kinship of spirit; as long ago as 1933 Barrault "choreographed" the battle scenes in Dullin's famous production of *Richard III;* again, in 1945, Barrault "designed" the battles in his own production of *Antony and Cleopatra.* To stylize a battle, he believed, was to move quite naturally in the direction of Chinese opera without necessarily imitating it. Barrault, it will be recalled, is a spiritual heir of Copeau and Dullin, both of whom expressed their admiration time and again for the suggestive, poetic, highly controlled dramatic arts of the East.

The acrobatics which so impressed the West are a relatively late innovation in the Peking opera; anecdote has it that they were included for the Dowager Empress, who was fond of watching her athletes perform their dazzling feats stripped to the waist. In contrast, the music of the opera, a much more essential part of the performance and present from the outset, has failed to interest us at all.

Parisian spectators commented with delight and astonishment on these particulars, but at the same time they were struck by the degree to which all facets of the performance were integrated, using every available resource of the theater. There were cries of dismay over the incompleteness of European dramatic art when compared with that of China, and critics evoked the great eras of the past, particularly of Greek theater which presents a similar synthesis of drama, pantomime, dance, music. Robert Kanters sums up critical opinion very neatly and makes some interesting suggestions for the Western actor and director. He deserves to be quoted at length.

> This is the great lesson and the great wonder for us, that there is no break between what is music-hall, theater, and opera . . . a spectacle at the same time heavier with meaning, more amusing, and even more realistic than the battle scenes at the Chatelet [spectacular operettas], or even those of Mr. Peter Brook. This is because each actor, each

supernumerary, is used from head to foot, with all his resources in every sense, as a single word or a single instrument. Ah! if M. Gérard Philipe in playing the scene of the Cid's narrative could have as well the arm and leg movements of Mme Tchang Mei-kiuan who juggles with an incredible number of javelins. . . .

Without going so far, it is obvious that we have a great deal to learn from the Chinese theatrical tradition, even if it is only that we should revive and maintain more faithfully the theatrical traditions of our Occident.[11]

Kanters' suggestions are not so heretical as they might sound on first hearing. One has only to recall the great theaters of the past to realize how drastically the modern drama has diminished theatrical resources. The names of Shakespeare and Sophocles are apropos here, and it is not surprising that dramatists like Claudel, who were influenced by Elizabethans and Greeks, were likewise receptive to the great theatrical traditions of the East. Indeed, following Kanters' pregnant suggestion, one has the impression that by employing some of the devices of the Oriental theater the masterworks of the Western past might be presented in a style much more similar to that of the original productions than are those of the productions one usually witnesses in the modern theater. The way is no doubt fraught with dangers, but the results would be worth the risk, particularly when one considers the mediocre performances of Shakespeare and Aeschylus one is often subjected to, performances that reduce the grandeur of theatrical giants to the readily comprehensible dimensions of the television studio or the picture-frame stage. A *Hamlet* staged in rehearsal clothes remains, no matter how grand the declamation or profound the characterization, a simple rehearsal of a drama whose immense dimensions must be achieved visually through color, costume, and movement. Through the Oriental theater, approaching the problem obliquely, we may be able to find an approach to those dimensions once more, expressed in a slightly different but meaningful way for us today. A careful study of the spirit and techniques of the Oriental theater will open new doors and may well make of our theater once more a true theater of feast.

ADVENTURES

Several outstanding experiments in Chinese theater for the West have been made in the past thirty years. I have selected four that represent varying degrees of abstraction from the original genre, approaching the problems of such a transposition in four different ways; the first two use Chinese operas and the last two adapt them completely into a Western key. These varied approaches suggest some of the difficulties encountered as well as some of the solutions found.

The first, *The Butterfly Dream*, is only slightly removed from Chinese opera itself, since the professional American actors who performed it were coached by Peking actors in the details of the Chinese style of presentation, under the able direction of A. C. Scott. The second, S. I. Hsiung's translation of *Lady Precious Stream*, which enjoyed great popularity in England and on the Continent, furnishes a text purporting to be faithful to the Chinese original. The third is made up of the writings of Bertolt Brecht which show the dramatist's contact with Chinese drama. The fourth, only indirectly related to Chinese theater, is formed by the plays of Jean Genet, which show an awareness of Oriental techniques and reflect his contact with Chinese opera in a completely transposed key.

The Butterfly Dream

In 1961 Professor A. C. Scott was asked if he would direct a production of a Chinese opera for the Institute for Advanced Studies in Theater Arts (IASTA). The distinguished author of five or six books on the Chinese and Japanese theaters and of numerous translations, Professor Scott was the obvious choice for such an undertaking. At first hesitant, he was convinced when he witnessed the successful production of a Japanese Kabuki play presented at IASTA and directed by the Kabuki actor Onoe Baiko.

IASTA was founded by Dr. and Mrs. John D. Mitchell, not as a showcase for actors' talents, but as an atelier where young professionals in American theater might become familiar with foreign theatrical traditions under the direction of a master of those traditions. Since 1959 they have performed, for a small invited audience, works in such varying traditions as those of Chinese opera, Kabuki, Indian dance drama, Spanish Golden Age theater, and French classical comedy and tragedy.[12]

Once he had accepted the challenging assignment, Professor Scott's first task was to select a play. Since music is an essential part of Peking opera, it was necessary to choose a play that might not lose too much by the omission of its vocal music, for young Western actors could not even begin to master Chinese singing techniques in the allotted rehearsal period of six weeks. *The Butterfly Dream,* an important play from the Chinese repertory, as a variant on the tale of the Matron of Ephesus, seemed a fitting choice.

When the musical problem had been solved by transposing the sung portions into blank verse, there remained the immense undertaking of imparting to the cast a knowledge of Chinese stage movement: walking, running, symbolic gesture, complex sleeve movements, facial expression, hair movements (including the beard), dance, and certain quasi acrobatics. The whole was set to orchestral music taped in Hong Kong and adapted to fit the smaller size of the Western stage, the differences in timing and rhythm between English and Oriental texts, the IASTA actors' skill in movement, and so forth. The entire experience is set down in entertaining fashion in Scott's article, "The Butterfly Dream," which appeared in *Drama Survey* in the fall of 1962. I wish here to stress only two or three points.

The text of *The Butterfly Dream,* Scott points out, is only a verbal framework: that is to say, the literary value of such a work is slight. Its entire value lies in the experience generated onstage and in the auditorium by clearly defined and artistically rendered stylization. Had the American cast decided that the intricacies of Chinese movement were beyond their capabilities, that the formalized gestures and grimaces were too difficult, their performance might have been amusing or quaint, but it would have lacked artistic value. What the actors were to learn was that there were no literary effects for them to hide behind, no rhetoric, imagery, verbal richness or suggestivity, no psychological complexity to mask a lack of technical mastery of style. The actor in all his nakedness was to be revealed before the audience on a literally bare stage.

If this is true of *The Butterfly Dream,* might it not be equally true of certain Western productions? How many great *roles* do we know which exist in texts scarcely worth our consideration? However absorbing the theatrical experience they furnish, plays like *La Dame aux camélias* and *The Bells,* even in the hands of a great actor or actress, can by no means be compared with the theater's literary classics. And yet generations applauded them wildly, not, I think, because our grandfathers had less taste than we do, but because the actors they beheld in these plays were the possessors of a highly developed technique, the creators of a style. The only way to achieve such a style—given that magic of "presence"—is through discipline. And this, I believe, is the second important lesson to be learned from Scott's production. His actors discovered what discipline means on the stage.

Way back in 1913, writing in Craig's periodical *The Mask,* the great Indologist Ananda Coomaraswamy reported a conversation he had had with Craig regarding the traditional Indian art of acting. Craig, he claims, expressed dismay that human beings should submit to such discipline. Coomaraswamy went on to reflect, with no little justification, that the "modern theater has so accustomed us to a form of acting that is not an art, that we have begun to think it is too much to demand of the actor that he should become once more an artist." [13] The experiment at IASTA shows that, given the will, the talent, and a great deal of work, even in a relatively short period of time, actors can acquire a certain amount of technique. Professor Scott was pleased with the skill his actors developed; he reports the surprise of amateur Chinese actors living in New York when they witnessed, performed by Caucasians hitherto unfamiliar with Chinese opera, a play they would have considered beyond their own capacities as amateurs. Some of them returned several times to see *The Butterfly Dream.*

More important than this tribute and other critical praise was the feeling that the actors themselves had profited immensely through their experience in an exotic form of theater. "Discipline was the vital lesson learned through this production," Professor Scott states. The actors learned to use the entire body within a rigidly fixed system of acting, and yet succeeded in imprinting their own personalities on the roles they performed. Something of the subtle differences enjoyed by Chinese connoisseurs could be savored in this American production.[14] Professor Scott, who came to the venture as a doubting Thomas, concluded that "the true essence" of the Chinese opera "was appreciated and came through." [15]

The imagination and the courage of the founders of IASTA have no doubt already begun to bear fruit in a hundred subtle ways of which we are as yet unaware: in the performances of the young actors who have had the enriching contact with "exotic" traditions, in the attitudes of these actors towards their discipline, and in the attitudes of directors and other theater people who have discovered new possibilities in theater through the workshop productions. The artistic integrity, honesty, and sincerity of these performances stand in stark contrast to some of the more facile commercial transpositions of Oriental plays which have served only to entrench us in our complacency, assuring us that the East is indeed mysterious, quaint, and picturesque.

Lady Precious Stream

Shih I. Hsiung, the translator of *Lady Precious Stream,* is the author of *The Western Chamber* and numerous other works written in Chinese. Before going to England he was a successful writer for the stage in Peking and managed a theater in Shanghai. Professor in Peking and lecturer at Cambridge, he translated several Shaw and Barrie plays into Chinese. He was well acquainted therefore with the theatrical conventions of East and West.

Lady Precious Stream was first performed in 1934 by the People's National Theater in London with immense success. When the news reached America, the play was produced in

New York and Los Angeles. It crossed the Channel and has known success in various countries in Europe. It is probably the most intelligent adaptation of a Chinese text for Western audiences, not for the scholar but for the theater, taking for granted that the actors will be unfamiliar with Chinese theatrical techniques. Needless to say, we cannot expect of such a work the degree of authenticity found in the IASTA production. If, as A. C. Scott quite correctly points out, the text of a Chinese play is simply the verbal framework on which the performance is hung, then a text like that of *Lady Precious Stream* cannot go very far toward giving us the true experience of Chinese opera. Fortunately Hsiung appends rather copious stage directions, so that anyone producing the play will not lose all touch with the correct production techniques. But of course the precise symbolic gestures, sleeve movements, gaits, and so on, can scarcely be indicated by description. Music is totally lacking, although the translator does point out where music occurs and whether it is soft or loud. Happily, he has translated the text itself into sensitive, intelligent English, without the excessive quaintness that mars *Yellow Jacket* and parts of the popular *Lute Song,* itself based upon one of the most famous (and lengthy) of Chinese operas.

Lady Precious Stream is the story of a Prime Minister's third and loveliest daughter who falls in love with and finally marries the family gardener, the repository of all possible virtues. Together they go to live in utter poverty. Soon the husband must go off to war under the command of his two villainous brothers-in-law, both generals. He is believed dead, but for eighteen years Precious Stream is faithful to his memory. He finally returns, now King of the Western Regions, and takes back his aging wife as Queen.

In order to compensate for our ignorance of symbols and techniques, Hsiung has furnished his play with a kind of chorus. In a first edition this part was incorporated into the text as stage directions. The more recent Penguin edition, however, gives these words to a reader who elucidates the exotica for the untutored spectator.

Presumably the text of *Lady Precious Stream* is not spiced for the Western palate, but is an amalgam of the various versions used in China. Hsiung says in his introduction that he has altered nothing: "The following pages present a typical play exactly as produced on a Chinese stage. It is every inch a Chinese play except the language, which, as far as my very limited English allows, I have interpreted as satisfactorily as I can." [16] If we are unable to attend an actual performance in China, then such a translation might at least give us some notion of what *Lady Precious Stream* would be like. The "authenticity" of any such production would depend upon how much the director and his actors know about the true Chinese manner of presentation. Even without using the precise gestures for a given moment, or in a particular play, with a bit of research it is not impossible to preserve at least the fundamental spirit of the original stylized movement.

Used in conjunction with some scholarly background and approached with taste and discernment, *Lady Precious Stream* might furnish an excellent introduction to many facets of Chinese theater. The function of the property man, for example, is important to understand. He is an indispensable adjunct to many forms of Oriental drama, but he has often become, in the hands of an unwitting Westerner, the focal point of the performance. His role is to help the performance in a self-effacing way, to hand objects to the actor when he needs them, remove them when they are no longer needed, and place the various chairs, tables, and other symbolic properties about the stage as required. For the Chinese theatergoer he is invisible; any Westerner who has attended a play in which the property man has a function will remember how quickly this factotum disappeared from his field of perception. When the property man begins bowing to the audience with a flourish or comforting the characters onstage, as he did in a recent production of *Rashomon*, he is following the practices of neither Japanese nor Chinese theater.

That an onstage property man is possible at all arises from the fact that Oriental forms of theater are invariably theatricalist and there is hence no attempt at creating an illusion of real life. The spectator is capable of focusing his attention on that part of the performance which is intended for him. As in Kabuki, the actor is considered the center of the theater and everything is done to help him show his talents and technique to best advantage. Since he is the center, it is also up to him to create for us the invisible elements of his theatrical poetry.

We are constantly reminded, in Hsiung's play, that the theater is a world in which the spectator's imagination has free rein. Like the Elizabethan, the Chinese theater creates decor and properties largely through gesture and movement. Obviously one cannot bring a mountain onto the stage, so it is considered more logical (and in a certain sense even more realistic) to let a chair or a table with two chairs stand for that mountain. When the hero climbs up on a chair, steps across the table and down onto the other chair, we can understand that he has crossed the mountain. The same kind of symbolism applies to city walls, houses, and other large scenery. "Doors are not interesting," someone has said, "but what goes on behind them." Therefore the door is not placed on the stage; it is created by a century-old gesture which suggests the opening of a bolt, and as the actor enters the room he steps across a high threshold.

Even a natural phenomenon may be suggested, and often in a way that strikes a Westerner as poetic and supernatural. Here is the description of snowfall in *Lady Precious Stream:* "Two old men with long beards wearing the Taoist garments and head-dresses, enter from the right and left. They have each a black flag rolled up in the right hand, and a horse-hair switch in the left. They are assisted to stand on chairs and then they unroll their flags, when small white pieces of paper fall from them. Having done this, they descend with help and retire by the same entrance by which they entered. The chairs are then removed." [17] Minister Wang then comments, "What a beautiful scene the snow makes!"

Though decor is sparse, costumes and makeup are not.

Hsiung gives some indication of his characters' dress and of their makeup as well. Minister Wang's long black beard and lack of makeup reveal that he is not the villain of the play. His two sons-in-law, both generals, appear in "fantastic make-ups and embroidered armor." With some research a producer might easily find the authentic costume for a general— 6-foot-long feathers rising from the head and numerous flags sprouting from the shoulders like wings. Yet in the 1937 Los Angeles production of *Lady Precious Stream,* the program shows that both generals were wearing the *sha mao,* a finned hat characteristic of civil officials; that they did not wear their customary "fantastic" painted-face makeup as Hsiung directed; and that Minister Wang lacked his black beard and was therefore unable to express his anger by puffing through it.

The rich theatricality exhibited by such texts as this, by productions like *The Butterfly Dream,* or by visiting Chinese troupes—whether in Paris, Moscow, or San Francisco—has suggested a variety of applications to Western dramatists, directors, and actors. Minimal sets and props; the ever-present but "invisible" prop men; acrobatic battle scenes; fantastic makeup; symbolic use of gait, gesture, makeup, space; exaggerated richness of costumes; movements rhythmically calculated and stressed by sounds and music—these and other techniques of the Chinese opera (and of other Oriental theaters as well) call to mind the experiments, and occasionally the successful re-creations, of men like Copeau, Dullin, Meyerhold, Barrault, Roger Planchon, Thornton Wilder, Bertolt Brecht, and Jean Genet. I should like to comment particularly on the last two.

Bertolt Brecht

With Brecht we leave any effort at imitation of Chinese theater. Taking certain Chinese techniques and plays as a point of departure, Brecht effects a complete transposition. In another sense, however, his work resembles both *The Butterfly*

Dream and *Lady Precious Stream,* for he is interested in text as well as in acting styles. For both, he owes a good deal to the Chinese theater.

Brecht's first contact with the Chinese theater was apparently through a free adaptation of the fourteenth-century text, *The Chalk Circle,* made by the Viennese poet and sinologist Klabund in 1924 for Max Reinhardt. The work exhibits few of the peculiarities of Chinese production and is quite Westernized in its use of decor and prose speech. Nor does Klabund point out any symbolic gestures. As a contemporary of Brecht, Klabund could, however, have acquainted the German poet with other important phases of performance in Chinese theater. Or Brecht may well have read some of the books or articles published by then; that he was interested in Chinese thought is clear from certain of his poems. He understood Chinese theater as a blending of the didactic with the artistic. Such a mixture could scarcely fail to appeal to the man who was several years later to write the *Lehrstücke* or didactic plays.

Gradually Brecht developed his concept of the famous *Verfremdungseffekt.* The first occurrence of this word in his writing is, interestingly enough, in an essay entitled "Alienation Effects in Chinese Acting," written in 1936 but not published until many years later. A note in the margin informs us that the essay was occasioned by Brecht's seeing Mei-Lan-fang's troupe in Moscow in May, 1935. In the article, Brecht compares the Western actor who "does all he can to bring his spectator into the closest proximity to the events and characters" with the Chinese actor who constantly keeps a distance between himself, his character, and the spectator. The Chinese actor achieves this, Brecht believes, by two means: he is aware of the audience and plays to it, and he is aware of himself and even looks "strangely at himself and his work." Consequently he never loses control of himself; his performance is constantly on a conscious, artistic level with all emotion transposed.

In addition to seeing the Moscow performance, Brecht apparently witnessed Mei-Lan-fang in a brief spontaneous presentation in a drawing room; with none of the customary theatrical paraphernalia, and wearing Western clothes, Mei-Lan-fang demonstrated the elements of the Chinese actor's art. "What Western actor could have done that?" Brecht asks. "By comparison with Asiatic acting our own art still seems hopelessly parsonical," he exclaims.[18]

Brecht tells how, one evening at a performance in which Mei-Lan-fang was portraying the death of a girl, the person sitting beside the German visitor exclaimed aloud at one of the actor's gestures. He was immediately shushed by the people sitting in front of him. And Brecht concludes: "They behaved as if they were present at the real death of a real girl. Possibly their attitude would have been all right for a European production, but for a Chinese it was unspeakably ridiculous. In their case the A-effect had misfired." [19] One must add that, if this is so, the "Alienation effect" often misfires for the Chinese spectators as well, for they react emotionally to the sad scenes in Chinese opera. One wonders whether Brecht's feeling of coldness in Chinese acting does not arise, rather, from his unfamiliarity with the chinese stage conventions. The unfamiliar always causes us to focus our attention on the exterior until we are capable of going beyond it to the emotions within.

The Chinese music, which strikes a Western ear disagreeably and as not even remotely expressive of lyricism or deep emotion, often serves precisely that function in the Chinese opera. Brecht, on the contrary, uses music to break illusion, to establish "distance." Techniques that at first seem similar are ultimately different, at opposite poles of dramatic intention.

The same might be said of the didacticism that Brecht admired in Chinese dramas like *The Chalk Circle*. The connoisseur of Chinese opera is most often oblivious to such moral content, for even when he can understand the Peking dialect used by the performers (in Taiwan subtitles are sometimes flashed on a screen), his interest is centered not on the lesson the play might teach him, but on the technique of the actors and, in Peking at any rate, on their vocal attainments.

57

Brecht's firsthand encounter with Chinese theater in 1935 showed him an age-old drama that appeared to use, for different ends no doubt, the same fundamental technique he had developed. The encounter corroborated his belief that such alienation could succeed in a vast, popular theater, but it did not, however, establish for him any spiritual kinship between the European and the Chinese theater—at least, not in terms Brecht understood. It seems to me that Brecht's true use of Chinese techniques was an unconscious one that arose, not out of intended imitation, but from years of experimentation in the direction of conscious theatricality. In his essay on Chinese actors Brecht dismisses many of the symbolic conventions of Chinese theater as impossible of export. And yet a catalogue of the various conventions and techniques he developed for his plays and productions might read much like a listing of Chinese opera conventions.

In his lucid discussion of "The Brechtian Theater," Martin Esslin [20] mentions the following seven concepts as characteristic of Brecht's plays; the reader will recognize many of them from our earlier discussion of Chinese opera:

1. The story develops episodically through a series of loosely connected scenes, which can sometimes be considered complete in themselves. Indeed, some of Brecht's plays (*The Private Life of the Master Race,* for example) are often presented in excerpt, much as Chinese operas are. The titles that Brecht often projects over individual scenes give them a sense of autonomy, so that through sufficient familiarity with all his plays, one carefully chosen act from each of three or four might furnish as *unified* an experience as the complete presentation of a whole play.

2. "Everything hangs on the 'story'; it is the heart of theatrical performance." Like Chinese opera, Brecht's drama is largely narrative. He wants us to feel the same relationship to his drama which medieval men felt toward the epic *recited* to them in the manor hall. Instead of human *nature,* psychology or character, we are shown human *relations* as they are revealed through actions and events.

58

3. "Each single incident has its basic gest." Esslin defines gest as "the clear and stylized expression of the social behavior of human beings towards each other." He goes on to suggest applications of such a theory in particular scenes of the plays, and adds that "Brecht wanted to arrive at a *Gestus* so simple and expressive that it could be quoted with the same ease as a well-turned line of dialogue is quoted." Brecht is no doubt recalling the evening when Mei-Lan-fang, standing in a drawing room wearing a dinner jacket, demonstrated the elements of his art. There is, of course, a sharp difference between the acting of, say, the Berliner Ensemble and that of the Chinese actor, but both reveal a clarity of line, a definition, a quality whose source is art rather than accident.

4. "The groupings of the characters on the stage and the movements of the groups must be such that the necessary beauty is attained above all by the elegance with which the material conveying that gest is set out and laid bare to the understanding of the audience." Realism is not sought, but an economy of means and an elegance that will reveal the relationships and the social meaning behind any given scene. Chinese opera clearly rejects realism in favor of style and elegance, but with an entirely different end in mind: that of entertaining the audience by the highly developed technique of the actor-singer-dancer.

5. "Brecht was against the use of lighting effects to create atmosphere and mood." Like the Elizabethans, and like the Chinese and Japanese, his stage was bathed in a uniform light; the coming of night was indicated by the use of objects such as lamps, or perhaps by the movements of the actors. Since there is no pretense of realism, the source of the lights may well be visible to the public.

6. Esslin quotes a poem by Brecht, "Die Vorhaenge," in which the poet describes the preparations for a performance:

> Leaning back in his chair, let the spectator
> Be aware of busy preparations, made for him
> Cunningly; he sees a tinfoil moon
> Float down, or a tiled roof

59

Being carried in; do not show him too much,
But show him something! And let him notice
That you are not wizards,
Friends, but workers. . . .

Here we see something spiritually akin to the visible property
man on the Chinese stage, who not only hands needed props to
the actors but sets up the scene for the next act while the actors
are still performing the present one.

Obviously there is a world of difference in the reasoning
behind these similarities. Brecht would have us constantly reminded of who we are and where we are, so that we may judge
coolly. He takes it for granted that the spectator will be
entirely aware of the change of setting that is going on. In the
Chinese theater, on the contrary, it is taken for granted that
the spectator will be able to concentrate upon the most interesting part of the performance, the actor, and will be entirely
unaware of the property man's movements. A similar philosophy is reflected in the Kabuki theater of Japan, where one
often hears hammering backstage while the actors are playing
onstage. This seems to bother no one but the foreigners.

7. The musicians are not hidden, Wagner-like, but must be
visible. Indeed, they are sometimes placed on the stage, where
the Chinese (and Japanese as well) feel they belong, sometimes in full view of the audience, sometimes off to one side,
perhaps behind a screen or light veil.

When Esslin points out that we must not "overlook the
large extent to which the Brechtian theater represents a return
to the main stream of European classical tradition," [21] he is
reminding us of the fundamental similarities that have always
existed among the great theaters of the past, whether Asian or
European. That we might mistake a return to the classical
tradition for an Oriental borrowing suggests that, by voyaging
through Asia, we may well find a way back to our sources and
to the strength and nutriment that implies; in the Orient we
will find a *living tradition* actually embodied in performance.
To use Oriental theatricalism need not result in slavish imitation, quaintness, or superficiality. Brecht has given us an example of what can be done when a strong, vigorous, independent

mind comes into contact with what is apparently a foreign tradition. He has made it his own by adapting Oriental devices to his own purposes, or by arriving at similar devices through his own search and meditation.

In a review of the Paris Drama Festival in 1956, Kenneth Tynan points out several important resemblances between Brecht's theater and the Chinese opera, both of which appeared at the festival. What struck Tynan was the richness of resources deployed by both, presaging "an era in which drama, ballet, and opera are no longer separate arts." Expressing regret that England has not yet discovered the genius of Brecht, he recognizes the validity of a Brechtian (and one might assume, a quasi-Oriental) approach to the classics. If English critics do not open their eyes, he claims, the "ideal way of staging *Henry IV, Tamburlaine, Peer Gynt,* and a hundred plays yet unwritten will have been ignored; and the future of the theater may have been strangled in its cot." [22]

The Brecht play Tynan witnessed on that occasion was *The Caucasian Chalk Circle.* It is one of Brecht's masterpieces, written in 1944–45, his last "great" play. Like *The Good Woman of Setzuan* and like *Lady Precious Stream* (and any number of Chinese classic plays), it is the story of a woman's suffering and of her virtue rewarded. Again like them, it ends in what is a standard denouement for many Brecht plays and countless Chinese operas: a scene of judgment during which long-suffering virtue is finally recognized and wickedness punished.

If both Brecht and the Chinese opera turned many times to a similar plot, it is not because they were unable to concoct anything more ingenious or original but because they were concerned with something other than suspense and peripeteia. Brecht obviously was out to convince us of certain basic truths as he conceived them. But beyond that he was interested in the theatrical form itself, and, whether we agree with what he has to say or feel that it was worth saying, we are bound to find his experiments with theatrical form of the deepest interest. The new directions that Brecht reveals may well shape the future of the theater or of a significant portion of it.

61

The Caucasian Chalk Circle is a model of epic theater and the epitome of Brechtian technical virtuosity, with its mingling of prose, verse, chorus, and song; its cool objectivity given by the device of using the Story Teller to describe much of the action as it occurs; the use of masks for those characters who are least human, unchangeable; the suggestivity of decor which may enter and disappear as needed. All these facets of *The Caucasian Chalk Circle* also remind us that the play was inspired by a translation, however loose, of an ancient Chinese play.

What is particularly interesting in this text, however, is the immense role that mime plays. Brecht rarely states that a character is to walk or to move in a certain fashion, but his manner of movement is established quite clearly in one of two ways: by the characterization of the person through his speech or through the Story Teller's description. Time and again one comes upon scenes that suggest a very specific type of highly stylized movement. This symphony of stylized movement (over which Brecht no doubt took great care in production, but for which there are few actual notes in the text) begins when the Story Teller takes his place onstage; his gestures tell us that he has told the story many times, and it is he who gives the signal for the scenes to begin, with an appropriate gesture. The first scene is one of great pomp and procession, with caricatured personages, whose very words seem to decree their stylized movement, against the background of the rabble whipped by soldiers. The flight of the Governor's wife is a grotesque ballet with servants crawling under the weight of trunks, and the wife searching for her silver dress, bobbing up and down, suffering her migraine, ordering her domestics by signs. Grusha's night vigil over the Governor's child is a touching dance of maternal love.

A scene that most clearly suggests a famous Chinese device takes place when Grusha, fleeing into the mountains, crosses over a deep chasm on a swaying rotten bridge. One of the standard Chinese operas, invariably performed by troupes abroad, is *The Autumn River* mentioned earlier. The movement of the boatman and the young girl crossing the river is suggested simply by the movements of the actors as they sway with the drifting boat. In the hands of a skillful actress, Grusha's crossing the bridge can become such a piece of visual poetry.

Although Brecht's plays often possess undeniable literary values, the attention he gave to the production style, and the very elements the text itself seems to demand, suggest something that the Oriental theater would seem to corroborate: great theater is not dependent upon great texts. One can imagine with a shudder *The Caucasian Chalk Circle* performed in naturalistic style. It would lose much of its magic, for here, as so often, what Brecht has to say is much less interesting than the way he says it. Many of his plays, particularly the *Lehrstücke,* stripped of any stylization would no more be worth serious attention than a Sunday School pageant. More than almost any other modern dramatist, in the performance of his plays Brecht depends upon the production as much as upon the words themselves. Realizing that the theater is more than a text, Brecht attempted to use many other facets which for some time had been ignored. He thus approaches total theater.

But in a spirit so different from that of a man like Artaud, for whom total theater meant magic and immersion, the renunciation of the logical faculty in favor of something "deeper, higher, more real." Brecht's famous phrase, "Truth is concrete," opposes him diametrically to such a magical concept of art. If the magical theater of Bali is particularly suited to the penchants of Artaud, the theaters of China and Japan might satisfy either him or Brecht; where the latter sees coolness and objectivity, Artaud might easily find the demon loosed among both actors and spectators. Genet apparently leaned toward the latter.

Jean Genet

In a 1954 edition of *The Maids,* Genet published a preface-letter in which he speaks of the fascination the Oriental theater had exercised on his imagination. But it was only an

63

indirect fascination, for he had never witnessed a performance, having only read about what he calls "the magnificence
of Japanese, Chinese, and Balinese theater." [23] From what he
had read, his fertile imagination had been able to create a
conception of a theater very different from the usual Western
performance. The Occidental theater struck him as crude, and
he dreamed of "an art that would be a profound tangle of
active symbols, capable of speaking to the public in a language
in which nothing would be said but everything would be
vaguely felt." [24]

In language that recalls Artaud, Genet speaks of actors who
would become signs bearing other signs or meanings. He
stresses the religious aspects of a theater which would require
of its actors not the techniques of conservatory training but the
devotion of seminary vows. This art would use texts, decors,
and gestures; it would aim at something beyond make-believe
and masquerade; it would attempt to become ceremony.

Genet's first two plays, *Deathwatch* and *The Maids,* take a
step in this direction, but the author was not at all satisfied
with what he had done. "In order to succeed in my undertaking
I should have of course invented a tone of voice also, a way of
walking, a manner of gesturing. . . ." In other words, becoming more than author, the total creator and *metteur en scène*
of his drama, he would have liked to reinvent Western theater.
Genet rejects not only his own work but that of other dramatists as well. Those who sought inspiration in the Orient had
done so in a superficial way, he felt, with no understanding of
the deeper spirit.

In 1955 Genet witnessed for the first (and so far as I know
the only) time an Oriental spectacle: the performances of the
Peking opera in Paris. The program included a good sampling
of Chinese opera techniques—among other pieces, the ubiqui-
tous *Autumn River;* the flamboyant *Trouble in the Heavenly
Kingdom* with its acrobatic battle scenes between grotesque
monkey figures and gods, featuring some of the fabulous
painted-face makeups; and *The Three Encounters,* described
thus in the notes: "Although flooded in light, the actors, by

their exaggerated symbolic gestures, give the illusion of a fight in total darkness."

Whether consciously or not, Genet felt the impact of these performances, for they were to act as a catalyst in his work. "I was very impressed," he writes in a letter (Jan., 1963). "As for its influence on me, it would be very difficult for me to distinguish it from my own preoccupations. At any rate, the extreme tenuousness (I mean subtleties) of the themes, of the constructions, of the modes of interpretation of the Peking theater interest me greatly." There has always existed a certain kinship between the spirit of Eastern theater and that of Jean Genet. In the plays written after 1955, however, this affinity becomes much more evident. There is a sharp difference between the visual simplicity, for example, of *Deathwatch* and *The Maids* and the richness of later plays like *The Balcony, The Blacks,* and *The Screens.*

The appearance of monsters, masks, exaggerated costumes, music, the stress on ritual and ceremony, all indicate a fundamental change in technique. *The Balcony, The Blacks,* and *The Screens* show the triumphant use of Oriental theatrical devices which, consciously or unconsciously, Genet has appropriated and made peculiarly his own, transforming them in a way that is meaningful and effective within the framework of Western drama.

While the decors of the early plays are meant to suggest solid masonry, stone, or Louis XV frills and lace, *The Balcony*'s set, with its false mirror reflecting what is obviously not in front of it, and its stable chandelier which remains when the scene shifts, establishes the stage as a purely theatrical milieu. Decor as decor is still present, however. In *The Blacks* we are confronted with the bare stage of Chinese opera, with the addition, however, of gallery, runway, and platforms. The catafalque in the center of the stage, we later discover, is, like Chinese stage walls, created by chairs and a sheet. In *The Screens* the decor is created from screens rolled on and off stage as needed, the set changing before the eyes of the audience. Often the screen is bare and the decor itself is drawn

65

upon the surface by the actors: as an orchard catches fire, the Arabs draw flames in yellow and red; when night falls, an actor quickly sketches in a moon.

Costumes and makeup again recall the theatricalism of Chinese opera by their sumptuousness, violence, and brightness. Particularly striking is a resemblance between the so-called figures of *The Balcony*—the bigger-than-life General, Bishop, and Judge perched on their cothurni, their shoulders built out to great breadth—and the generals of Chinese opera, their figures enlarged by the banners rising from their shoulders, a high headdress topped with two 6-foot-long feathers. Warda, the great hieratic whore in *The Screens,* is equally impressive. Genet describes her thus: "Dress of very heavy gold lamé, high-heeled red shoes, her hair coiled up in a huge blood-red chignon. Her face is very pale [it is in fact painted white]. . . . Warda has a very long and very thin false nose." [25] As the scene progresses Warda's feet and hands are painted with lead white, and blue veins are drawn upon them. The other characters wear equally unrealistic makeup: "If possible, they will be masked," Genet writes. "If not, highly made-up, painted (even the soldiers). Excessive make-up." [26]

Genet often adds notes to his text regarding the production. It is interesting to compare the advice regarding actor's movement in his first play with that given in the last. In *Deathwatch* we are told that "the actions of the actors should be either heavy or else extremely and incomprehensibly rapid, like flashes of lightning." [27] In other words, the author wanted to draw attention to the movement as an integral part of the performance by treating it in a stylized way, but his ideas regarding the stylization were quite vague. By 1960, although there are few specific indications, the directions to the producer indicate that the dramatist has given up the "incomprehensibly rapid," in order to stress the significance of each movement: "The Acting: To be extremely precise. Very taut. No useless gestures. Every gesture must be *visible.*" [28] It is plausible to think that the choreographic, highly controlled, economical, and suggestive movement of the Chinese actor revealed to Genet a way of moving and gesturing toward which he had been tending, but which until then he had perhaps not succeeded in clearly visualizing for himself.

Two scenes in *The Screens* (13 and 15) are quite clearly indebted to the Peking opera, particularly to *The Three Encounters*. As in the Chinese play, night scenes are presented in bright stage light and darkness is suggested by the actors' movements. Genet thus describes the General and the Lieutenant as they enter in the night: "They will advance slowly, bent forward, one behind the other, groping. All their gestures must make us feel the darkness." In a later scene, as the soldiers talk: "The actors are to speak as if they do not see each other. Their gaze never meets that of the person they are addressing. They are to give the impression of being in pitch darkness." Following the Chinese, Genet is here giving back to the actor the central role in the drama, a role often usurped from him by the decorator and lighting technician. He is also putting more faith in our imagination, forcing us to find a childlike creativity we seem to have lost.

That such techniques recall great theatrical epochs of the Western past, as well as our heritage in primitive theater, is part of the point I wish to make. Different as Chinese opera and other Oriental forms of theater may be, they stand today as a living monument of a kind of theater we too once enjoyed. The productions I mentioned in the early part of this chapter show some of the dangers we encounter when attempting to find encouragement and inspiration in an exotic form of theater—or in our own past, for that matter. But the works of Brecht and Genet suggest that the trap of quaintness and picturesqueness can be avoided and that the "Chinese" features, actually as universal as theater itself, can be successfully integrated into Western theater. The spirit and the techniques of Chinese opera can be transformed to meet our needs, and can at the same time exercise a transforming power upon the plays and the playwrights who have the good fortune—and the wisdom—to consult them.

III Three Visions of Noh

> The Noh is a sublime form of dramatic
> art which can bear comparison with the
> supreme Greek tragedies.
>
> P. Claudel

> [Zeami's *Secret Tradition of the Noh*]
> revealed to me a theatrical technique
> reminiscent of Aeschylus. And yet it is
> an extremely modern book which I would
> recommend to the closed minds of the
> West.
>
> E. Ionesco

> [To his Japanese hosts after witnessing a
> performance of Noh]: You must preserve
> this.
>
> Ulysses S. Grant

THE TEXT OF NOH

China has given us more than 200 years in which to compound misunderstanding and misinterpretation, but Japan was
wiser: it was not until 1856 that she opened her doors to the
West. Then, she opened them with a vengeance, eager to learn
from the West and to make up in a few decades for the 250
years of isolation imposed by the Tokugawa shogunate. Westernization was even more a rage in late nineteenth-century
Japan than *japonisme* was in *fin de siècle* Europe. We were
beginning to admire woodcuts, the kimono, and the charming
musume, but we were not nearly so adventurous in the theater,
preoccupied as we were with the naturalistic revolution and a
reaction to it. The more daring Japanese were attempting to
"modernize" their theater along the same lines we were following in Europe, a program that almost resulted in the disap-

pearance of traditional Japanese forms, particularly in the popular Kabuki theater.

The Noh drama had long been associated with the shogunate, and when the Tokugawas were overthrown in 1868, it seemed that the stately drama was doomed to extinction. The great Noh artists disbanded, some fleeing to the Shogun's place of exile. Only a relatively humble practitioner, Umewaka Minoru, whose family for centuries had played the tertiary roles of *tsure* (followers), remained in Tokyo; it is largely owing to his courageous efforts that Noh survived. When General Grant, in 1879, viewed Noh in Tokyo, he perhaps failed to realize how seriously his admonition to preserve the form was needed. Most visitors to Japan in the 1880's were not so fortunate as Grant, and few of them even mentioned the Noh. It was only in the first decades of the twentieth century that this most austere of dramatic genres was brought to the attention of literate Western readers through the notes of Ernest Fenollosa, an American who had taught for many years in Japan and was largely responsible for reminding the Japanese that their own art forms were as deserving of study as were the newer ones from across the sea. Ezra Pound organized Fenollosa's notes and gave new poetic beauty to his translations of the Noh plays; in 1916 the fruit of this collaboration, *Noh, or Accomplishment,* was published. An introduction by William Butler Yeats attempted to elucidate some of the possibilities offered the West by so elevated and exotic a theatrical form.

Scarcely ten years earlier an English scholar, W. G. Aston, in the first—and even today the only—history of Japanese literature in English, described the Noh drama as decadent, deficient in lucidity, method, coherence and good taste; as drama, he claimed, it had little value. Although not so outspoken, he seemed to agree with A. B. Mitford, who pronounced the Noh "wholly unintelligible." [1] Fortunately there were other more perspicacious and penetrating scholars: Noel Péri's brilliant studies and translations (begun in 1909 and carried into the twenties) permitted cultured Europeans a

69

deeper understanding of this ancient art, as well as an opportunity to read a number of its important texts.

Arthur Waley's *Noh Plays of Japan,* published in 1921, offered twenty translations and the first extensive discussion of Zeami's recently (1908) discovered works, which were to correct a number of misconceptions regarding the development of Noh. Zeami was the creator of Noh and the first to formulate its theory into laws for theater.

Péri, Waley, Fenollosa, and Pound discuss the Noh performance in detail, and Waley stresses the fact that English versions "can at best be little more than makeshifts." Yet, despite their goodwill, it was impossible for these men to present the Noh as an experience, except as it was suggested through the text. Fenollosa, who studied Noh dancing, singing, and music for twenty years, tells us time and again that we must read the texts as if we were listening to music. But how is the reader who has never witnessed a Noh play to imagine this music, or to visualize movements so unlike any kind of "dance" known to the West? Can he be blamed for tending to focus his attention on the text?

The Japanese enthusiast, on the other hand, seeks to go beyond text, actor, and idea to what might strike us as a mystical mindlessness, thereby arriving at a fuller, deeper experience of the Noh. Without special study, the modern Japanese cannot readily understand the text of a Noh play with its archaic vocabulary, obsolete forms, deformed diction, and convoluted sentence structure wrenched out of coherence in order to satisfy the strict requirements of Noh prosody. The Noh libretto is a kind of gongoristic dialogue made up of verbal elegance; obscure literary, historical, and religious allusions; and frequent quotations from the Chinese (which, by the way, often deserve much of the credit for the lyrical beauty of the text). A translation can scarcely do justice to such a libretto. Without denying the Noh texts' literary value, I agree with the Japanese critics who claim that it is not necessary to understand the text fully in order to appreciate the Noh.[2] It was Zeami, the greatest dramatist of the genre, who advised, "You should not discard even bad plays; the actor's care will bring them to life." [3] After averring that "the writing of Noh texts is the lifeblood of our art," Zeami adds immediately that brilliance is not requisite, for dexterity alone will lead to a good Noh. Zeami takes this point of view because, as actor-director-composer, he does not look upon the Noh as a literary genre, but as a theatrical art. Although there was certainly scope for the dramatist with literary talents, "the basic requirement," Professor P. G. O'Neill points out, "was rather the skill to blend together old songs, poems, and stories dealing with a suitable literary or historical figure or famous place." [4] Professor O'Neill further notes that Noh plays tend to be so ungrammatical that in the eighteenth century a thorough revision was undertaken.[5] Conservative forces dominated, however, and the texts soon reverted to their original irregularities.

When W. B. Yeats undertook his ambitious adaptations of the Noh form to Western drama, it was perhaps inevitable that he should use a textual approach, for he had never witnessed a Noh performance. He had been able to observe a young Japanese dancer in London,[6] but this is scarcely reflected in his plays. In a penetrating study, "Yeats, A Poet Not in the Theater," William Sharp strikes at the heart of the matter when he observes that Yeats, in his *Four Plays for Dancers,* has given us only words, and it is as pure text then that the works must be evaluated: "Even the argument that it is not a play 'in the traditional sense' but makes 'dramatic sense' in its music and dance is not valid when one remembers that there are no dance steps, no musical notes. As far as Yeats the dramatist is concerned there are only words, and it is on words that one must base his conclusion." [7] In other words, there is no concept of a style. Yeats, in his Noh-like plays, is writing not in a relative vacuum, created by his rejection of a drama for the masses and his espousal of an aristocratic theater, but in a *total* vacuum, for no one but Yeats himself knows what he has in mind or could successfully embody it in production. Despite his love of the Noh texts and

7I

the hieratic drama they suggest, despite his use of such correct adjectives as "distinguished, indirect and symbolic," despite his understanding that the Noh actor's art must suggest reality and yet "find it all in the heart," Yeats betrays a radical misunderstanding of the Noh when he declares that once he has written and has had performed, for "friends and a few score people of good taste," several plays inspired by the Noh, he will "record all discoveries of method and turn to something else." He adds in a manner that seems strangely detached and dilettante to those acquainted with the years of training and discipline implicit in the life of a Noh actor: "It is an advantage of this noble form that it need absorb no one's life." [8] It is difficult to repress the idea that Yeats regards Noh drama as something terribly picturesque and exotic for the aesthete to dabble in, but to which the dramatist is, after all, not ready to give more than momentary interest.

Traditions are not created in a day, nor do they grow without devotion, sacrifice, discipline, consecration. It was a mistake for Yeats to believe that he could give us anything resembling the Noh drama when he was writing so completely out of context for an audience that, no matter how select, would also be out of context. Whatever the poetic virtues of *At the Hawk's Well* and *Calvary*, they do not capture the spirit of Noh, because it cannot be caught in words alone. The strongest impact of the Noh is not even to be found in a perfect harmony of words, dance, and music, for this would be only the exterior form. The essence of Noh lies elsewhere. "We work in pure spirit," said Umewaka Minoru.

In one of the most discerning of all articles devoted to Yeats and the Noh, Mrs. Yasuko Stucki points out how completely Yeats failed to grasp the approach to spirituality embodied in the Noh. On all levels of the play—meaning, imagery, character, story—Yeats's work is diametrically opposed to that of the Noh. While the Noh presents an experience, which may be colored by the Buddhist philosophy of its creator, Yeats's dance plays present symbols that point to occult concepts. One might say that the Noh experience radiates outward in ever-growing concentric circles, whereas the Yeatsian version of the Noh is turned in upon itself, leading from surface symbols to specifically intended, if not too clear, meanings. The Noh begins with an unmistakable meaning embodied in an experience and thereby sheds light, not on some occult doctrine, but on the human predicament itself. Yeats's plays, Mrs. Stucki says, "stand on two levels of presentation, one sensual and the other intellectual. However, a Noh play has only one level of presentation in which our passions and material world are presented in unity. . . . What is symbolized is not *Yūgen* (the secret depths) as a concept but as experience." [9]

The spirituality of Noh derives from its religious origins, from the influence of Zen Buddhism, and from the genius of its classic creator, Zeami. Noh took on something like the form we recognize today toward the end of the fourteenth century. A blending of several earlier forms, both native Japanese and Chinese transplants, Noh drew chiefly upon *dengaku* and *sarugaku*. The former was at first a folklike dance associated with rice planting and harvesting. During its long history it became more and more refined, and was gradually dissociated from the rice cycle; by the fourteenth century it had become a courtly dance. *Sarugaku* began as a variety-type popular entertainment incorporating mime, acrobatics, juggling, music. By the fourteenth century it had moved in the direction of *dengaku*, which had in turn borrowed certain elements from the *sarugaku*. At that time troupes of players were associated with various shrines and temples, performing the *sarugaku* in connection with religious festivities. It was at one of these, in 1374, that the seventeen-year-old shogun, Yoshimitsu, witnessed a performance by Kannami, the most skillful performer of his day. Captivated by him, as well as by his twelve-year-old son Zeami, the young Shogun invited them to become part of his household. In this capacity Kannami and his son, who succeeded him as head of the troupe upon Kannami's death in 1384, exercised an immense influence on the other *sarugaku* performers in Japan. It had been Kannami's brilliant idea to incorporate into the *sarugaku* elements from the *kuse-mai*, a

73

dance that related a story through movement at the same time that the dancer chanted the tale. The story, which usually centered on a priest, a temple, or a famous locale, rendered the performance more dramatic by giving it some slight narrative thread, and stressed its religious aspects by associating the play with a sacred person or event.

Kannami's device was probably taken over by other *sarugaku* troupes, and by the performers of *dengaku* as well. In texts of the fourteenth century it is often difficult to ascertain exactly what kind of performance is being referred to, for there was apparently much borrowing. It is clear from Zeami's writings that *sarugaku* and *dengaku* used similar types of plays. Zeami, referring to the Noh, sometimes uses the word "Noh" but often uses *sarugaku* or *sarugaku no nō*. Professor O'Neill, who discusses this question brilliantly in his fascinating study, *Early Noh Drama,* makes it quite clear that there is no one moment at which Noh begins to be written. As with other art, a gradual development leads to a form, which then assumes a particular name. It is only by looking backward from the *fait accompli* of Noh that one can begin to discern the various threads contributing to it, for, since Zeami's day, the Noh has been frozen in a precise, fixed form.

"Noh," Professor O'Neill states, "is best considered as a serious entertainment form containing three main elements—mimicry, song, and dance." [10] Such a description, which equates each of the elements with the other two, suggests the distance between the Noh drama as theater and the texts, which for many years were our only means of approaching it. Mimicry (or imitation) originally was a separate element in the performance; Noh was born on the day when mimicry—and the dramatic incident it implied—was integrated with song and dance.

Noh plays, as developed by Kannami and perfected by Zeami, fall into one of five categories: god, warrior, woman, frenzy, and demon plays. A full Noh performance includes all five plays in that order, which conforms to the aesthetic rule of *jo, ha,* and *kyū,* or introduction, development, and conclusion.

The introductory play must be simple, formal, even monotonous. The next three plays, those belonging to the development section, must be elegant, graceful, slightly more complex than the introductory play, leading through the fourth play to the quickened tempo of the finale in the demon play. The rule of *jo, ha,* and *kyū* is applied within the three plays of the second section, and also to the structure and feeling of each play individually.

Whether Noh plays belong to the first, second, or third category, they are much alike and usually constructed along the same lines; inevitably, each play uses the same characters, who are thought of as actors presenting the characters rather than the personages themselves. There is only one true actor in the performance, the *shite,* who impersonates the central character. The *waki* or secondary actor is actually the catalyst of the event and a passive observer of it. The event, however, is rarely an action presented to us as it takes place; instead, it is the evocation of some past action, relived through dance and song. Professor René Sieffert gives the following concise formulation of Noh: "The Noh is the poetic crystallization of a privileged moment in the life of a hero, detached from its spatiotemporal context and projected into a dream universe evoked and revealed by means of a witness who is the *waki.*" [11]

After the "orchestra," consisting of two drums and a flute, and a small chorus take their places onstage, the play begins when the *waki* makes his entrance down a bridge that leads from the backstage area to the upper right corner of the stage. After introducing himself, and perhaps voicing some pious thoughts concerning the transitoriness of life, the *waki* states that he is traveling to some famous shrine or village. There follows a *michiyuki* or traveling song that describes his voyage, symbolically represented by a few steps. Having arrived at his destination, he sits at the *waki*'s pillar, downstage left. This part of the play is the introductory or *jo* section, and is characterized by its simplicity.

The second of the three parts of a play, the *ha* or development, is made up of three sections which again show the *jo, ha, kyū* structure. (1) The *shite* enters and sings a song stating the themes of the play, his own preoccupations, life, or work. (2) The *waki* converses with the *shite* and asks him to relate the tale for which the locale is famous. (3) The *shite* relates the tale briefly and reveals that he is in reality its protagonist. This last moment of revelation corresponds to the *kuse-mai* or story dance.

After an interlude in which a *kyōgen* or comic character recapitulates the story in less elusive terms, the finale or *kyū* begins. This section is characterized by a more rapid tempo as the *shite,* who had exited backstage, returns in his true identity, now a ghostly apparition of the legendary figure he had described. Accompanied by a chanting chorus, the ghostly figure relives his moment of anguish or struggle through a slow, stately, evocative dance which is the climax of the performance. The Buddhist sentiments voiced by the *waki* and chorus; the contrition expressed by the central character (whose speeches are often delivered by the chorus); the story of eternal unrest, rebirth, and suffering—all point to the religious beginnings and temple-centered existence of the *sarugaku* and the religious subject matter of the *kuse-mai.* The piety expressed textually may strike us as somewhat thin, particularly when we remember that a large segment of the modern Japanese audience cannot understand the text and often resort to following it in a libretto. Such textual piety, however, is dramatically embodied in the underlying action of the play which visually portrays the eternal rebirth and suffering of a once-living being.

There is a more spiritual aspect to the Noh, however, which arises not so much from the content of the play as from its performance. Zeami, who brought the Noh to its peak of perfection, grew up at the court of Yoshimitsu, a supreme aesthete who was at the same time the military ruler of Japan. The Shogun's warrior courtiers admired Zen Buddhism for its extreme physical and mental discipline. Noh drama, embodying the virtues of restraint, austerity, quietness, suggestivity, formality, is closely akin to the other quasi-mystical arts, which developed at the same period and grew out of the Zen way of life: ink painting, flower arrangement, landscape gardening, tea ceremony, and archery. Like its sister arts, Noh is concerned with essences and attempts to suggest the core of a situation or event in the simplest terms, reducing the whole to a highly controlled experience within clearly defined artistic limits. If Peking theater and Kabuki are the grand opera of the Orient, the Noh is its chamber music. Or, perhaps a better analogy, Noh is a Bach double violin concerto which, contrasted with a symphony, strikes us as bare.

For many Westerners the Noh is a ceremony rather than a drama. After reading the texts and being thrilled by their theatrical possibilities, we are disappointed or bored by the way they have been embodied on the stage. Our reaction is at least partly due to our unfamiliarity with the spirit, techniques, and vocabulary of the Noh art. One of the most sensitive interpreters of Oriental theater, Camille Poupeye, warns us that there is in the Noh an "ensemble of visual and auditory sensations which we would be wrong to deny simply because they escape us." And he adds wryly, "We are after all only barbarians from the West." [12]

Until we have had the opportunity to educate ourselves through a prolonged contact with the actual performance of Noh, it seems to me that Westerners will find the most enriching approach to Noh not through the texts themselves but through writings about those texts and about their performance,[13] and most particularly through the writings of Zeami.[14] Such an approach would allow us to glimpse at least the spirit of this drama, whereas our reading of the texts serves only to confirm us in our own Western approach to dialogue. If, as René Sieffert suggests in his preface to a brilliant new translation of Zeami's *Tradition Secrète du Nô* (1960), we are able to supplement reading by the use of films and commentated recordings, we might be in a position to appreciate the contribution Noh can make to Western drama. The specific content of a Noh play, he points out, is too peculiarly Japanese to serve us:

How can Japanese music, choreography, and texts several centuries old be appreciated as they should by people belonging to a civilization absolutely foreign to the conditions prevailing at the birth and development of Noh? Therefore it cannot be a question of creating a European Noh, or even of adapting translations of authentic Noh plays to the Western theater. . . . At the risk of disappointing the Japanese devotees of Noh, I believe I can say that, for the Occident, Zeami the theoretician of Noh is more interesting, and more important, than Zeami the composer of Noh plays.[15]

A glance at Zeami's writings will help us, then, to enter the unfamiliar world of Noh, revealing perhaps fertile new perspectives in dramatic art. It will also make us aware of universals we share with this drama, which manifests itself in a way utterly unlike our own.

ZEAMI AND THE THEORY OF NOH

Zeami's so-called *Sixteen Treatises* (twenty-three have actually been found, although the authorship of some is in doubt) span a period of at least thirty-six years. In 1400, at the age of forty, recognized as the chief exponent of his art, Zeami set down for his disciples what he intended to be the secret precepts of the Noh as they had been developed by his father, Kannami. Zeami is modest, and no doubt many of the ideas he ascribes to his father were his own. During thirty-six years his ideas grew and changed, so that it is difficult to give a single interpretation to certain central concepts of Zeami's art. He was a man of the theater, and like all supreme dramatists he worked *in* the theater as composer, director, teacher, actor. His treatises reflect a thorough acquaintance with the practice of the drama and a profound psychological insight. For those who think of Noh as an esoteric, aristocratic form, it comes as a surprise to learn that Zeami was an eminently practical man; he would, no doubt, have agreed with Jouvet, who said that only one question need be asked about a play: Is it successful? But Jouvet and Zeami meant success through artistic means, not success through facility, vulgarity, and an appeal to the baser instincts.

In the training of the Noh actor, lifelong study is taken for granted. Zeami points out at the start that one cannot expect a youth of twelve to show the same coloring in his performance which one would find in that of a young man of twenty, or an adult of forty. Each age has its particular charm and skill; it is a mistake for the master to attempt to foist his own interpretation upon the young actor. From the first page of his first treatise Zeami reveals so keen an understanding of human nature that he seems modern five and a half centuries after he set ink to paper: "At first he [the apprentice actor] should be allowed to act as he pleases in what he happens to take up naturally and follow his own inclinations. He should not be instructed in minute detail, or told that this or that is good or bad. If he is taught too strictly he will lose heart and also become uninterested in the Noh and forthwith cease to make any progress in performance." [16] Since Zeami, like the finest Japanese actors today, looked upon acting as an art that requires many years of study, there need be no rush to inculcate principles; at first, the student is allowed to feel his way naturally into the world of the Noh theater. With each period of training new approaches are added, but, Zeami reiterates, the old actor must never forget his earlier stages of development, while constantly broadening his field of performance in accord with his particular talents and his age. Humility is essential: "The self-conceit of even an expert will cause his performance to retrogress." When we see someone less expert than ourselves who excels in some aspect of the Noh, we must be modest enough to study his method.

Zeami divides the stages of an actor's development into seven periods: first, up to 12; second, from 13 to 17; third, from 18 to 24; fourth, from 25 to 34; fifth, from 35 to 44; sixth, from 45 to 50; seventh, beyond 50. Only by the time he has reached the fourth period, from 25 to 34, is the actor considered a beginner. At this crucial stage the young man must study the art of mimic with particular attention, meditate assiduously, and must apply lucidly to himself all he has learned from the masters of the past. If he should analyze his own talents and degree of development incorrectly, he is irretrievably lost. It is interesting to note that Zeami's first four divisions correspond to those that prevail in today's Western education for the professions. The first stage, up to 12, corresponds to elementary school; the second, 13 to 17, to high school; the third, 18 to 24, to college and university; the fourth, 25 to 34, to graduate studies and professional training.[17]

The fifth period, from 35 to 44, should reveal the peak of an actor's powers. If he has not yet attained renown and public favor, it is probably because he does not deserve it; for such an actor, the fortieth year will no doubt mark the beginning of a decline. But every actor faces real severity in the fifth period, for at this time he must not only have mastered the material of the past, he must look toward the future as well, to determine what artistic means he will enjoy.

After forty-five the artist must modify his acting, preferring what is simple and restrained to what is complicated and violent, for the latter would reveal his weaknesses. With rare exceptions, all physical beauty has faded and the charm of an actor over forty-five must be found elsewhere. One of Zeami's focal ideas is that of the *flower* (*hana*); he means a quality, possessed by an actor, which is interesting, unusual, and hence particularly appealing to an audience. It is the *flower* that holds the interest of the public. For a child of ten, childish grace is sufficient, and, for a young man, adolescent beauty may suffice. But by the age of forty-five all these qualities, which were flowers of the moment, have disappeared; if the actor is sufficiently gifted, this last period is the time for the true flower to appear. Only the master actor arrives at this stage of accomplishment. He arrives there through a thorough understanding of his métier, of course, but equally essential are lucidity and understanding of the self: "Knowledge of self belongs to one perfected in the Noh." [18]

After fifty the actor is generally condemned to *noninterpretation,* by which scholars understand not inaction, but the acting of roles that do not require much movement or brilliance. The great actor, however, within a small and simple repertoire may still reveal the true flower made of spiritual strength and awareness, more fascinating for the connoisseur than the momentary flowers which have now disappeared. Zeami points to his father as an example: several days before his death at fifty-two, Kannami had presented a particularly brilliant performance, which had been praised by high and low alike, "for his Flower came from true perception so that it remained blooming on the tree of Noh until it became an aged tree with few leafy branches left." [19]

Zeami has organized the actor's training in various ways. There are *three facets:* exercise, study, meditation; these correspond to training of the body, the mind, and the spirit. In the perfection of these three facets lies the road to the true flower. One cannot help reflecting here that Western training methods tend often to neglect one, and sometimes two, of these facets. On the other hand, we remember with satisfaction great teachers of acting like Stanislavski, Copeau, and Dullin, who would subscribe fully to Zeami's tripartite division; in their own practice, however different it may have been from that of the Noh, they insisted upon the importance of the spiritual and intellectual equipment of the actor.

The *two elements* on which the actor's training will focus—and here we are far indeed from Western approaches, since the form of the Noh is so radically different—are song and dance. Song includes such elements as diction and emotional tone. These elements are applied to the *three types* that dominate the Noh drama: old man, woman, and warrior. In his approach to character the actor aims not at psychological complexity and reality, but at formal beauty and spiritual depth. This is expressed in the concept of bone, flesh (muscle might be a better translation), and skin. Bone gives strength; it is the native talent and the spiritual backbone. Flesh contains the spirit, the dance and song that, when mastered, give a sense of security. Skin covers and decorates the flesh; it is that subtle beauty emanating from a healthy skin. [20]

If the actor must know himself, he must also know his public; Zeami deemed it of the utmost importance that an actor be constantly aware of the needs of his audience, and that he answer those needs. René Sieffert sees this concordance between actor and audience as the central idea of Zeami's philosophy. Kannami, we are told, was most exemplary in this, for he was able to appeal to the peasants in far-off corners of Japan as well as to the refined aesthetes of Yoshimitsu's court. Obviously the noble is of more importance than the peasant, since he is able to appreciate the fine points of the actor's art and to grasp the spiritual core that is its essence. In an important passage Zeami gives an example of the skillful actor adapting his playing to the late arrival of a noble. We have seen that a complete Noh program of five plays must follow a structure from introduction (*jo*) through development (*ha*) to climax and finale (*kyū*). Only certain kinds of plays and certain manners of playing are adapted to each of these moments. If, however, a spectator of importance enters during the development (*ha*) or the climax (*kyū*) of the program, he would not be receptive to the emotions peculiar to these parts, since he has not yet passed through the introduction. Because of his importance, his arrival will tend to distract the spectators who have viewed the performance from the start. The actor must be able to counteract such an event, not by returning to the opening or to an introductory style, but by interpreting the *ha* or *kyū* passage with his spirit turned slightly toward the introduction. Although already at the development or climax of the performance, he will thus capture the attention of the tardy noble, giving him the feeling of completeness from beginning through the middle and to the end.

There are different kinds of Noh—play and performance—to appeal to different levels of understanding. The connoisseur, Zeami observes, sees with the spirit, whereas the beginner sees only with his eyes. Beginning on the lowest level of sophistication, there is the Noh that appeals to the sense of sight; it includes the more violent plays and more spectacular elements of performance such as fast dances, impressive and colorful costumes, immense wigs. On a slightly higher level is the Noh that speaks to the sense of hearing; it is made up of chant, song, drum and flute music, and the words themselves. On the highest level is the Noh that speaks to the spirit; only the greatest actors can embody it, only the most refined spectators can appreciate it. Here we are on a level close to mysticism, in which the very stillness of the actor, his *frozen dance,* can communicate something deeper, more meaningful, and more beautiful than the more readily perceptible beauties of the other orders. Woe to the actor who judges the level of his audience incorrectly, for he is sure to fail, no matter how skillful he may be.

Zeami divides the accomplishment of the actor into a scale of nine degrees. The actor begins in the middle, attempts to develop to the top, and only then attempts the three lower degrees which might corrupt him if he approached them too early. The lower degrees stress movement, violence; the central degrees stress style, art, skill, and the beginning of the flower; the higher degrees stress the true *flower,* spiritual prowess. Starting from the bottom the degrees are:

9. The violent and corrupt style
8. The powerful and violent style
7. The powerful and meticulous style
6. The superficial but ornamented style
5. The ample and precise style
4. The style of the genuine flower
3. The style of the serene flower
2. The style of the flower both high and deep
1. The style of the marvelous flower

The growth of the actor is clearly related to a spiritual journey, an ascent from the purely physical aspects of an art to its spiritual core, through a constant purification and paring away: an ascesis. The lessons of reflection, discipline, and concentration inhere in such a journey.

It would be a mistake, however, to assume that the spectator is to focus his attention on the spirit, for spirit can only be experienced. For the beholder to become aware of the actor's spirit as the controlling factor would be for him to become aware of the method behind the experience, thus disrupting the experience. Nor are emotions to be overlooked, particularly in all but the highest degrees of Noh. Unlike the Noh audience of today, in Zeami's day people were expected to react quite strongly and emotionally. If the actor playing the part of a madwoman succeeds in moving his audience to tears, "we recognize in him supreme skill," Zeami declares. He later tells us that when a skillful actor dances and chants before an audience, people give free rein to their emotions. The actor who can capture the unconscious emotion of the public is the one who will attain universal renown.[21]

The modern Noh has taken on the atmosphere of what Professor Sieffert calls a *chapel* to such a degree that only with difficulty can we imagine anyone weeping at a performance. It is even more difficult to imagine the spectators, "nobles and commoners alike," uttering cries of admiration or saying to one another, "Yes, indeed, how true, how true!" Zeami's description of such audience reaction can give us some indication of the distance that separates contemporary Noh performances (at least from the audience's point of view) from those of the fifteenth century. Today the elegance and restraint seem to have all but eclipsed any pretense of imitation, and yet the concept of *monomane* or imitation is one of the two fundamental pillars of the Noh.

Zeami and scholars since his day pose two polar concepts as fundamental to Noh: *monomane* and *yūgen*. The first, translated "imitation," "truth," or "realism" (but not of the nineteenth-century variety), attempts to grasp the exterior resemblance; the second, *yūgen*, or "what lies beneath the surface," attempts to soften, to stylize, and to find some hidden essence. Influences from the *monomane* and from the *yūgen* concepts correct each other, and should achieve a dynamic balance. Zeami warns his followers, "Be careful not to turn into a devil or fall into a dance posture." In other words, avoid the extremes of violent realism on the one hand and aestheticism on the other. *Dengaku*, one of the protoforms of Noh, disappeared through hypertrophy of its *yūgen*, for it lost touch with reality and imitation, falling into aestheticism and ultrarefinement. Zeami laments the fact that his own age seems to demand a good deal of *yūgen* in their Noh, but, according to the principle of concordance, he must give them what they require. One wonders whether Zeami's fears have been borne out, for the Noh has continued in the direction of elegance and refinement, losing touch with realism which was an essential part of it in Zeami's day. One wonders too if Zeami's belief that his public required *yūgen* was the result of his court-centered existence. Professor O'Neill reminds us that there were many Noh performers in the fourteenth century who did not give such importance to *yūgen,* but stressed *monomane* and a more "full-blooded style." [22]

For Zeami, imitation of the exterior is a path that leads to an understanding of the character's feelings. Too literal an imitation, however, leads to ugliness and vulgarity, he claims; it also strikes him as old-fashioned. Imitation must be corrected by beauty and elegance, thus giving it the "flower" of interest. Zeami is speaking here of stylization. His approach to the role of the old man is illuminating. Rather than imitating an old man, the actor should simply slow his movements so that each is slightly behind the beat. Zeami observes very neatly that an old man would like to be young, and attempts to give the impression of youth through his movements. Therefore the actor should use youthful movements. But since the character is actually old he cannot quite keep up the tempo, and it is through this slight syncopation that his age is suggested. Such a technique gives pleasure to the audience because it is unusual, unexpected, interesting: "It is as if flowers were blooming on an old tree." [23]

A further check on realism is the expressionless face of the Noh actor. Since the *waki* is simply catalyst to the story of the *shite,* his face must show no emotion whatsoever. The *shite* must express character and emotion through his bearing and movement, for his face too is expressionless or, more often, covered by a mask. The masks are works of art which, depending upon the movement of the actor and the way the light is cast, show varying emotions, although surely fewer now when electric light is used than was possible when sun- and torch-light illuminated the performance.

The difficult term *yūgen,* suggested by the stylized beauty of the mask and the spiritual reality behind it, has been translated in many different ways; indeed it is difficult to pin down, for Zeami used it with differing meanings over a period of thirty-six years. The primary meaning of *yūgen* is "the occult," or as Waley translates it, "what lies beneath the surface." Other meanings, which give the reader an idea of the breadth and complexity of the term, are transcendental phantasm, fathom-less sentiment, transcendental insight, elegance, gracefulness, the subtle, the hint. Sieffert suggests "subtle charm." And Zeami expresses the concept metaphorically by "a white bird with a flower in its beak." *Yūgen,* no doubt, attempts to de-scribe something it can only suggest. If its essence cannot be defined, its results can at least be experienced by those with sufficient sensitivity and background. *Yūgen* results in beauty of many kinds: physical grace, elegance, quietness, and the like. At one point Zeami goes so far as to say that beauty of attitude is the supreme accomplishment. Charm, beauty, and elegance must never be confused with softness, for, without the strength of bone and the firmness of the flesh beneath, the beauty of the skin would not be visible.

The subtlety of *yūgen* results is a highly suggestive perform-ance, in which the spectator must become a part so that he may create what is merely suggested by the actor. The actor's gesture should never supplant the ideal gesture. Zeami phrases this principle very effectively when he advises, "Move your spirit 10/10, move your body 7/10." This graphic formula sug-gests the strong control that the spirit must exercise, leading the body in its movements, yet always contributing more than the body, so that the spectator, following the spirit, will be able to complete the movement himself. Such a technique might well lead to the true *flower,* the unusual and interesting.

The concept of the *flower* comes as something of a surprise to anyone who has seen much Noh today; the actors, having for centuries followed traditions to the letter, now allow little if any room for individuality or surprise.[24] And yet Zeami states that, despite the inheritance of a predecessor's style, "there are some kinds of performance which come from your own ability." [25] Nogami even goes so far as to say that Zeami wants to create suspense, a sense of bafflement. There are many flowers of the moment, which charm and interest an audience, but there is only one true flower: something quite special, in contrast with *yūgen* and *monomane,* which might even be *wrong* if done by someone without proper training and skill. Zeami describes it as "an oasis in the desert." I think Western theater may provide something like the one true flower in the great moments we remember as profound experiences, which startled us by their daring and yet struck us as absolutely right. Such moments, which in the hands of anyone but a great artist would have shocked us by their incongruity, have been transformed into an experience terrible and beautiful: Yonnel's cry of "Malheur!" in *La Reine morte,* Judith Anderson's "What's done cannot be undone" in *Macbeth.*

The actor who has attained the flower follows the norm but he gives something more, something of himself. Only after long discipline and preparation is liberty allowed. Zeami speaks of the actor who has attained the highest art as existing beyond words, for his role is as spiritual as it is dramatic. He has arrived at unity, at the ideal form, the model suggested by spirit; he stands now outside technique. Such a metaphysical goal at the summit of Noh art, coupled with its search for beauty in form, rhythm, and music, explains to some extent the fascination it has exercised and continues to exercise for Westerners. Since the middle of the nineteenth century, Westerners have been following a parallel route in the poetic search for an absolute, for the unity of a lost paradise, and for the evocation of, in Poe's words, "supernal loveliness."

Professor Sieffert no doubt supplies a healthy corrective when he warns us that many seemingly esoteric or mystical interpretations of the *Treatises* originate in linguistic uncertainties in the text arising from the condition of the manuscript and the differences in usage between past and present-day Japanese. The *secret* tradition of the Noh is secret, not because it is abstruse and esoteric, but because it was meant to be kept only for the members of the school—their "tricks of the trade," so to speak. After these sobering suggestions Professor Sieffert recognizes the religious purpose of the Noh, an effort to "translate a reality more real than vain appearances, a 'surreality.'" Its language, he remarks, is sometimes strangely similar to that of the surrealists.[26] A dreamlike atmosphere and sense of timelessness, as well, relate it to that movement.

The Noh has probably changed little in its fundamentals since the time of Zeami. What I have said regarding the *Treatises* is largely true of today's Noh. As I suggested, however, three or four changes have occurred; all these can be ascribed, I believe, to a respect for tradition and a feeling that after several hundred years the Noh has become something holy, something that cannot be changed without damaging its spirit. Such an attitude has, paradoxically, brought about four notable changes, some of which I have already remarked upon: The balance between realism and *yūgen* has been lost and the scale has gone far down in favor of the latter. A relatively pliable tradition has become frozen into a rigid traditionalism hard to break. The audience, which once apparently reacted with some emotion, is now expected to sit in sacred—if not somnolent—silence. Most important of all: the tempo of the performance has slowed excessively. A Noh performance in Zeami's day took perhaps half the time it requires today.[27]

Obviously there is no reason for the Noh today to stick hard and fast to Zeami's rules or to the fifteenth-century form of the Noh simply to follow tradition. But Zeami was an extraordinarily intelligent man of the theater, and one wonders whether the Noh might not profit from a fresh reading of Zeami's texts and a fresh consideration of the needs of its audience today.

Despite the many centuries that separate us from Zeami, his

theory of the drama offers us the same kind of rich food for thought we find in Aristotle's *Poetics*. The reader has perhaps found meaningful perspectives for himself in the foregoing exposition of Zeami's system. Here I would like to recall one particularly rewarding use made of Noh in the West, an experiment carried on by a man who had never witnessed a Noh performance, but whose personality and genius allowed him to absorb a good deal of its spirit through a study of texts and theoretical works: Jacques Copeau.

Jacques Copeau is at the source of many of the new vistas opened to the theater in the twentieth century. Indeed, without Copeau and the disciples he inspired, it is unlikely that we should have witnessed the flourishing of the French theater between 1930 and 1960. Giraudoux, Anouilh, Montherlant, Beckett, Ionesco, and Genet are inconceivable without the work accomplished by Copeau and the Cartel des Quatre.

Jacques Copeau was one of the first to become aware of the rich training possibilities offered by the Noh and other forms of Oriental theater. His notebooks preserved at the Bibliothèque de l'Arsenal show the extent of his interest. There are pages of notes devoted to books and articles on the theaters of Asia, suggesting fertile comparisons with more familiar forms. With his predilection for a theater that was refined, highly stylized, religious in essence, Copeau was prepared to appreciate the Noh. It is a theater, he points out, that accommodates the Japanese need for idealism, unreality, and poetry; such theater is carefully guarded from "the logic that has depoetized our Occidental theater." In a letter dated August 9, 1946, he establishes analogies between the Catholic Mass and the Noh drama. The Introit, he observes, corresponds to the passage on the bridge where the *waki* makes his entrance, "like a prologue that expresses the general sentiment." The travel song and the climactic dance are fixed moments in the ceremony, just as the actors themselves are fixed into the functions of *waki, shite* and followers, priests and acolytes. Instead of altar, choir, pulpit, we have the fixed forms of the Noh stage: background of painted pine, the *waki*'s pillar, the *shite*'s pil-

lar, the *metsuke-bashira* or pillar on which the actor fixes his
eyes, and so forth. As in the Church, the Noh program observes the seasons of the year, certain plays being performed
only in autumn, others adapted to winter, spring, or summer.
And the schools of training are more like seminaries than
conservatories.

In March, 1924, the students of Copeau's School at the
Vieux-Colombier were to present a Noh play; unfortunately
one of the principal actors fell and sprained his knee, and the
performance was never held. The rehearsals, however, had
been of immense value to the students and had resulted in an
impressive final rehearsal. Granville-Barker, present at the
last rehearsal, congratulated the performers: "Until today I
didn't believe in the virtue of dramatic training, but you have
convinced me. Henceforth, you can hope for everything."

In 1931 Copeau explained why the school had undertaken
the production of a Noh: "Because this form is the strictest
one we know and requires of the interpreter an exceptional
technical preparation." [28] It was not Copeau himself who had
prepared the production, but his colleague and friend Suzanne
Bing. Madame Bing's work notes are preserved among the
Copeau manuscripts at the Bibliothèque de l'Arsenal. During
the summer of 1923, using the books of Arthur Waley and
Noël Péri, Mme Bing and her students had made a study of
the Noh theater. They were struck by the similarities between
its dramatic "laws" and those Copeau had begun to discern in
his own work: "The Noh appeared to be the application of the
musical, dramatic, and plastic studies upon which, for three
years, we had nourished our students, so much so that their
various improvisations, the goal of these studies, was related
in style to the Noh much more than to any contemporary
work." [29]

The play chosen was *Kantan*, a well-known work sometimes
attributed to Zeami, but probably of later vintage. It relates
how Rosei sets out from his village in search of fortune. In the
town of Kantan he sleeps upon a famous pillow that causes the
sleeper to see his entire future in a dream. When Rosei wakes

a few minutes later, the dinner put on to cook before he went to sleep is not yet ready, but in his dream he has lived his whole life. Concluding that "Life is but a dream," he returns home to his village.

Madame Bing was wise enough to realize that an imitation of the Noh style by young French students, for a French audience, and with French teachers, would have resulted in something highly artificial. Equally to be avoided was an adaptation and deformation of the work according to European dramatic conventions:

> We would present as best we could the work as it is, seeking our inspiration in the Noh and in the style of Japanese art. We would attempt to see just what this art and this style are made up of. We would take as the base of our movement and our *mise en scène* all the traditional restrictions instead of rejecting a single one; we would confine ourselves within their narrow limits, rather than attempting to escape them. It is within this framework, depending upon this solid base, that we would allow ourselves the liberty of transposition.

The translation was made with full knowledge of the importance of rhythm and continuity in such a play. Since the Noh takes its point of departure from truth (or *monomane* as Zeami calls it), the actors began by using natural inflections. Because the Noh speech is actually declaimed and chanted, however, they transposed the natural rhythms and inflections to music and wrote them down with musical notation. Particularly lyrical or emotional moments were aided by the flute, while two drums (one dull, the other very sharp) gave a subtle, natural rhythm which, according to Mme Bing, seemed to command the movement of the actors and the very breathing of the spectators. Following the Japanese practice, all the solo parts were played by men. The small number of men available, however, required putting some women in the chorus; the female voices, Madame Bing perceptively notes, changed the intonation and volume of the chorus. An assistant was on stage to hand the necessary props to the actors, arrange their costumes, and perform all the functions assigned to a Noh prop man.

I should like to quote at some length Mme Bing's notes on the acting style itself. Her comments and the preceding notes indicate what a surprising degree of authenticity of feeling, if not of precise gesture, was achieved by this group of serious, devoted students of theater before they could have seen a Noh performance or even, in all probability, have heard a record of the music.

> Faces are impassive, gestures slow and solemn; a fine discretion, a fine control order the expression, so that the simple gesture of a father posing his hand on the shoulder of his lost son gives enough intensity of emotion to bring tears to the eyes. We chastened our gestures.
>
> We ennobled our postures, attempting to make of them a melody of noble and beautiful poses, one engendering the next according to the logic of the drama. A little more daring and obedience, and we composed the dances, one slower, another faster, as required.
>
> The Noh actor must never forget that he is *acting* a poem; he must refuse to call on facile personal emotion, which works directly on the emotion of the audience. The emotion must arise from the poetry itself, a hard discipline for very young actors full of the impatient ardor of self-expression. The Noh actor leaves the stage exhausted by this constraint.

The measure of success of this experiment, so distant in spirit from many facile "adaptations" we have seen or heard of, lies not in the praise of Granville-Barker or others who saw the final rehearsal. It lies in Copeau's judgment, for Copeau himself was never one to be easily satisfied: "This Noh, as I witnessed it in its final rehearsal, for its depth of scenic understanding, control, style, quality of emotion, remains for me one of the jewels, one of the secret riches of our production at the Vieux-Colombier." [30]

The lessons of restraint, control, meaningful movement, inner strength, concentration, and sacrifice which such a production can impart have borne fruit in the thought, teaching, and performances of the outstanding French directors and actors who were Copeau's disciples. Charles Dullin often spoke of his admiration for the Oriental theater, and admitted a great debt to the ancient Japanese theater: "it was by studying its origins and its history that I consolidated my ideas about the renewal of the theater," [31] he claimed. The West cannot simply imitate, there must be a process of transposition, Dullin goes on to say. But we cannot afford to ignore the examples of realistic and poetic transposition presented by the Japanese theater, and the effects it obtains from rhythm and *la plastique*. In training actors to move, Dullin liked to use a half mask, for it depersonalized the actor once he had learned to develop his own personality, thereby imposing a new discipline. Dullin believed that the actor, instead of using either a personalized or a depersonalized approach to his characters, might approach them from the inside and from the outside at the same time, thus creating a more complete and more theatrical characterization. Like the Noh actor who sits in front of a mirror studying his mask before he enters the stage, feeling his way into the part, Dullin's masked actor must find his movements no longer through his own senses, but through the personality imposed by the mask covering his true face. In training, moreover, the mask helps the student to relax, to overcome his timidity, and perhaps most important of all, it makes him use his entire body as an instrument of expression, since he cannot depend upon facial expressiveness.

Dullin's colleague, friend, and biographer, Lucien Arnaud, now director of the Ecole Dullin, tells how one year Dullin used a Noh type stage for his production of François Porché's *Tsar Lenine*. Dullin did not attempt to imitate the construction and design of the Noh stage, but used a stage that was bare except for four pillars and thus was reminiscent of the Noh; the place of action was suggested by words and movements rather than by decor of any kind. In the first act, the center of the stage represented Paris, the edge, Russia. Time, too, was compressed. Like the *waki* of the Noh, an actor could take three steps and be across the continent, a few seconds corresponding to a voyage of weeks. "The *mise en scène* at the Atelier," said one reviewer, "has first of all this superior virtue: that since it is destined for the theater, it is purely

93

theatrical. . . . In the center of the stage [in Act II], among four wooden columns, in a decor without backdrop, without *trompe l'œil,* is Petrograd." [32]

Jean-Louis Barrault, Dullin's most famous student, recalls the days at the Atelier when Dullin inspired in him and his fellow students a great love for the theater of the Far East, and particularly the Noh. Despite his knowledge of the Noh, Barrault was unable to witness a performance until the Kanze troupe came to the Théâtre des Nations in 1957. At that time he was surprised to feel utterly untouched by the performance. He was not alone, for almost every review of the production stressed the feeling of strangeness, bafflement, confusion, and bewilderment experienced by the European audience, surely less prepared than Barrault for such a spectacle. Gabriel Marcel declared that he had never felt so Boeotian in his life, and Georges Lerminier admitted that the Parisian spectator could only stand on the threshold of such an experience. He wisely added: "Let us not give in to our Occidental prejudices. . . . This is a privileged theatrical place, not a vulgar 'scenic apparatus,' but a ciborium, where artists, like priests, are celebrating a ritual for initiates." [33]

Most Westerners are not afforded the opportunity to study Noh ceremony on its home ground, to attempt to become a member of the faithful. But Barrault, during a tour of the Orient in 1960, was able to witness another performance of Noh, this time in a setting eminently conducive to an understanding of the form. In his *Journal de bord* describing the tour, he devotes a chapter to the Noh, remarking on several interesting aspects. As might be expected, Barrault—disciple of Artaud that he is—was struck by the intimate blending of dance, music, mime, text, chant, which makes of the Noh a total kind of theater. Particularly fascinating, however, is Barrault's sensitivity to the symbolism of the fan and to the inwardness of the Noh experience. For him the fan is not simply the symbol of sword, brush, bottle, or branch; it is much deeper than that, for it represents the very thought and inner life of the character. Reading Barrault's description is almost like reading Artaud's evocation of the living hieroglyphs which were the Balinese dancers:

> The *shite,* strikingly immobile, has opened wide his fan. His inner life is there offered to all: his soul unfolded. While the Chorus chants the torments of his character in unison, he makes his fan undulate and tremble. We have the impression that these emanations from the soul literally come from the object itself. The soul quivers. Our eyes are riveted on the fan. The actor's power of concentration is such that, from a distance, he can direct our attention upon this determined point. There is no lighting, yet it seems that the entire stage is plunged into darkness and only the fan is luminous.[34]

While our attention is centered on the fan, the apparently immobile actor has moved, but so subtly that we are unaware of it. So concentrated is the acting, so intense the emotion for Barrault, that he wishes the actor would move even more slowly. The movement, rather than being imposed from the outside, seems to be a result of the actor's own inner intensity, the spirit moving 10/10 and the body only 7/10. Summing up the moving, dreamlike ("a dream one could have touched") experience, Barrault writes, "I had never seen anything so beautiful, so internal, so magical. It seemed to me that I had lived physically inside a soul." [35]

Although Barrault has not attempted to produce any Noh plays or to use any specific Noh techniques, he was clearly most impressed by them. In an interview on June 10, 1964, he spoke of the importance of the physical manifestations of theatrical experience. "Everything must be channeled through the physical," he said, "and at that moment theater comes into existence." Such a physical experience is precisely what Barrault is sensitive to in the Noh production. While many Westerners seem to feel that the Noh is so spiritualized that it has become almost immaterial, Barrault is able to project himself into the intensely concentrated inner world of the actor.

For many years, Barrault confessed, the Zen archery book was his *livre de chevet.* This work teaches that technique is more important than hitting the mark; that once you learn this truth and perfect your technique, you almost unconsciously hit

the mark. With his particular leanings and theatrical background Barrault was better prepared than most of us for
grasping the spirit of the Noh. But beyond that he is tremen-
dously interested in specific techniques. His dream, he said, was
to spend several years studying the various forms of Oriental
theater; then he could train his own actors to use Oriental
techniques in his own theater.

THE EXPERIENCE OF NOH

Until now we have spoken chiefly of Noh drama as text and
as theory, realizing all along that nothing can replace the
actual experience of Noh in performance. Before 1945 or
1950 few Westerners had had the opportunity to see a Noh in
Japan. Since then, however, a number of factors have made it
possible for many of us to receive a firsthand impression of
Noh: increased world travel, cultural interchange, and most
particularly the visits of the Kanze troupe to the Théâtre des
Nations in 1957, and the performances directed by Sadayo
Kita at the Institute for Advanced Study in Theater Arts
(IASTA) in 1964. Unfortunately, these experiences have
rarely been more than superficial, since visits tend to be brief
and spectators are not too well prepared. But at least steps
have been taken in the direction of a thorough understanding
of one of the world's major theatrical genres. From this understanding have grown several experiments with profound implications for Western dramatic art, for they point to new directions that lead forward to innovations on an ever-broadening
horizon, and at the same time back to earlier, all-but-forgotten
forms of theater.

We have already spoken of the Chinese drama, *The Butterfly Dream,* performed at IASTA in 1961. Since its foundation
in 1958 the Institute for Advanced Studies in Theater Arts has
been studying the theatrical traditions of many countries. Its
purpose has been double: to make American theater aware of
other theatrical traditions which may help our search for a
more meaningful, comprehensive, and artistic theatrical style;
to enrich the background and training of young American

professional actors by allowing them the opportunity of working with the finest directors and artists the other traditions
afford. In 1964 IASTA brought from Japan a leading actor of
the Kita Noh Troupe, Sadayo Kita, and his assistant Akiyo
Tomoeda. With a group of young actors they undertook to
present *Ikkaku Sennin,* a Noh play belonging to the demon
play category, the final section of a complete Noh performance. This play was chosen for two main reasons: first, since a
Kabuki drama based upon *Ikkaku Sennin* had been presented
at IASTA several years earlier, the differing treatments of the
same story facilitated a comparison of the two theatrical techniques. Second, the demon play is more dramatic than the
other types of Noh, and at the same time, since it *is* violent,
it lacks *yūgen* which is so difficult to define and even more difficult to instill in non-Japanese actors.

The stage of the IASTA theater was completely rebuilt as a
Noh stage; it was made just slightly larger than those in
Japan, to allow for the somewhat larger bodies of American
actors. It is a tradition in Japan for the aspiring young Noh
actors to polish the mirror-like floor of the Noh stage by
scrubbing it with leftover bean curd early in the morning.
When Kita and Tomoeda found that the young American
actors were willing to do this job, they were hopeful that these
Occidentals would be able to capture the spirit of Noh.

Costumes and masks for the performance were made in
Japan. The Noh actors and musicians taped the entire performance in Japanese for Radio Corporation of America;
then the musicians made a second tape, taking their cues
through earphones so that only the music would be on the tape
used in the American performances. The American actors
were to learn the same intonations and chants that the Japanese used. This posed a particularly difficult problem in preparing the text. Using Frank Hoff's translation, IASTA's playwright in residence, William Packard, undertook to adapt it so
that it would correspond syllable for syllable to the Japanese
text. Furthermore, since certain syllables are elongated and
others are pronounced in a rapid staccato manner, it was neces-

sary to take care to put in such places English syllables capable of elongation or staccato. That the Packard adaptation was made, and that the American actors undertook to learn the traditional voice patterns and inflections of the Japanese text, are symptomatic of the spirit of seriousness and authenticity at IASTA. This unusual, and very successful, adaptation was published in *Players Magazine* (March, 1965); the Hoff translation, the original Japanese text in Roman letters, and the Packard version are set next to one another in three columns.

Just as they attempted to reproduce the sounds, the American actors studied for many weeks to reproduce the movements of the Noh actors. The first four weeks of rehearsal were spent simply in drilling the actors in basic movement, a movement so unlike any in the West that even the trained dancers had trouble. In fact, Kita finally found that those who had not had any Western dance training were better able to learn the Noh techniques, for they were more willing to learn an entirely new approach. The manner of walking in Noh, for example, requires that the actor slide his foot along the floor, raising only one part at a time. Sitting in the usual Japanese fashion is extremely painful for a person who has had no practice, particularly when he must assume the position for twenty or thirty minutes at a time.

The prominent American choreographer and director Jerome Robbins, fascinated by the Noh, witnessed many rehearsals. He spoke of them enthusiastically, and particularly of the new perspectives they had given him on American theater: "It has thrown a whole new light on theater for me, particularly on American acting styles. Our acting is limitless, casual, sloppy, anything-you-want. But this style refines and refines and refines movement." [36] Elsewhere he summarized his impressions of the Noh rehearsals thus:

It is like turning on a light that illuminates another terrain of the theater. Through extreme disciplines and limitations of space, costume, voice, action, expression, gestures, music and pitch; through the distillations of the essence of drama; and through an awesome, tender,

and religious love of the theater, its props, costumes, and the very
surface of the stage itself, a final poetic release of beauty is achieved.[37]

Only after basic movements had been imparted was the
actual play undertaken, and only after the movements of the
play had been learned was the attempt made to go inward to
find the spirit of the play. That the actors succeeded to some
degree in adding the mysterious flavor of *yūgen* to the play is
indicated by Kita's comment: "I think that in learning how to
add *yūgen,* the actors really acquainted themselves fully with
Noh." [38] Before leaving, Kita expressed his amazement that
Western actors should have been able to perform a Noh play
so successfully. "I had been disturbed by the fearful thought of
spoiling all the fragrance and depth of the Noh form but,
after several weeks' rehearsing with the American actors, I am
looking forward to seeing how the American people will absorb and utilize the technique, spirit and *yūgen* that is Noh
theater." [39]

It is no doubt too early to see the effects of such training, but
we know that Jerome Robbins has said that a Noh project he
had had in mind would become a reality. William Packard,
writing in *First Stage* (Summer, 1965), reports: "Those
members of the theatrical profession who were searching in
their own work for something beyond mere naturalism were
especially delighted by this reproduction of an acting style
which was so poetic and controlled. Many commented that
they intended to use the principles behind this production in
their own future work." Since the project was largely aimed at
giving American actors a new dimension in training, the reactions of the actors are of special interest. One performer,
Virginia Blue, was impressed by the manner in which the Noh
actor invites the audience to participate intellectually as well as
emotionally. Instead of delivering a message as we tend to do
here, she claimed, a suggestive technique is used which forces
the audience to exercise both imagination and reason. Peter
Blaxill, who played one of the leading roles, said he had
learned to use nuances of which he had never been aware: "I
think already my brief acquaintance with Noh has heightened

99

my acting power and given me new tools with which to
work." [40] "Another actor," Packard tells us, "stressed the self-
less spirit of the Noh, as opposed to the egotism in the
American theater." [41] A devastating comment on New York
theatrical agents, by the way, is the fact that some agents
prevented their actors from getting into the IASTA production on the grounds that the actors might be masked and
therefore unrecognizable: the performance would not serve as
a showcase for them. [42]

The IASTA production featured a true Noh performed by
Occidentals in a style approximating that of the original work.
No one claims that the young Americans achieved in six weeks
the depth, beauty, and perfection that Japanese actors take
years to attain, but the experiment was obviously beneficial to
the performers. It was beneficial to the audience as well, not
necessarily as a perfected artistic achievement, but as a revelation of what Noh strives for in performance. The vast majority of the people at the production were not specialists in
Oriental theater and had learned about Noh drama only
through texts and theoretical works.

A different approach is embodied in those Western dramatic
pieces that take the Noh drama as their point of departure and
transpose its elements into a mode more meaningful for modern, Western audiences, while hoping to remain faithful to the
spirit, of Noh. Few of these have been successful. We have
already referred to Yeats's creations. Some more recent adaptations deserve brief mention here, if only to point out that
they are adaptations in every sense of the word, since they take
their point of departure in the Noh drama itself, but arrive at
something quite different in spirit. Bertolt Brecht and Yukio
Mishima use these old plays, much as Anouilh or Cocteau used
Greek tragedies, as an accepted form within which to cast their
modern perspectives.

Brecht's *Yea Sayer* and *Nay Sayer,* two short didactic pieces
that recount the same story but with different endings, are
based upon *Taniko,* as translated into English by Arthur

Waley. Elizabeth Hauptmann, using Waley's translation, adapted *Taniko* and translated it into German; it was she who drew Brecht's attention to the play. Brecht's first version, presented in 1930 with music by Kurt Weill, follows Waley's text almost word for word, making only the changes necessary to adapt it to the particular lesson Brecht had in mind: that the individual must sacrifice himself to the good of the whole. In the Japanese play, a youth leaves his sick mother to accompany a group on a ritual climb into the mountains, there to pray for his mother's recovery. But he falls ill along the way, and the Great Custom decrees that he must be hurled into the valley below. The pilgrims, "sighing for the sad ways of the world and the bitter ordinances of it," toss the boy to his death. In Brecht's play, the boy goes off with the group to seek medicine in a neighboring valley, but with the same dire results to himself.

When this "learning piece" was played for young students, they objected that the boy was foolish to have agreed to his own murder. After giving the matter some thought, Brecht apparently decided they were right, and that the play should actually teach that Great Customs are not right just because they are venerable: we must change the wrongs of our world. Accordingly, Brecht uses the developments in the earlier version, but then has the boy turn to the pilgrims and refuse to let them throw him below, teaching them that we are going to institute a new great Custom: to think anew in each new situation.[43]

Brecht's operas, closer in spirit to his other *Lehrstücke* than to the traditional Noh, lack the spirituality, sense of ritual, intense inner concentration, and poetic suggestivity identified with Noh. If they must be compared with any form of play, they resemble the Sunday School pageants that teach in no uncertain terms the lessons our elders deem wise.

Yukio Mishima's *Five Modern Noh Plays* are striking for the skill with which the author has succeeded in finding modern equivalents for the situations in the traditional plays. They do not, however, preserve either the outer form or the inner spirit of Noh. The form Mishima has given his little dramas is entirely Western, and reflects the changes effected in Japanese drama since the middle of the nineteenth century. In his introduction to the English translation, Donald Keene makes two statements that point up the fundamental differences between the two forms of theater. "There is no question," Professor Keene states, "but that these plays have in their own right an immediate and powerful appeal even to people who are normally indifferent to Japanese drama." [44] This is tantamount to saying that, unlike the Noh plays, this kind of drama requires no preparation, no discipline from the audience; like Brecht's plays it reaches out to them with its explicit meanings, rather than working in a more subtle, poetic manner. It cannot be denied, however, that Mishima's plays do preserve some of the overtones of the supernatural so essential to the Noh, but seen in a modern perspective and often in scientific, psychiatric terms in which everything somehow seems logical and explicable. As Professor Keene notes, "Inevitably we feel that the story makes better sense as told by Mishima." This is no doubt why such a treatment appeals more immediately to our hypertrophied logical faculties. Our preference for the modern version also indicates the amount of richness and poetry that have been lost in the transition.

Another element has been lost as well, an element of vital importance to the Noh—style. For these dramas are meant to be presented in a modern, representational style. That *The Damask Drum* was performed in traditional Noh style in 1955, and that *The Lady Aoi* was sung in 1956 as a *Western*-style opera, do not alter the fact that these are modern Western-type plays rather than Noh plays of any kind, either in structure or in spirit. Once this distinction is understood, one may appreciate *Five Modern Noh Plays* for what they are, extremely clever and occasionally moving treatments in modern terms of tales also used as bases for Noh dramas.

The most successful "modern Noh play" has not been the work of a Japanese but of an Englishman, Benjamin Britten. While in Japan some years ago Britten, following the advice of a friend, had gone to see a Noh performance. He was so impressed by one play he saw, *Sumidagawa*, that he returned to see it again, and determined to write a version of the story treated in terms of his own musical idiom. He asked William Plomer, the friend who had sent him to the Noh in the first place, to write a libretto based on the play *Sumidagawa*. Plomer follows the story, and even the dialogue, of the Noh play very closely; so similar are the texts that one can quite easily follow the English work by reading the translation of the Noh play, which has sometimes been taken word for word.

Plomer changed the setting from Japan to the fens of East Anglia on the banks of the Curlew River. It is here that a woman, mad with grief over the loss of her son, kidnaped a year ago, comes, asking the Ferryman to take her across to the other side of the river. During the crossing the Ferryman explains the crowd gathered on the far side of the river: just a year ago a man and a kidnaped child came along this way. The child, weary from traveling, died here and was buried, and the folk have gathered now to pray for him on the anniversary of his death. The Madwoman realizes that the Ferryman is telling about her son. After crossing the river in a highly stylized, symbolic fashion, they disembark. The Madwoman, approaching the grave, weeps, and finally joins the others in praying for her son. The child's ghost emerges from the grave and the mother seeks to embrace him, but they inhabit different worlds, and as the ghost disappears the mother is left to her loneliness and despair.

When the British Broadcasting Corporation presented *Curlew River* in 1964, the commentator stressed two things. First, Britten's work, although written for singers, is not to be thought of as an opera. It is rather "a parable for church performance." This points, I think, to an interesting parallel with Noh. Although Noh is secularized to some degree, it still retains strong religious overtones and almost inevitably carries a Buddhist message. Britten was apparently aiming not at an opera for the general public, but at something that would be meaningful in a Christian context, for the *faithful,* much as a

Noh play is meaningful and accessible only to those who are "initiated," so to speak, in the way of Noh.

Second, the BBC commentator stressed that *Curlew River* is not to be thought of as Oriental in any sense. Like the Noh, it employs extreme stylization, a sense of stillness, quiet, and formality. But this parable for church performance is a re-thinking of *Sumidagawa* in Christian terms and for a Western, Christian audience. "Memory of this play has seldom left Britten's mind in the years since he saw it in Japan," we are told.[45] Seeking parallels in English drama, Britten found them in the medieval mystery plays. The setting by the riverbank might well have served for a mystery play; the simple staging might have been used in a church. A moral story about human suffering, enacted by an all-male cast of ecclesiastics with a limited instrumental accompaniment seemed to suggest striking similarities to the manner of presentation of a Noh play. After eight years of thought and meditation, *Sumidagawa* was transmuted into *Curlew River*. Using music and sentiments that might be meaningful to a Christian, Western audience, Britten has successfully created an experience similar to that of the Noh for a Japanese.

There are four soloists in *Curlew River:* the Abbott who is a kind of chorus leader; the Ferryman who corresponds to the *waki;* a Traveler (the *waki*'s follower); the role of the Boy; and the Madwoman, who plays the role of the *shite*. The latter is sung by a tenor, the spirit of the Boy by an alto, while the others are sung by bass and baritone. The music is extremely simple, based chiefly on an old plainsong, "Te lucis ante terminum," which is sung by the chorus at the beginning and at the end of the performance. One is never aware of an aria; rather, the vocal line resembles a chant, at times almost monotonous. Dissonances frequently occur, and the soloists use slow glissando and portamento to give the impression of passing over quarter tones.

The Noh orchestra is composed of two or three drums and a single flute. Britten's accompaniment is extremely sparse, but he has made allowance for Western musical taste in composing his score. Seven musicians play: flute, horn, viola, double bass, harp, chamber organ, and percussion. The latter is made up of five small untuned drums, five small bells, and one large tuned gong. Like the vocal line, the accompaniment is often extremely simple, although occasionally it becomes quite "musical," melodious, and particularly at entrance passages, notably rhythmical.

The costumes are simple; at first, all the actors appear in monk's habit. Later, the soloists change to appropriate costumes. Such a change corresponds to the change that usually takes place before the second half of a Noh play.

Britten's parable strikes me as astoundingly successful in re-creating for us a quasi-ritual, quasi-theatrical experience very much in the spirit of the Noh. An important element here is, I believe, the stylization imposed by the music. If Britten had simply adapted the words of the play, *Curlew River* could not have left us with the feeling that it is a ceremonious performance. But once Britten added music with a strong ritual flavor and deep emotional overtones for a Westerner even remotely familiar with the Christian religion, then stylization in performance had to follow. As a musician, Britten was no doubt more sensitive to the musical, tonal aspects of the Noh than he was to the ritualized movement. But the style and tempo of his music show that he was aware that a certain kind of movement was necessary. Had he been able to secure singers who were at the same time dancers able to find the visual correspondent to his plainsong score, then he would have found as perfect a "Noh for the West" as one might dream of.

Curlew River, which Britten calls a "parable," may help us to understand a little the so-called didactic element of the Noh. In both genres, the spectator is struck by the emotion transposed to an aesthetic level; if a didactic element is to be felt, it must come through the general lines of the story and through what the observer already knows of its content or dialogue. In the parable for church performance, as in the Noh, the words are often so distorted for aesthetic and emotional purposes that they are incomprehensible. It is almost ironical that one can understand what is happening and being said in Britten's "Christian transmutation" by referring to the strictly Buddhist text of Motomasa. The Christianness of the transmutation is largely due to the music from the Christian tradition and to the costumes, which recall the Christian Middle Ages. In any work that is faithful to the spirit of the Noh, meaning comes to us not through the words alone, or even primarily, but through other aural and visual means.

If *Curlew River* is an anomaly among Britten's works, there is another Western writer who has consistently written dramas that, although very different from the Noh, present curious parallels to the austerity, simplicity, and concentration of Noh. Samuel Beckett has said, "I am not at all well acquainted with Noh drama or Oriental theater in general and have made no attempt to use such techniques in my plays." [46] He is familiar, however, with the plays of William Butler Yeats, and is perhaps acquainted with the Fennolosa-Pound volume, *Noh or Accomplishment.* Whether or not there is any influence from the Orient, direct or indirect, what is striking here is the degree to which Beckett's plays embody certain elements of the Noh theater. Indeed, the critical reception accorded the Noh troupe at the Théâtre des Nations was not so different from that given Beckett's plays earlier. Robert Kemp (*Le Monde,* June 27, 1957) was bored by the Japanese work, and spoke of the torpor, the slowness of the performance, and the insignificance of the subjects. One can well imagine him making the same comments after seeing Beckett's plays.

A more adventurous and perceptive critic, Marcel Ginglaris, comments: "It would not be so paradoxical if some day an Occidental author should speak of Noh as an ultramodern theatrical technique." [47] Ginglaris was aware of the point of contact between the old and the new, the classic and the experimental. The avant-garde, Ionesco has said, is not only seeking new forms of theater; it is also attempting to return to primitive (but not elementary) theater as well. Beckett's work, in the context of the Noh, is a good example of such a return. The fact that Beckett is today recognized as one of the most

Rangda attacks the prince in the Balinese Rangda drama. The monster's brightly painted mask features horrendous tusks and bulbous eyes. Her attendant, wearing a comic buck-toothed mask, watches from the background. (*Photo:* author)

The Rangda play. Above. The Prime Minister, a comic character, is assailed by Rangda's attendant. The latter features the same pendulous breasts and dangling intestines that decorate Rangda. (*Photo:* author) *Below.* The dramatic encounter between the evil monster, Rangda, and the benign monster, the Barong. Rangda holds a magic cloth which renders her invincible. (*Photo:* author)

The Beautiful Bait, presented by the Foo Hsing. *Above*. The evil Prime Minister. Again the human features are stylized by symbolic makeup, and the theatricality is stressed by colorful costume, impressive headdress, and patently false beard. (*Photo:* Foo Hsing Opera School) *Below*. A fight scene. The four flags and pheasant feathers indicate that the young man is a general. The fight is stylized in acrobatic fashion. (*Photo:* Foo Hsing Opera School)

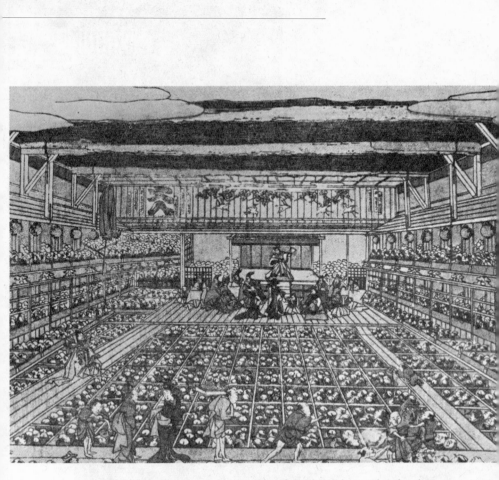

An Edo theater about 1802. Considered the finest form taken by the Kabuki theater, this structure exhibits striking parallels with Elizabethan playhouses, and corresponds in many ways to the ideal of Antonin Artaud. Note that each member of the audience is near at least one acting area, and that many are entirely surrounded by the hanamichi. At left an actor poses, at right a vendor sells food, while at the rear people enter and a fight appears to be going on. (*Photo:* Waseda University)

Above. Onoe Baiko as the monster in the latter half of *Momiji-gari* (*The Maple-Viewing*). Wig, costume, and pattern are enlarged. Note the stylized makeup which, unlike Chinese makeup, does not obliterate the features but stresses them. (*Photo:* Shochiku) *Below.* Onoe Shōroku as Tadanobu in *Yoshitsune Sembonzakura* (*Yoshitsune's Thousand Cherry Trees*). The curtain has closed at the end of the scene, and Tadanobu (in reality a fox who has taken on the shape of a loyal retainer) makes an impressive *roppo* exit which reveals his joy and his animal spirits. Aragoto makeup stresses muscular structure of body and face, while the movement shows almost unbelievable strength and tension. (*Photo:* Shochiku)

Onoe Shōroku as the defeated General Tomomori in *Yoshitsune Sembonzakura*. Preferring death to shame, the general ties an anchor about his waist and tosses it into the sea. Anchor, rope, costume, and wig are all exaggerated and grotesque. (*Photo:* Shochiku)

akamura Utaemon as the *oiran* Yatsuhashi in *Kagotsurube*. The hero of the play, the pock-marked Jirozaemon, is struck dumb with love at his first view of the beautiful courtesan. Gorgeously blossoming cherry trees, and splendidly bedecked courtesans who, because of their high geta, must steady themselves on the shoulders of attendants, are standard sights in the colorful licensed districts of the Kabuki stage. (*Photo:* Shochiku)

TERAKOYA. Above. The late Ichikawa Danjūrō in a heroic pose. The pines on his robe stand for his name, Matsuomaru. The fur hat represents hair that has grown long because Matsuo has been ill. Note the total use of facial muscles. (*Photo:* Shochiku) *Below.* Matsuo threatens Genzo. Because Genzo is a schoolmaster, the samurai disdains to draw his sword. Such poses are frequent in heroic Kabuki plays. (*Photo:* Shochiku)

BENTEN THE THIEF at the University of Hawaii, directed by Earle Ernst. *Above*. Act I, before the Lotus Temple. (*Photo:* Stan Rivera, Honolulu) *Below*. Final tableau from Act III, scene 1. After a ballet-like fight with the police, the five thieves pose victoriously. Note the wide, shallow proportions of the stage, the decorative upper fringe, and the hanamichi. (*Photo:* Stan Rivera, Honolulu)

THE MONSTROUS SPIDER at Pomona College. *Above.* The priest Chichu appears mysteriously on the hanamichi and announces he has come to pray for the ailing Lord Raike. (*Photo:* Lapp) *Below.* In reality the priest is a monstrous spider-demon. In the second half of the play he appears in his true form. (*Photo:* Lapp)

Above. Benten the Thief, Act II, at Pomona College. Benten has disguised himself as a woman in order to rob a cloth merchant. When his true identity is discovered he fiercely announces himself and bares his shoulder to reveal the fancy tattoo typical of thieves. (*Photo:* Lapp) *Below.* The production of *Narukami* by the Institute for Advanced Studies in Theater Arts (IASTA). The evil priest makes advances to the princess sent to seduce him. The princess is here played by a man; an American *onnagata!* (*Photo:* IASTA)

Jean Dasté's production of Gabriel Cousin's *Drame du Fukuryu-maru*. *Above:* In a scene presented largely in mime, the fishermen at sea are surprised by the appearance of a strange sun in the middle of the night. (*Photo:* Comédie de St-Etienne) *Below:* Matsuyama, disfigured by the atomic blast at Nagasaki, visits the mother of her boyfriend, the fisherman Urashima. (*Photo:* Comédie de St-Etienne)

significant dramatists of our era seems to indicate that even so exotic a form as the Noh may not be so inaccessible as it at first seems. Perhaps it is *not,* as Gabriel Marcel claimed, really from another planet! The most striking resemblance between Beckett's drama and the Noh lies in the sense of compression and concentration which one experiences, for example, in *Hagoromo,* or *Sotoba Komachi, Endgame* or *Krapp's Last Tape.* One has the impression that these plays have been reduced to their essence, pared down to almost skeletal proportions, with muscle and sinew, but surely no excess fat. What Ionesco (judging from his latest play *Thirst and Hunger*) has not learned from reading Zeami's writings, Beckett has learned without reading them.

The action of a Noh play is always reduced, so much so that Claudel contrasted Noh with Western drama by saying that in drama some*thing* comes about, while in the Noh some*one* comes about ("quelque chose arrive / quelqu'un arrive"). Perhaps it is pushing things too far to say that in Beckett's theater "someone comes about." Even in so "static" a play as *Endgame,* however, we note a structure remarkably similar to that of the Noh. *Endgame* is not, of course, an imitation of a Noh play, and is somewhat more complex structurally, but the major outline is surprisingly similar.

As the play opens the secondary character, Clov, performs a kind of ritual voyage about his small universe, opening trash cans, unveiling Hamm, peeping out the windows. He then almost chants the theme of the play: "Finished, it's finished, nearly finished, it must be nearly finished." Finally, stating the goal of his voyage, "I'll go now to my kitchen," he leaves. After this simple but eloquent introduction (*jo*) which stresses monotony by its repetitive movements, we witness the awakening of the major character, Hamm. In a few suggestive words he asserts himself as master, depicts his solitude and misery, and restates the major theme of a world drawing to its close, enriching the meaning of "it's finished" with a secondary theme of illusion and reality. The major part of the development (*ha*) of the play is devoted to the cruel dialogue between

Hamm and Clov, in which they indeed relive the past, evoke what has happened before, interrupted by the comic-pathetic appearances of Nagg and Nell in their ash cans. As the *shite* acts out his story before the *waki,* so Hamm must perform for an audience.

Ruby Cohn has described *Endgame* as the presentation of the "death of the stock props of Western civilization—family cohesion, filial devotion, parental and connubial love, faith in God, empirical knowledge, and artistic creation." [48] If her analysis is correct, then there comes a moment when Hamm is reduced to nothing other than himself, divorced totally from any meaningful relationship with people or even with objects—a terrifying revelation. Clov has left him, or so he believes, and in the finale (*kyū*) of the play Hamm performs what might well be called his farewell dance, once more going through the trivial motions that were his life, but now only for himself, and in anything but rapid tempo. Unlike the Noh plays, *Endgame* carries no suggestion of release or of any kind of happiness, attained or attainable.

If Beckett's characters—in *Endgame* more than in *Waiting for Godot* and in the later plays more than in *Endgame*—are turned toward the past, constantly reenacting the events of a life already lived, it is because they, like the Buddhist ghosts of the Noh, are tied to the wheel of life, unable to escape the effects of their past, unable to free themselves from a cycle that has become meaninglessly repetitive. Only the kind of faith possessed by the priests and ghosts of old Japan, but so tragically lacking in Beckett's world, could bring some cessation to the suffering of his pathetic protagonists.

Arthur Waley speaks of the Noh story as creeping "at its subject warily." Since the action is presented as a memory evoked by a dead man "we get no possibility of crude realities; a vision of life indeed, but painted with the colours of memory, longing or regret." [49] Such a description applies to *Krapp's Last Tape* and *Embers,* in which the protagonists are ghosts and the action is evoked, for it took place long ago. One has some reservations regarding "no possibility of crude realities," however; if Beckett's theater paints with the "colours of memory, longing or regret," what he paints is often scabrous, unpleasant, or disgusting. It strikes me that Beckett's inclusion of "naturalistic" phenomena in his plays is somehow close to the more primitive forms of theater which preceded the Noh. The first *sarugaku* performance, recorded in the twelfth century, included a part in which a performer "appeared in shabby clothes, rolled up his skirt, and trembling with affected cold ran ten times round the courtyard fire exclaiming, 'The night deepens and I grow cold. I will warm my scrotum at the fire.' " [50]

Zeami advocated a balance between *monomane,* imitation, and *yūgen,* the mysterious "subtle charm" translated in a score of different ways. If Beckett's balance between *monomane* and *yūgen* would have shocked the courtly Zeami, we cannot deny that there is nonetheless a balance. Perhaps each audience perceives the *yūgen* it is capable of seeing. If our puritanical propensities make us overly sensitive to the scabrous elements in Beckett's drama, our materialistic leanings make us singularly insensitive to his spiritual depth.

We are not alone to blame for our inability to see *yūgen.* Rational and scientific revolutions have divorced our drama from its spiritual roots. The Noh drama exists within a precise tradition, perhaps too much so, while Beckett's work, even more than most modern Western drama, stands outside traditional theater as we have known it.

By using certain ritual rhythms, gestures, word patterns, and images, however, Beckett succeeds in establishing a dynamic, if subconscious, rapport with Western religious tradition. Inherent in ritual is the concept of the symbol: a physical manifestation—a gesture, a sound, an object—that points to some deeper, perhaps more universal (therefore more vague) reality. Like the Noh actor, then, Beckett's actor must assume a certain degree of stylization, for each movement stands for something beyond itself. Hamm's ride around his room is something more than a ride around a room, just as his garbage cans are not merely garbage cans or his sexless dog simply a dog. We see here, in the symbolic use of movements and objects, the same compression and concentration that Beckett uses in portraying character and action.

Needless to say, since Beckett works outside an established theatrical tradition, he cannot depend upon an accepted symbolic vocabulary, as could Zeami. And yet, with incredible skill and imagination, the Western playwright has managed to fill his scripts with objects and movements as meaningful to the modern man as was the fan or the twig of the Noh character to the Japanese. What Beckett cannot do is to give his actors a highly stylized mode of moving and speaking. Our theater has moved so far from the concept of the dramatist who is also actor and director that the actor now almost resents any interference from the dramatist. Beckett, we are told, is keenly interested in the *mise en scène* of his plays, and takes great pains, if he attends rehearsals, to indicate precisely what he wishes. Indeed, his scripts are quite exemplary in this regard, and become more so as his dramaturgy develops. Scenic indications in *Godot,* while plentiful, cannot compare with those in Beckett's latest drama, *Play.* Divorced from a tradition that would allow the actor to know precisely how to intone the text or how to move, Beckett has clearly attempted to compensate for this loss by detailed stage directions.

Beckett's texts offer parallels to the Noh texts also. The latter, in addition to a certain poetic beauty, are characterized by numerous quotations from Chinese and early Japanese authors, and by a multiplicity of the kind of puns and playing with words possible only in Japanese. Beckett's texts feature a sparse, suggestive poetry coupled with outrageous wordplay, and in some plays at least, frequent quotation. *Happy Days* is the best example.[51] Often the text speaks to us more effectively through its suggestivity or its music than through its apparent meaning. In *Play,* although there is no music, the dialogue is spoken so rapidly that it is unlikely the audience can grasp much of it. Like the Noh, Beckett depends for effects largely upon nonverbal elements in the theater.

There is quite clearly a kinship between Beckett's plays and the Noh drama, but there is just as clearly no true influence. If I have made this excursion it is not in an attempt to show influence where there is none, but to suggest that Beckett's drama, like that of some of his fellow writers, has made us sensitive to forms of theater that fifteen or twenty years ago might have struck us—as they did Robert Kemp—as slow, insignificant, and dull. *Waiting for Godot* seemed static in 1953 partly because the action it embodies is unlike any action we had witnessed on the stage before. In the years since that most important premiere, we have learned to look for other things in our theater; we have broadened our dramatic horizons, sharpened our perceptivity, and deepened our understanding. Beckett has shown us that a drama may at first strike us as strange, exotic, difficult, even undramatic, and upon closer acquaintance, prove to be a meaningful addition to our aesthetic and human experience.

IV Kabuki

Inroads in the West

If these young men in their mistaken zeal
succeed in driving Kabuki out, they will
then in my opinion have destroyed the
finest theater existent today.

PAUL GREEN

The long hours I spent at the Imperial
(Kabuki) Theater, following with deep
emotion the unfolding of the heroic epics
of the Genroku period, were for me a
veritable professional school of dramaturgy.

PAUL CLAUDEL

Neither so esoteric, hieratic, or aristocratic as the Noh, nor so
"operatic" and acrobatic as the Chinese Peking theater, the
Kabuki is no doubt the Far Eastern dramatic form that most
resembles the Western theater. At the same time it is a new
and entirely different world, employing techniques of acting
and production as yet unused in the West.

Kabuki began its development in the early seventeenth century when Okuni, an attendant and dancer from one of the
shrines, began to present dance programs in a dry riverbed in
the capital, Kyoto. She attracted large audiences, particularly
after she added several women to her troupe and began to
perform as a man. There are many stories about Okuni; it is
difficult to separate legend from history. By 1629 many
troupes, composed chiefly of women, were performing in the
capital, and using their performances as a means of enticing
men to buy the wares the actresses might offer them after the
dances were over. The Tokugawa shogunate soon outlawed

this immoral state of affairs, which they feared would corrupt the samurai and might serve as a means of breaking down the strictly structured society of the period. When women were forbidden to appear in Kabuki (the name is derived from a verb meaning to behave outrageously), the roles of the young ladies were taken over by handsome young men who had begun training more than ten years earlier. By mid-seventeenth century the young men were causing as much corruption among the samurai as the women once had, and they in turn were outlawed.

It was then, in 1652, that Kabuki as an art came into being; no longer able to count upon the good looks and charm of the performers, the *Yaro* or men's Kabuki had to develop other skills to hold its audience. For a time music and dance were banned; as a result dialogue and dramatic development assumed an important role. Shortly thereafter music and dance were reinstated; the Kabuki (now dignifying its name with three characters meaning song-dance-skill) incorporated them into the dramas that had developed. These troupes developed a more realistic approach to theater than that used by the Noh, inventing makeup, styles of movement to suggest femininity and masculinity, falsetto voices for the men playing women's roles, and gorgeous costumes (periodically prohibited by the government). In 1664 the first long play was performed. Within the next twenty years curtains and scenery were introduced, and the two most creative actors of early Kabuki appeared and founded the two major currents of Kabuki which survive to this day: Sakata Tōjūrō reflected the elegance and realism of Kyoto (the Emperor's court) and of Osaka (the commercial center); Ichikawa Danjūrō originated the heroic and flamboyant *aragoto* style reflecting the tastes of the general public in Edo (Tokyo), capital of the military rulers of Japan.

With its vitality and its themes, reminiscent of the great ages of Occidental drama, Kabuki offers a particularly accessible point of contact for the theaters of two hemispheres. Many men of the theater have remarked on the rich theatrical possibilities offered us by Kabuki, but little has yet been done to take advantage of these treasures which, according to Paul Green, "so many yearning playwrights have dreamed about." [1] The task is complicated by the fact that Kabuki, like other forms of Oriental theater, cannot be thought of simply as a text. The goodwill of authors will not suffice, although it is a necessary factor that would contribute to a successful transposition, since at present there are few modern texts that lend themselves to a "total" treatment. Western actors and directors have had little time to devote to a study in depth of the Asian theaters; most of the work accomplished in this field has been done by scholars, necessary spadework that can bear fruit only when the actual workers of the theater have the time, the talent, the imagination, and the will to devote themselves for a minimum of several years to the disciplined study of a particular genre.

We have already noted the difficulties of any real contact between artists of East and West, since each is preoccupied with developing his art on home ground. The brief visits of Oriental troupes have simply given us a tantalizing taste of their art, and little more. In the case of Kabuki, difficulties have been increased by the fact that a tour necessitates transporting many people and much paraphernalia. There is not only a large group of actors, but each major actor brings with him a world of disciples and students who, according to the medieval hierarchy of Kabuki, are still a requisite adjunct. Many dozens of backstage helpers are required to change sets and to manipulate the complicated stage machinery, which is not easily available in European and American theaters. Whereas Noh and Chinese opera have no setting to speak of, Kabuki requires very elaborate decors. Many costume changes, layers of clothing for one costume, elaborate wigs, large stage orchestras—all compound the difficulties of a Kabuki tour, which is seldom financially feasible.

Consequently Westerners have rarely had the opportunity to witness this exciting drama, and have had to depend upon reports, a few films, and troupes either of inferior quality or not truly representative of the Kabuki their name implied. Kabuki troupes have made only three brief tours to the West: to Russia in 1928, to the United States in 1960, and to Europe (Berlin, Paris, Lisbon) in 1965. But before these major experiences, there had been minor moments of revelation.

EARLY INTIMATIONS

Japanese culture was first revealed to the West at the Paris Exposition of 1867. Only fourteen years before, in 1853, Admiral Perry had sailed into Tokyo Bay and reestablished official contact between Japan and the outside world. In 1856 Townsend Harris, the first American consul, went to Japan; in 1862 the first Japanese embassy was established in Europe. In 1868 began the remarkable period of Westernization in Japan known as the Meiji, named after the Emperor who was, in that year, restored as the actual, as well as nominal, ruler of the country.

As an Oriental nation new to the West, Japan was quick to jump to the fore; with the energy and skill we have witnessed time and again in the twentieth century, she set up an admirable exhibit at the Exposition of 1867. The French found her porcelains, bronzes, and sculptures of an "incredible delicacy," and declared that of all the Asian exhibits the Japanese one was without contradiction the most complete and the most brilliant. At the same time two groups of Japanese acrobats were appearing in Paris and received rave reviews from Théophile Gautier.[2]

By 1860, Sardou, a king among constructors of the well-made play, had already introduced fan, parasol, and double suicide into a play, and in 1861 Baudelaire was receiving prints from Japan; but this was nothing compared with the Japanophilia that broke out after the Exposition. Verlaine reported that he had woodcuts and a wall hanging, the Goncourt brothers wrote their studies of Hokusai and Utamaru, Zola surrounded himself with woodcuts, and the Impressionists and post-Impressionists followed the lessons of Japanese art. Saint-Saëns and Lecocq composed "Japanese" operettas, Heredia wrote his sonnet "Samurai," and Loti evoked a false but picturesque Japan full of affectation and diminutives in *Madame Chrysanthème.* Judith Gautier wrote dramas with such names as *Yellow Princess, The Cherry Trees of the Suma, The Vendor of Smiles,* and *Princess of Love,* while at the department stores the bourgeois housewife could purchase any number of vases, dolls, and cheap trinkets made in Japan for export.

The spuriousness of this understanding and appreciation of Japan may be largely summed up in two things, a picture of a kiosk and a play, *La Belle Saïnara.* In an illustrated booklet on the Exposition of 1867 there appears a startling engraving of what is called the Japanese kiosk; it is a cross between an Indian mosque and a Thai temple, and is surrounded by elephants, samurai, and Victorian ladies. The play, the work of a minor Parnassian poet, Ernest d'Hervilly, knew the glory not only of a production at the Odéon in 1876, but of a revival at the Comédie-Française in 1893.[3] The charmingly quixotic behavior of the incomprehensible Japanese was manifested in this play by a character named Musmé, which in Japanese (*musume*) is not a name at all, but a noun meaning girl, daughter, maiden. Musmé is given to frequent and inexplicable pirouettes. Her behavior, however, is no more curious than the house in which she lives, for d'Hervilly indicates that there are "flowers everywhere in bronze or porcelain vases." Anyone with even a superficial knowledge of Japan realizes that the essence of Japanese flower arrangement is simplicity and austerity, just as the essence of Japanese poetry is brevity, succinctness, concision. Yet the hero of *La Belle Saïnara* announces at curtain rise that the poem he is writing "will have no more than ten thousand verses"! Needless to say, it is written in the standard, twelve syllable French verse form, the Alexandrine.

At the same time that Europe was developing this highly artificial concept of Japan, European travelers were visiting the country itself, and were witnessing theatrical performances. What struck them most was the "realism" of such performances. In the Europe of 1875 neither realistic texts nor acting styles were as prevalent as they are now, so it is scarcely surprising that Westerners, accustomed to the more stylized performances of Bernhardt, to say nothing of the French tradition of restraint, should note particularly the way in which Japanese actors reproduced certain kinds of behavior in detail. Georges Bousquet, writing in 1874, hoped that the young realistic writers of his day would see some of Kabuki's "lugubrious exhibitions" of prolonged suffering and death, so that they might learn "how tiring the unlimited application of their theory might be." [4]

Time and again we find Kabuki described by such expressions as "naturalness of acting," "exact representation of nature," "truth of feeling," "sincerity of detail and of mores," "excessive reality of properties." "Realism" as it is used at the end of the nineteenth century is not always a term of praise. Indeed, critics seem inconsistent about its meaning. One wonders whether it was not sometimes used simply as a term of opprobrium, for scenes of violence and exaggeration called "realistic" would strike us today as distinctly stylized. Alexandre Bénazet, who finds Kabuki's dominant characteristic in its realism, tells the story of an actor who was working on a demon role. He succeeded in creating a facial expression so terrifyingly realistic that his wife, returning home unexpectedly, took him for a real demon and died of fright on the spot!

What seems to bother the commentators is not so much the reality represented as the extremes to which the actor would go in presenting it. Almost to a man they complain that Kabuki plays were too dramatic, the emotions aroused too violent. Accustomed no doubt to the anodyne productions of nineteenth-century Boulevard or Broadway, they were unprepared for a theater that was a real experience, and hit at levels that seemed not quite decent. The French preferred a "polite" production of Racine, and Racine is surely one of the least polite of French dramatists, if one goes beneath the polished surface where many spectators prefer to remain. They found the creations of Shakespeare to be disquieting and mysterious, so quite naturally they placed Kabuki near the "Shakespearean monstrosities." Only recently have the French found it possible to think of the Englishman as anything other than a barbarian of genius.

Strangely enough, Georges Bousquet, who claims that in Kabuki "everything passes as it does in life itself," goes on to relate that he once asked an actor why he uttered such heart-rending cries and made such immense gestures in his tragic roles. It scarcely struck the Frenchman as the way a lord or a soldier would really behave. The actor replied that if he behaved like just anyone, the audience would scarcely recognize him as a hero. Clearly this actor, and many of his fellow artists, were seeking some kind of idealization, a character with greater nobility and strength than the man of everyday flesh and blood; their creation was a theatrical transposition rather than a realistic imitation. This, at any rate, is the way we would describe it today.

Motoyosi Saizu, writing in a French periodical twenty years later (1894), relates an entirely different approach to Kabuki acting, and one tantalizingly close to what has come to be called "The Method." The students of a certain actor, Dengorō, hated their master because of his cruelty to them; unable to abide his behavior, they decided to kill him during an on-stage fight. Dengorō, however, was too good a swordsman, so they could not even succeed in wounding him. After the performance he congratulated his students on their admirably vigorous, courageous, and truthful performance. When they admitted the truth, the master declared that it was sometimes necessary to have recourse to such methods when one could not find the necessary emotion any other way.[5]

The truth is that Kabuki contains extremes of both realism and stylization. Whether one is struck by one or the other depends upon his own background, the particular program he sees, and the actors who are playing. The play of middle-class life (*sewamono*) tends to resemble our own realistic plays in many ways, while the period (*jidaimono*) and dance (*shosagoto*) plays are highly stylized productions. The Osaka school specialized for many years in *sewamono* and a more realistic style of acting, while the Tokyo actors were given to the flamboyant exaggerations of *jidaimono*. Toward the end of the nineteenth century one of the leading Tokyo actors, Danjūrō IX, attempted to give more historical accuracy and verisimilitude to Kabuki plays. Fortunately his efforts were short-lived. It is likely that the French observers of the period had seen some of Danjūrō's performances, or perhaps, like to-day's tourist, they were unable to sit through the many hours of a Kabuki performance, and based their impressions upon a superficial viewing of a single (perhaps atypical) play. Even today one of the most knowledgeable writers on Japan, Edwin Reischauer, can say that "Kabuki stressed realism of action and setting," [6] while one of the great authorities on Kabuki theater, Earle Ernst, calls it a "nonillusionistic, uncompromisingly theatrical form." [7]

Whether we call it theatricalism or realism, the violence and drama of Kabuki were apparently too much for our grandparents, and they preferred to dismiss it as the monstrous creation of "a nation of children." This condescending attitude, adopted by A. Lequeux, author of the first book devoted to Japanese theater (1889), is reflected in most writers of the period, including Bousquet, who concludes with fatuous provinciality: "The Far East, we must recognize, has not known the simple, naked beauty of the Greeks: a prerogative of the Aryan race, the conception of a superior world has, for the Oriental, always taken the shape of a formless exaggeration of reality. Beyond daily triviality he has found only the monstrous." [8]

The Japanese victory in the Russo-Japanese War a few decades later was to show Europe that the Japanese were more than charming children, and that their ancient civilization was worth serious study on its own grounds rather than as a quaint curiosity for the delectation of dilettante Europeans. After 1905 Europe learned to take Japan, her people, and her cultural manifestations seriously, and began the study of Japanese institutions.

But before Europeans had discovered much about Japan, another revelation took place. At the International Exposition of 1900 the fabulous Sada Yakko blazed for a few months like a comet out of the East, dazzling the French public with the skill, emotion, and theatricality of Japanese dramatic art. Reports of her acting had preceded her to Paris; she was received as the most illustrious living Japanese actress, a kind of Duse of Japan. Reading the newspaper reports of the day, one would almost believe she had come alone, but she was in fact accompanied by her husband, Kawakami, and a troupe of Japanese actors, the first ever to visit Europe. In England, Sada Yakko performed before Queen Victoria. Ellen Terry embraced her warmly, crying out, "What a great lesson in dramatic art this has been for me!" And Irving is quoted in the French papers (in their own savory English version) as saying, "I never had an idea of such an acting." [9]

Sada Yakko and Kawakami performed a number of plays; their programs usually included a European curtain raiser or a group of dances by Loie Fuller. None of the plays were true Kabuki plays, but they gave the European spectators a real taste of the strong Japanese acting style. Most of the pieces were fantastic melodramas that allowed Kawakami to indulge his skill in swordplay and Sada her talents for dancing and for the portrayal of madness and death. The most famous of these vehicles was *The Geisha and the Chevalier,* a story of love and jealousy in old Japan, with a denouement reminiscent of the Kabuki play, *Dōjōji Maiden.* Sada was given the opportunity to dance for the temple priests in order to gain access to the temple where her husband was in hiding with his lover. Afterward, transformed into a demon, she was able to deploy her talents in a fight with the lover, and finally to die in a most strenuous way.

The critics remark on Sada's loveliness and charm; her light, simple movements; her dramatic intensity; her caressing little voice, which is compared with that of a wounded bird. But most of all they are impressed by her death scenes, calling them

. . . an incomparable spectacle. Without contortions, without grimaces, she gives us the impression of a death that is physically progressive. We see life slowly abandoning the little body, almost second by second. . . . Our Sarah Bernhardt herself, who so excels in dying, has never given us a stronger feeling of artistic truth.[10]

After her temptress smiles, what eyes deep with anger! Her nose dilates, her cheeks become hollow, fright convulses her whole frame, and she dies with a sort of supernatural realism.[11]

Whether they see her as contorted and grimacing in her death, or as extremely subtle and interiorized, critics agree that the theater Sada Yakko exemplifies makes our own seem timid in comparison. Her style of acting struck them as both barbaric and refined; when a Japanese residing in Paris wrote that Sada Yakko and Kawakami were not at all representative of traditional Japanese theater—indeed, were noteworthy for their adoption of everything modern and Western—the critics could reply that Sada was still surprising and unusual to a European. And this no doubt was true. One would like to have seen her not only in the famous geisha role, but also as Portia in the judgment scene from *The Merchant of Venice* which she offered at the Athénée in 1901, or in the *Dame aux camélias* which was translated into Japanese for her. In various newspaper interviews Sada described her pleasure at seeing the great European actors of her day, and announced her intention to return to Japan, with the million francs she had earned in France, in order to build a modern theater for the performance of the works of Corneille, Molière, Hugo, Shakespeare, and other European classical writers.

Sada Yakko and Kawakami were anything but classical Japanese actors. Sada, in fact, had never been on the stage in Japan, and her acting in the West had come about as an accident. In Japan, Sada Yakko had been a geisha before her marriage to Kawakami. She had therefore received training in the traditional Japanese arts and was an accomplished dancer. Her husband, an unsuccessful politician, had turned to the theater and achieved a certain amount of fame as a teacher of acting. In 1898 he and his troupe decided to make a study tour of the world. They did not intend to perform, but simply to study Western theater on its home ground in order to "modernize" the theater in Japan. When they arrived in San Francisco, an impresario asked them to perform. At first Kawakami was hesitant, but the impresario was so insistent, and the offer so remunerative, that he finally agreed.

At that time, in Japan, mixed troupes were forbidden by law; therefore, all the roles in Kawakami's troupe were taken by men. When, on the afternoon of the performance, the young man who was to play the part of the heroine fell ill, Sada offered to take the role. It was a surprising idea, but Kawakami acceded to the wishes of his wife, and the performance turned into a personal triumph for the diminutive woman. She was called back for ten curtain calls.

After this performance Sada Yakko began to study acting seriously, and appeared with her husband's troupe across the United States. When she finally arrived on the East Coast, she was congratulated by the Japanese consul general there, but also given a stern warning: her behavior was illegal in Japan; when she returned home, she would surely be prosecuted. The troupe went on to England. When Queen Victoria witnessed Sada Yakko's performance, she was so moved that she asked if she might do something for Sada. The young actress asked her to request the Emperor to allow her to perform with her husband, not only in Europe, but on the stage in Japan. In a few days it was a *fait accompli;* since that time the strictures against men and women appearing together on the same stage have loosened. It is piquant to think of Victoria as responsible for this "immoral" state of affairs.

Only after her triumphant Western tour did Sada Yakko become well known in Japan, where she performed the works of Shakespeare and other Western writers. In 1908 she and Kawakami were back in Paris, where they performed a modern Japanese play, the ever-popular *Geisha and the Chevalier,* and an adaptation of a Kabuki play, *The Maple Viewing* (*Momijigari*), which, like *The Geisha,* allowed the actors to display all their most striking techniques.

As the first Japanese actors to perform in Europe, Kawakami and Sada Yakko were important. Their performances revealed to Western audiences an actual example of the forceful, emotional, intensely "realistic" theater most Westerners had only read about. It is interesting that critics were not in accord about the degree of realism or of stylization in Sada Yakko's performances, and were capable of coupling two words like "supernatural" and "realistic." Critical comment and audience reaction stress several important points. First, the truth embodied in the Japanese productions was not a lifelike but an artistic truth, a transposition of life into a more theatrical key, both dreamlike and true. Second, the fact that every critic comments on Sada's ability in the death scenes points to an awareness of the technical aspects of her performance. Let us hasten to add that critics and public were equally aware of Duse and Bernhardt as great technicians. This is precisely the point; before the heyday of realistic acting methods and psychologically integrated productions, actors and actresses were allowed their moments of technical display, and no one was any the less moved. For virtuosity in performance was theater, frankly recognized as such.

"What a spectacle for the imagination, what a feast for the eyes," exclaims one critic.[12] After the somber fare of the Naturalists, and the frothy comedies of the Boulevard, the Japanese actors must have kindled the imagination of the Parisian public, and thrilled them with a performance that spoke as forcefully through the eyes as it did through the ears.

Except for Sada Yakko's return in 1908, and a few visits of dancers like Hanako, Europe waited thirty years for another full-fledged theatrical troupe from Japan. In 1930 the critics drew on a similar vocabulary of superlatives for the troupe of Tokujiro Tsutsui. Although Tsutsui's actors were not authentic Kabuki actors any more than those of Kawakami's troupe had been, Tsutsui's repertoire did include several plays from the Kabuki theater, most noteworthy of which was *Kanjinchō*. Since his specialty was adventure plays with a good deal of swordplay, Tsutsui's approach to Kabuki masterworks was not

particularly traditional. Several newspaper articles by Japanese pointed out that the troupe was not one of the best, that it
had arranged the classics for its particular ends, mingling new
and old, literary and popular. One Japanese, however, agreed
that the Tsutsui performances could "give Westerners an
elementary idea of the classical Japanese theater." In 1930,
even an elementary idea was needed. Dithyrambic reviewers
cried out, "This is theater, truer than truth itself!" Here was
a frankly nonrepresentational theater using stylized movement, dance, music, acrobatics, and yet it seemed to reveal
life as it is: truth revealed through artificial conventions and
a highly developed technique.

Maurice Rostand was struck once again by a death scene,
"so stylized and yet so real, touching at once the highest
poetry and the most poignant reality." He praises the actors,
and lucidly points out that through their talent a play that is
essentially a melodrama (in Western terms) is raised to the
level of profound psychological drama. He ends his review
with some sage advice to the actors of his own day, advice that
actors today might well listen to: "How many French actors,
partisans of the easy way, afraid of too much work, would
derive benefit from listening to the advice of these Japanese,
their prodigious art, as different from a realism without beauty
as it is from a romanticism without truth. How far we are
here from our usual fare, and how deeply this deserves
reflection." [13]

The French theater between 1900 and 1930 witnessed the
usual number of pseudo-Japanese operettas and plays, as well
as several more serious efforts. Two of these deserve mention,
one for its absurdity and the other for its honesty and sincerity. *L'Honneur japonais* was performed at the Odéon Théâtre
de France in 1912. Written by Paul Anthelme after a brief
visit to Japan, *Japanese Honor* is a retelling of the most
famous tale of heroism and loyalty, *Chūshingura*. The same
story furnishes the material for one of the most enduring
masterpieces of Kabuki theater. The play was directed by
Antoine and was lauded for its noble theme, for its elevating

sentiments, and for being a fine spectacle. Curiously enough—
and this should have been a danger signal—the public, according to one critic, "prized particularly the French qualities of
the author, clarity, logic, restraint, precise eloquence, rapidity
of action." [14] That is to say, the audience appreciated what was
most distinctly un-Japanese in the play. The "tragédie cornéli-
enne" which some saw in *Japanese Honor* did not prevent
others from claiming that its Japanese character had a "truth-
fulness that the most knowledgeable connoisseurs of Japanese
legends and life could find no fault with." [15] Despite such
praise and such assurance, despite Paul Anthelme's Japanese
sojourn and the "highly Japanese" theme of the drama, *Japanese Honor* contains the usual affected character names—
Chrysanthemum, Little Smile, and Dame Prune!—and what is
more serious, a total ignorance of Japanese life and even of
Japanese geography. This blindness is all the more curious
when one recalls that Antoine, so dedicated to an accurate
reconstruction of real life, was in charge of the production. He
apparently did not even think of consulting a Japanese to help
him in his *mise en scène*. The results:

> Act I takes place in Osaka with a view of Mount Fuji in the
> background, a geographical impossibility.
> The son of the Prince of Sendai makes Sayemone a knight by
> striking him on the shoulder in good European fashion.
> Old friends greet each other by shaking hands.
> The Prince of Osaka's *seppuku* (hara-kiri) is performed before a
> large audience.
> Shoes are worn inside the house.
> A princess wears the headgear of a high-class courtesan, surely a
> very theatrical and impressive piece of decoration, but here full of
> comic implications.
> This most tragic of Japanese tales ends happily because the Em-
> peror *happens to drop by* for an evening call.

Almost at the opposite pole was *The Mask Maker* pro-
duced by the distinguished pioneer of international theater,
Firmin Gémier, in 1927 at the First International Theater
Meeting, which he organized. *The Mask Maker* by Okamoto
Kidō is one of the best-known modern Japanese plays. Written

in 1911, and considered a modern Kabuki play, it tells the story of a sculptor of masks who has carved a mask for his lord, but feels he has failed, for the mask seems to wear a look of death. The artist's daughter marries the impoverished lord, and when the latter is attacked in battle, she puts on his mask so that she can fight to save him. Both are killed. As the play ends the mask maker, sorrowing at the death of his daughter, is yet happy to know that he is still the greatest sculptor of masks, for the look of death he had carved into his lord's mask was death itself. Always the artist, as the curtain falls he takes his brush to sketch his dying daughter so that he may immortalize her features in a mask.

The great virtue of Gémier's production was its honesty and authenticity; it cleared the European stage of the false "japonaiserie" of colored lanterns, cherry blossoms, and mincing maidens, and put in its place a true and human Japan. Rather than seeking inspiration in the superficially colorful, it attempted to cope with Japanese theatrical techniques. An indication that Gémier approached his task with a sense of responsibility and seriousness lies not only in the reviews. We have seen them err often enough. But one glance at the program tells us that, unlike Antoine, Gémier turned to Japanese artists, dancers, and musicians in order to give a true Japanese coloring to his production. The music was reconstituted from Japanese themes, the settings were designed by Fujita, the costumes by a Yanagi. Although Gémier himself took charge of the production in general, all the "Japanese *mise en scène*" was done by a M. Omori.

The play was simple and sober, but not without color. Most of Act II was devoted to a village festival made up almost entirely of dance and mime. Several Japanese actors were in the cast, lending an air of authenticity but also helping the other actors in their movements. The reviewers particularly noted a M. Urin who danced and mimed the role of a madwoman to great effect. Against the austere, rough, gray-toned backdrops, the actors in their poses reminded more than one reviewer of Japanese woodcuts.

The critics agree unanimously that Gémier's production was a model of fidelity and taste, and his own acting so scrupulously prepared that no Japanese actor could have been more Japanese than he.

LATER VISITATIONS

Until 1928 it was necessary to visit Japan in order to witness a performance of authentic Kabuki. The few theater and dance troupes traveling across America and Europe gave only the vaguest idea of what an actual Kabuki performance was like. In 1928, however, a troupe of Kabuki actors headed by Ichikawa Sadanji performed in Russia, where they aroused no little interest. The influence of Japanese theater had already been recognized in Russia by theatricalist directors, most notably Meyerhold who praised Japanese use of suggestivity, total actor resources, contact with the audience. Indeed, Diaghilev's Ballets Russes, introduced to the West in 1909 in Paris, had already suggested a similar synthesis of the arts and had revealed the dramatic effects to be derived from dance.

One of the artists most struck by the Kabuki performances in Moscow and Leningrad was the young film producer, Sergei Eisenstein. In the Kabuki he saw a brilliant example of effects that might be achieved through the camera. In an essay showing his imagination and genius, he points out some of the lessons offered us by Kabuki, the most important perhaps being the achievement of unity. Eisenstein calls Kabuki a *monism of ensemble:* "Sound—movement—space—voice here *do not accompany* (nor even parallel) each other, but function *as elements of equal significance.*" [16] The Kabuki actor, Eisenstein notes, appeals to every level of the spectator simultaneously, creating what may be called synesthesia, for the actor's movement can correspond to music or to the sound of wooden clappers; it can take place in space, be accentuated by sound or by a flat surface moving at the back of the stage, or it can correspond to some intellectually conceived convention. [17]

Eisenstein recalls for us the old opera singer who assured his theater director that "whatever notes I can't take with my voice, I'll show with my hands." But the Kabuki actor does not choose between one or the other; he uses both simultaneously: "And we stand benumbed before such a perfection of—montage." [18] Well grounded in Japanese culture, Eisenstein makes apposite comparisons with similar phenomena in other phases of Japanese life. In writing, for example, the Japanese is accustomed to using a phonetic syllabary (actually *two* of them), and at the same time he expresses many of his words and ideas in characters that belong to an entirely different order from phonetic symbols. The character itself, like the Kabuki actor, exists on many levels at once; each character has two, three, or even five or six different prounciations and meanings, depending upon the context. In some contexts the character stands as a symbol for a meaning almost independent of any phonetic value, while in others it stands as a symbol for a sound entirely unrelated to the meaning that it would otherwise convey. The complex unity of Kabuki playing levels is apparently inherent in the entire web of Japanese culture.

Thirty-two years later, in 1960, the troupe from Tokyo's Kabuki-za made its highly successful tour of the United States. Americans who were unprepared for Kabuki may have left the theater bewildered, and even a trifle bored, but those who had acquired the necessary background, and possessed the requisite insight, carried away with them a sense of revelation from their contact with the traditional Kabuki theater. There was no doubt of its popular success either, for every one of its twenty-four New York performances was sold out, and it was felt that the three-week stay could have been extended almost indefinitely. Noted American theater people haunted the City Center where the Kabuki actors were performing; at that time there was a strike against most New York theaters, which gave the "vacationing" actors leisure to view the Kabuki as often as they wished. Faubion Bowers recalls seeing both Irene Worth and Anne Bancroft there almost every night. In a highly informative article in the *Nation*,[19] he relates how Greta Garbo went backstage for the first time in her life, so eager was she to see Utaemon VI, who played the major female parts during the tour. Bowers quotes Garbo as saying that Utaemon was "the greatest single theatrical experience" of her life.

Bowers, one of the most knowledgeable people in the United States when it comes to Kabuki, or Oriental theater in general, is also acquainted with the Western theater world. He feels quite sure that someday elements from these Kabuki performances will be incorporated into our own theater. One playwright, Arthur Penn, he tells us, has already admitted "borrowing from Kabuki" for his play *A Death in the Family*.

One of the inspiring lessons we can derive from such a viewing of Kabuki is the use of stylization. True stylization is, as Eisenstein noted thirty-two years earlier, not grafted on from the outside; it grows from within. When we think of stylization in the West, we perhaps tend to envision the kind of quaint poses we see in turn-of-the-century photographs of Bernhardt, or of buxom opera singers. Their air of artificiality and decorative exteriorization strikes us as anything but moving, unless we are moved to laughter. The Kabuki appearance here in 1960 surprised many American actors because it revealed that emotion can be communicated through stylization.

The scene of ritual suicide in *Chūshingura*, which as Brooks Atkinson points out would have been completed in a few moments in a Western play, here took fifteen or twenty minutes. The twenty minutes, he reports, were not long and tedious, but "almost unbearably dramatic." The slowing down, the extreme formality, were apparent in all the plays. Shōroku's portrayal of the loyal samurai in *Chūshingura* again shows the blending of stylization and realism which is one of the earmarks of Kabuki: "Although the style is elaborate, measured, and formal, the emotions he expresses are real." [20] And in *Kanjinchō* the critic again notes a combining of strongly contrasting styles: elegance and bravura.

Paris had to wait for five years before it was allowed to see the remarkable artists of the Kabuki-za. Until 1965, when the Kabuki-za appeared at Jean-Louis Barrault's Théâtre de France, the Parisian public had seen only the productions of

Kawakami and Sada Yakko, of Tsutsui, and of a number of Japanese dance troupes. One of these, the Azuma Kabuki, had appeared at the Théâtre Hébertot in 1955 and had been warmly received. Unfortunately, the name "Kabuki" gave the French the impression that the Azuma performance was indeed an example of the Kabuki theater, whereas actually it was a series of dance excerpts from certain Kabuki plays. The Azuma also departed from Kabuki tradition in that some roles were danced by women. The company is highly professional and extremely skilled, but it is not a Kabuki troupe.

In 1958 the Kabuki Hanayagi appeared at the Théâtre des Nations. Like the earlier visitors, it was a dance group featuring classical Japanese dance, including several from the Kabuki repertoire. The inaccurate name again gave rise to erroneous ideas regarding Kabuki, and several critics concluded that the gentle, restrained, picturesque world of cherry blossoms and drizzling rain in Hanayagi's production was typical of all Kabuki. Obviously, they wrote, Kabuki lacks the epic grandeur of Chinese opera; its expression is less concrete and its psychology more hermetic. A careful consideration reveals that both Kabuki and Chinese opera possess epic grandeur; the former is more concrete and its psychology is more comprehensible to the Westerner.

In October, 1965, in the same theater where Anthelme's travesty, *Japanese Honor,* had been enacted fifty-three years before, several scenes from *Chūshingura*—the Kabuki play on which *Japanese Honor* was based—were performed. Public reception of the Kabuki troupe at the Odéon Théâtre de France was warm and enthusiastic, although most reviewers, apparently put off by the exoticism, the unfamiliar techniques, and the slow rhythm, failed to reflect this enthusiasm in the press. They praise the artistic rigor of the performers, the beauty of the production, and the total theatrical resources employed, but only Gilles Sandier in *Arts* shows a real understanding of the form, and an awareness of the possibilities it offers the West. Quoting Genet, he lauds Kabuki's suggestive symbolism, its religious quality, and the discipline of form and actors alike. He salutes this extremely stylized theater as a vehicle that carries us to the heart of reality. Through actors who are "human pieces of architecture" in their enormous costumes and wigs, engaged in the "eternal ballet of desire, vengeance, humiliation, struggle, friendship, sorrow, and death," we begin to see ourselves, for each character is an immense abstraction, or rather a character reduced to its essence:

> When one sees the wife of the enemy chief coming out from the end of the hanamichi, as though out of a magic lantern, amid strange stridences, it is the birth of Woman (voice, gestures, bearing, walk) which we feel we are seeing. It is indeed a birth that is taking place each time a character comes out of that Pandora's box, as though he had sprung from human imagination fully armed: the birth of mythical beings, charged with the weight of a reality written in capital letters, The Widow, The Warrior, The Friend, and so forth.[21]

We stand too close in time to these recent Kabuki visits to be able to see what Western writers, directors, or actors have learned from them in a concrete way. That there is something to be learned is apparent. Indeed, there are already several texts that not only permit, but encourage, a Kabuki approach to production. Clearly they owe something to their authors' acquaintance with the Japanese theater. I should like to mention two, one by a well-known dramatist, a major figure of twentieth-century theater, and the other by a poet-playwright who, coming only recently to the theater, has created some astonishingly original and significant works: Paul Claudel and Gabriel Cousin.

Claudel was one of the first eminent European writers to discern the richness that Kabuki offers to Western drama. As ambassador in Tokyo from 1921 to 1927 he frequently attended the Kabuki theater, which he called "a veritable professional school for the dramatist." The music, the acting techniques, the physical disposition of stage and audience—all struck him as having distinct possibilities for the West. Although he wrote very little drama after the middle twenties, and therefore did not utilize his knowledge of Kabuki in his own composition, he did write a short mime drama, *The Woman and Her Shadow;* it was performed in 1923 with no small success at the Imperial Theater in Tokyo, one of the major Kabuki houses at the time. *La Femme et son ombre* was revived in 1929 at the same theater. The music for this dance play was written by a well-known composer of Kabuki music, Kineya Sakichi, and plays an essential role in the production. With real understanding of Kabuki, Claudel effaced himself before the movement of the actors and the music that underlines it.

As the play opens a samurai comes to a solitary wild place marked as the "Frontier between the Two Worlds." Here he comes to meditate on his dead wife, whose shadow appears to him behind a screen of mist. At the same time, a living woman enters and tries to entice the warrior. The live woman sings, and when she stops a voice behind the screen continues. As she dances the shadow reproduces her movements. Finally, the warrior takes his sword and cuts the invisible bond between shadow and woman. As he does so, the living woman falls to the ground. The warrior pursues the shadow and as he plunges his sword into the screen, the flesh-and-blood woman utters a cry and dies. Reeling with terror, the warrior leaves, and from behind the screen we hear a few notes on the samisen and the laughter of a woman.

This poetic and suggestive play depends upon the visual effects created by the actor-dancers, and the music that accompanies them. The first version is only a scenario and contains no dialogue. A second version, a half page longer than the first (two and a half pages in all), indicates a few evocative verses to be sung by a chorus that speaks in place of the woman.

Claudel is probably the only foreigner ever to have written a "Kabuki play" presented by professional Kabuki actors. It is not surprising that he should have been so distinguished, for Claudel's theatrical quest was ever broadening, and was never restricted to the imitation of everyday reality which dominated so large a segment of Western drama during his lifetime. His last, and according to many his most powerful, play, *The Satin*

Slipper, parallels Kabuki in its vastness, breadth, color, thematic variety, complexity, and blending of "realism" with stylization. *The Satin Slipper* was completed during the author's sojourn in Japan, and it may well be that he was influenced in its writing by his experience at the Kabuki theater.

Gabriel Cousin is as passionately humanitarian as Claudel was passionately Catholic. A teacher of physical education at a lycée in Grenoble, his first writings were devoted to physical education and culture among the working people. After writing several volumes of poetry, he turned to the theater in 1951, when his oratorio-pantomime, *Officina*, was produced in Italy by Jacques Lecoq. A year of drama study in 1944–45 and a season of performances with Les Compagnons de la Saint-Jean gave him the practical theater experience reflected in his work. All of Cousin's dramas show an experimental turn of mind as well as a thoroughly developed social consciousness. *L'Aboyeuse et l'automate* (1959, *The Barking Woman and the Automaton*), which exists in two versions, as a tragedy-farce and as a ballet-pantomime, deals with the dehumanization of the individual in modern society. *L'Opéra noir* (1961, *Black Opera*) is a terrifying tale of racism in the southern United States, employing jazz, song, and dance, and rising to a climax of terrible irony when a white man disguised as a Negro is murdered by white racists, while his Negro fiancée, disguised as a white, stands by helplessly. Two of Cousin's plays use Japanese themes as their sources. *Le Voyage de derrière la montagne* (1962, *The Voyage behind the Mountain*) is based on an old Japanese legend that served as the subject for a famous Noh drama, *Obasuteyama*. In a certain village it was the custom to take the old people who had lived past the age of usefulness, and to expose them on the mountains. Cousin uses this story to illustrate his theme that there is hunger in a world where two-thirds of the population do not have enough to eat. Using a slow tempo and theatricalist techniques that recall the Noh (a narrator, music, choreographed movements), the dramatist sets his play in an unspecified country, since he hopes to awaken us to the plight of starving men everywhere.

Le Drame du Fukuryu Maru is one of Cousin's earliest dramatic works (1954–1957) and remains one of the most interesting. The author calls it an epic drama, and it is indeed epic in its implications, and is related structurally and thematically to the epic theater of Brecht. It was accepted by Jean Vilar for performance at the Théâtre National Populaire, but, largely because of the death of Gérard Philipe, it was not shown. Instead, it was Jean Dasté who first produced the work in 1963. Inspired by the story of the Japanese fishing vessel, *Lucky Dragon,* which was hit by fallout from atomic experiments off the Marshall Islands, Cousin's play tells the story of a young couple whose lives are destructively twisted by the atom bomb. Matsuyama, disfigured by the bomb at Nagasaki, loves a young fisherman, Urashima. The latter is hit by atomic ash and comes home to die. Matsuyama, not realizing he will die, takes advantage of an offer to have her face restored by plastic surgery, and returns just at the time of her fiancé's funeral ceremonies.

The major theme of the play is that atomic energy poses a threat to mankind's happiness and survival. A second theme has to do with love in a society aware of class differences. A third theme, suggested to the author by an essay of Einstein's he read while doing research for the play, deals with the conflict between old and new ways of thinking. The latter theme is evoked through the contrast between Urashima, outspoken representative of the workers, and Matsuyama, member of a wealthy family attached to the traditions of old Japan, and through the chorus of workers and women as contrasted with Michizane, Matsuyama's grandfather. Cousin has invented fictitious characters and situations, but the play is based in fact, and all the details about the atomic explosion are true.

Although *Le Drame du Fukuryu Maru* is a moving and important *human* document, I wish to stress the play's theatrical aspects. Cousin has miraculously succeeded in creating a play that lies close to the spirit of Kabuki—miraculously, because he has never had the chance to witness a Kabuki performance. Before writing *Fukuryu Maru,* Cousin had had

preoccupations." [22] For Cousin, like the authors of Kabuki (or of past epic eras of Western theater), is writing what the French call "théâtre populaire," which does not mean "popular theater" in the sense of frothy comedies that would have a broad appeal to the most frivolous public. *Théâtre populaire* is theater for the *people, le peuple,* the workingman, the masses. And as such it should appeal to those who would agitate for social reform, as well as to those who simply want to be amused by a colorful spectacle. Kabuki, too, has at times been outspoken in its criticism of social injustice, but in concentrating on a social message has never lost its appeal to the senses. Kabuki is theater of "feast," the word Cousin likes to use in describing his play: "It should also be . . . like a feast, and feasts should be neither boring nor too austere. We can relax the spectator and delight his eyes in a play where the intensity of the drama and the gravity of the situations might—for some people—be almost unbearable." [23]

Cousin has been fortunate in having intelligent directors for his plays, and what is more, directors who are oriented toward a total kind of theater. Dasté, Lecoq, Mendel, Maria Piscator were no doubt attracted by the theatrical possibilities of the plays, and also by Cousin's willingness to allow the director his margin of freedom. Again in the tradition of Kabuki (and of Artaud as well), Cousin seems to understand that a play must be created *in* the theater and not simply on paper; thus, a large contribution is made by director and actors. It is therefore up to them to determine in what direction to push certain elements of the text as given by the playwright: "Between the written and the performed text, there is a margin that it is compulsory to cross. In fact, the writing in the theater must submit to the imperatives of the staging and the playing of the actors. It is on the stage therefore that the 'performed' text will be born collectively and definitively." [24] Gabriel Cousin, aware of the problems of the theater, as he is of the problems of mankind, is creating a drama not for yesterday, but for the men and the theaters of today and tomorrow.

V Kabuki for the West

The Kabuki theater is universal and time-
less and reaches the core of man.
                    JOSHUA LOGAN

We also are slightly Kabuki! But not
sufficiently!
                    SERGEI EISENSTEIN

Kabuki's position, halfway between realism and stylization,
makes it an accessible and profitable meeting point for the
theaters of East and West. Less obviously balletic than the
dance drama of Bali, less obviously operatic than the Peking
theater, less obviously ritualistic than the Noh, it offers striking parallels with Western realistic drama as we know it
today, and with our more highly stylized forms of theater
from the past.

In 1925 Zoe Kincaid, in the first extensive study of Kabuki
written in English, expressed the conviction that Westerners,
"groping their way to find a new method to unite the independent arts of the theater," [1] might find some surprising answers
in Kabuki. Almost fifty years ago Kincaid wrote: "The Western theater, possessing the traditions of the Greeks and of
Shakespeare, has yet to discover the Eastern theater, a sphere
of human endeavor that remains unexplored and unexploited.
Out of the theatrical wisdom of the East may come a force to
produce a new era of creativeness in the West." [2]

In 1966 Kincaid's words continue to apply to the greater
part of Western theater. Happily, there have been exceptions,
and exceptions of genius, which have brought fresh air into our
theater, breaking down, not only a fourth wall, but also all the
others. The experiments of Claudel, Brecht, Genet, Barrault,

138

Planchon, IASTA, and other imaginative playwrights and producers have taken important steps toward a meaningful dialogue between East and West. But so much remains to be done, our theater is still so provincial in its overwhelming devotion to the worn-out forms of several decades ago, that Earle Ernst is justified when he writes in 1959: "As our stage works its way out of the cul-de-sac of realism and looks for wider avenues of expression, the techniques of the Japanese theater . . . may be helpful in suggesting how the Western theater can get on with its somewhat neglected but requisite business of being larger than life." [3]

Kincaid was a pioneer, and Ernst is still a pioneer, for only theatrical vanguards have ventured so far afield as the Orient. Professor Ernst's book, *The Kabuki Theater*,[4] is obligatory reading for anyone involved in the theater. A careful study of this volume, written by a theater man for other, as yet uninitiated, theater men, will open up a new world of possibilities to directors, actors, dramatists, and teachers of drama. Other excellent volumes, somewhat less technical in approach, are A. C. Scott's *The Kabuki Theater of Japan*, Faubion Bowers' *Japanese Theater*, and the Halfords' *Kabuki Handbook*.

Few texts of Kabuki plays have been published in English or in western European languages, but since so little is understood of Kabuki production techniques, perhaps this is fortunate. A Westerner reading a Kabuki text is likely to conclude that the play is worthless because the text as such offers very little in the way of literary, psychological, philosophical, or sociological interest. We tend to judge plays by the written version rather than by the production in the theater; with any form of Oriental drama, this kind of judgment is impossible. The text is actually a pretext and, as Gabriel Cousin so lucidly acknowledges in his notes to *Fukuryu Maru*, the play takes its true shape only in the theater, in the hands of director and actors. One exception in Japan is Chikamatsu, a writer recognized as the most distinguished national dramatist. Some of his plays, in very playable translations by Donald Keene, exhibit the textual qualities Westerners expect to find; therefore, a Chikamatsu play may have a certain appeal on paper, although the impressions obtained from reading are only a small dimension of the play. Other significant Kabuki texts have been edited or translated by Scott, Ernst, Watanabe, Richie, Motofuji, Muccioli, and others.[5]

Strangely enough, despite the curious deformation of *Chūshingura* at the hands of Paul Anthelme, and the somewhat less absurd adaptation by John Masefield (*The Faithful,* first performed in 1915 at the Birmingham Repertory Theater), there is no modern version of this perennial Kabuki favorite, which relates the tragic and heroic story of the faithful forty-seven masterless samurai who avenge the death of their master. *Chūshingura,* which Claudel considered "one of the great works of mankind," does exist in a 1910 translation, and in a partial translation (four scenes from the first section) made by Miyoko Watanabe and adapted by Donald Richie at the time the Kabuki-za toured the United States. The visit in 1966 of the Japanese puppet theater, Bunraku, allowed American audiences to see three of these four scenes performed by the puppets for whom they were originally written; after being performed by puppets, the plays were frequently adapted for living actors of Kabuki.

Through the numerous studies of Kabuki in English, and the few texts of the plays available, the Western reader may gain some idea of the Kabuki theater. But only by viewing the productions can he really understand and appreciate it. In this chapter I wish to treat Kabuki theater not as a form itself— since this has been done so admirably by others—but in its possible relations to the Western theater, stressing the aspects that strike me as offering the best opportunity for meaningful transposition in the Occident. Several Western productions of Kabuki will serve as guides for possible directions.

PROSPECTS

One of the most striking characteristics of the Kabuki theater as it exists today is the *hanamichi,* or runway that connects the stage to the rear of the auditorium. Beginning at the

KABUKI FOR THE WEST

downstage right area, the hanamichi runs straight back to the rear of the house, allowing space on both sides for people to sit. It is a special acting area used to great effect for important entrances and exits, for processions, climactic poses, dance sequences, and the like. True to the spirit of Kabuki, the runway presents the actor to his public in the round, and permits a particularly intimate contact between actor and audience. In the highly theatricalist Kabuki form, there is a constant tendency to bring actor and audience together, and to push the actor, not backward *into* a realistic decor, but forward *out of* a decorative background and toward the public.

Many Western observers have been aware of the dramatic effectiveness of the hanamichi. Claudel declares that we in the West would do well to imitate it. In 1910 Max Reinhardt had already used such runways in his productions of *Oedipus* and of *Sumurun,* a Near Eastern fantasy-pantomime. The runway contributed not a little to the charm and success of the latter play, Robert de Flers tells us. Meyerhold followed suit in his 1924 production of Ostrovski's *The Forest,* but here the runway, instead of beginning at downstage right, swooped forward in a semicircle from the rear of the stage out into the audience. S. Mokoulski comments that "people will never forget the ingenious ending of this performance: the slow departure of Piotr and Aksouscha along the runway, to the sound of the accordion. To this day, neither the Russian theater nor even the European theater has seen such a thing." [6]

The Kabuki theater, frequented by Claudel and other observers in the early twentieth century, was somewhat different in structure from the one we see today. Under the influence of Western theater architecture, and the economic pressure that dictated more seating or standing room for patrons, a secondary hanamichi to the right of the spectator has disappeared, as has the *naka-no-ayumi,* or runway joining the two hanamichi at the rear of the auditorium. At one time, the Kabuki actor could enter at the rear left of the audience on the major hanamichi, stride down to the stage, cross downstage from the audience's left to right, step onto the smaller hanamichi, and,

141

going clockwise, return to his point of entrance. The use of a single hanamichi suggests exciting possibilities, but impressive beyond the scope of any Western construction are the effects available when the audience can be surrounded by one or more actors and included in the dialogue passing over their heads, as communication is made from one area of the house to another. It must be remembered that the hanamichi, whether used in its simple form as it exists today, or in a more complex form with two or three runways and connecting bridges, is always a special place. The hanamichi cannot be compared with Western forms of central staging, or with Western uses of the theater aisles or even with the strategic placement of theater seats for interaction among actors in different parts of the auditorium and/or on the stage, because the hanamichi is always a platform related to, but set apart from, the stage. It does not put the actor on the same level as the spectator, thus destroying the actor's distance and glamor. The Kabuki runway brings the actor into very close rapport with the audience, but it guarantees him at the same time his own place as artist and creator of theater magic.

One constantly comes back to Antonin Artaud in speaking of modern experiments in theater. One wishes that he had had the opportunity to view the Kabuki, for he would surely have found much in it to admire. In his "First Manifesto of the Theater of Cruelty" he describes the physical disposition of his ideal theater. While it is not precisely like the late eighteenth-century Kabuki theater, it presents certain striking similarities. In the direct and exaggerated fashion that is part of his genius, Artaud begins by overstating his case: "We abolish the stage and the auditorium and replace them by a single site, without partition or barrier of any kind." [7] A bit later, however, he points out that, while the audience will be placed in the middle of the auditorium rather than at one end, the actor will still have certain places that are especially his. The action may take place in any corner of the room; galleries will run around the periphery of the hall permitting actors to go from one part of the hall to another; several actions may take place at the same time. Finally, Artaud says, a central position will be reserved to "permit the bulk of the action to be concentrated and brought to a climax whenever necessary." [8]

Admittedly, the Kabuki structure is too formal for Artaud, but it certainly comes closer to realizing his dreams than any other theatrical construction the world has ever devised. Indeed, the form that the Kabuki theater exhibits in the first three or four decades of the nineteenth century, which Japanese scholars believe to be its finest,[9] corresponds very closely to Artaud's ideal. The stage, which today has been pushed back behind a kind of proscenium, at that time still jutted out into the audience, very much in the fashion of Shakespeare's stage. Looking at a print of an Edo (Tokyo) theater about 1802 (see picture in illustration section), we see that the audience almost surrounded the stage, sitting on all sides of the platform, which juts out into the auditorium, and to the rear of the platform as well. The only place free from spectators is the central upstage area, which forms a kind of inner stage, usually placed on a platform and representing the interior of a house. A large part of the audience, in the section corresponding to "orchestra seats," is entirely surrounded by the two hanamichi and the bridge joining them near the rear of the house. Most of the rest of the audience, although not surrounded by, is at some point in close contact with, one hanamichi.

In this old print we see quaintness rather than theatrical possibilities, because we cannot abstract the local color from the structural peculiarities. And yet one of the most lauded modern theater structures in America is built on similar principles, the Guthrie Theater in Minneapolis. As in the old Kabuki theater, the stage projects well into the house; decorations are largely in the form of backgrounds, against which the actor plays, rather than walls that envelop him. Entrances and exits are made not only from backstage, but from doors underneath the audience areas, as though the actors were belched forth from the bowels of the earth. The peculiar shape of the

143

seating area reflects again the attempt to bring each spectator into as intimate a contact with the stage as is technically possible.

But the Guthrie Theater is obviously not a Kabuki theater. The "subway" entrances lack the dramatic effectiveness of the hanamichi and do not possess its varied possibilities for use, since they are not part of the stage, not platforms, but simply doorways, allowing access to the stage without the possibility of exhibiting the actor. The hanamichi, as I suggested before, is not simply an entryway; it is a stage that has importance in itself. One of its vital functions is to show us the emotions or personality of an actor as he enters. When the actor arrives at the *shichi-san* (a point called 7-3, meaning 7/10 from the rear of the auditorium, 3/10 from the stage, the most effective playing area of the hanamichi), he comes fully into character, pauses, and often strikes a pose that sums up his feelings or attitudes at this moment in the play.

Kabuki plays upon all the senses; the pleasures connected with the hanamichi are not only visual. At the back of the runway there is a door covered by a curtain whose metal rings hang on a metal rod. Before each character enters, the screeching of the rings on the rod tells the audience that someone of importance is about to emerge; almost as one body, the public turns to the rear, eagerly anticipating the dazzling appearance of some monstrous or pathetic figure. For the Kabuki habitué, the grating sound of the curtain opening becomes so closely identified with the pleasure of a major hanamichi scene that the sound itself is a pleasing sensation.

Professor Ernst contends that the use of the hanamichi in modern Western theater "would probably produce mild discomfort among most of the audience (as did the wedding procession in *Our Town*) and very little intimacy."[10] I disagree strenuously. At this point in Western theater development, the hanamichi cannot be used in all kinds of plays, but if it is used with taste and judgment, there is, I think, no reason for the audience to feel discomfort. Actually, discomfort is experienced only because people are unused to turning in their seats and dislike the effort of turning their heads. We are so accustomed to having everything handed to us in the theater that we resent making an effort of any kind, whether it be mental or physical. Once the strangeness of the hanamichi has been outgrown, a feeling of intimacy and habitualness will arise quite naturally.

As for the discomfort caused by the wedding procession in *Our Town*, obviously the actors made the audience feel that their privacy had been invaded; suddenly, the actors were in the aisles, reduced from their fictional height to the same level as the public, to the level of Aunt Mary sitting next to sister Susan. This change may have created some of the feeling of intimacy that Wilder hoped for, but in the state of the Western theater today, this kind of intimacy is not possible, particularly in a play with so homey a flavor. A vital relationship between actor and audience is possible only so long as each keeps to his own level. It is not the people involved who must interchange levels; it is the two levels that must be brought into intimate contact.

The Kabuki actor, blessed with a theater that can show off his virtuosity to great advantage and in close proximity to the audience, is a total actor. That is to say, he acts, as Eisenstein pointed out, in such a way that he "makes a full one hundred per cent appeal." The Western actor, inhibited by his realistic and psychological approach to acting, might learn a real sense of freedom from the Kabuki actor: freedom not to do anything at any time, but to use body and voice within a much broader range than Western theater practice permits. Once again, such techniques could not be used indiscriminately, but there are certain kinds of plays within the Western tradition—and among them many of the plays we have come to call great—which lend themselves particularly well to Kabuki techniques. Indeed, they *demand* a similar treatment, and it is only our timorousness, lack of imagination, and conformism to the prevailing modes of realism which keep us from producing them as they deserve to be done. The plays of Shakespeare and Marlowe, of almost any Elizabethan or Jacobean playwright, of the Greeks, and of the Spaniards of the Golden Age—any such play presents a bigger-than-life concept of the theater, a heightened vision of reality which rejects mere imitation and is eminently adaptable to what might be termed a "Kabuki for the West" style. Kabuki is extremely varied; somewhere along its spectrum from the relative realism (but only relative, for it is stylized when compared with Western realism) of the middle-class tragedies (*sewamono*), through the dance plays (*shosagoto*) to the exaggeratedly heroic period plays (*jidaimono*), there are elements that could be profitably adapted (after due transmutation) into almost any kind of Western play conceived before the realistic period.

The basis of the Kabuki actor's technique is dance. But Kabuki dance, except for its sense of rhythm and control, does not resemble Western dance in any way. Whereas Western dance tends to pull away from the ground, to rise in the air, and to become abstract, Kabuki dance in harmony with gravity is tied quite firmly to the earth, and takes as its point of departure the natural movements of everyday life. Its very essence lies in its gestures, each of which holds a specific meaning. By nature a dance drama, Kabuki converts words into gestures. Rather than emphasizing movement, it stresses the grace and the dynamic tension of poses; Kabuki has been described as moving from pose to pose.

To say that a Kabuki actor dances rather than acts every role, is to give an erroneous impression to the Westerner. It would be grotesque for Macbeth to fly across the stage in a *grand jeté*, or even to move in the more earthbound manner developed in recent Western dance styles. The Kabuki actor's movement can be as obviously choreographed as the movement in a dance play, like *Dōjōji*, but it can also appear to be as natural as it is in a *sewamono*. But even in the latter case, the movement is closely controlled, every gesture dictated by the aesthetic principles of economy, suggestiveness, grace, and intensity. There is no wasted motion, and no gesture without preparation, development, and resolution.

146

The nonrealistic form of presentation in Kabuki allows the actor to use a wider range of gesture than is available to his Western counterpart. Even in our most "stylized" productions, we rarely see a performer reach out with his hands to the extreme limits above and around him. Nor do we see expressive uses of the feet and legs. The Kabuki actor has, over a period of two hundred years or more, developed highly specialized techniques that use the area about him, and take advantage of the meaningful and expressive possibilities of the limbs. One of the most exciting and suggestive of these techniques is the *mie,* an incredibly dynamic pose that expresses the emotions of a character at a climactic moment in the play. The mie, one of the high moments of every performance, is accompanied by audible effects which attack the spectator through the ears at the same time that the actor launches his attack through the eyes. Often an acceleration in pace, or an intensification of emotion and of vocal effects, will lead into the mie. At the crucial moment, the actor steps forward, describing a kind of arc with his advancing foot, which seems to pause in midair and then come to the floor with a loud bang. A pattern of controlled intensity is described with one, or both, arms; at the end, one arm, with a flip of the wrist, often comes to a stop above the head. As the actor's head begins to roll, rotating on his neck, from one shoulder to the other, the wooden clappers announce with two or three sharp whacks that the climax of the mie has arrived. As the head reaches the shoulder, it pauses, and then whips over to a final position, sometimes slightly to one side, sometimes straight ahead; the actor often accompanies this movement by a crossing of one or both eyes, and a frightful sneer. This example is only one among many different kinds of mie, all capable of dozens of variations.

The mie is a very specialized technique developed for Kabuki, and it may strike us as folly even to attempt to emulate it on the Western stage. And yet, at one time, Western actors too struck poses, stamping the floor with their feet. While there are other ways of posing besides the mie, it offers an example of a harmonious and dramatically effective pose that might serve effectively for heroic or gigantically exaggerated and rough characters in stylized Western plays.

Japanese dance movement as used in Kabuki, both in its more obvious and in its attenuated forms, suggests that the actor's body may be totally expressive, and in a way that does not disturb the emotional and psychological elements of the performance. Rather than emphasizing dance as abstraction, Kabuki stresses heightened and economical treatment of natural movement.

Movement is a corollary of meaning and emotion, and in Kabuki emotion is always reflected visually. Laurence Olivier has said that there is no such thing as overacting, since all acting is overacting. The Kabuki actor embodies this theory, but not at every moment of the performance. His normal state is immobility; he acts only when it is his *turn* to act, and when his acting will not detract from some more important moment onstage or on the hanamichi. Unlike the Western actor, he does not feel the need to react to everything that is happening onstage. Or rather, he does not feel the need to react immediately. He waits until the audience has grasped the major situation and is ready to observe the reaction, and then he reacts in a way that makes our Western manners seem timid indeed. For he gives a theatricalized transposition of the normal reaction, and as such it is heightened, made larger than life, and sometimes even modeled on the stiff movements of the puppets whose repertoire the Kabuki has assiduously plundered. When a grief-stricken woman stumbles and falls, her fluttering hands clawing the air, the Kabuki actor reveals more than the comparatively staid Western actress would in the same part, and does so in a distinctly theatricalized, nonnaturalistic way.

Eyes, lips, and even nose may be as dramatically expressive as the hands and arms. The Kabuki actor, like the Kathakali dancer of India, or the Balinese dancer, has a large vocabulary of eye, eyebrow, and lip movements to show fear, worry, courage, anger, sorrow, and the whole range of emotions.

Sounds are as eloquent as gestures. We have already noted

the screeching curtains at the back of the hanamichi, and the sharp wooden clappers which accompany the mie and other exciting moments of the performance. Drums and other instruments add to the auditory experience, too. But it is the actor himself who produces the most exciting sounds. The Kabuki actor's voice, like his body, is a total instrument and is used to reflect emotion through timbre, pitch, intonation, as much as or more than it serves as a means of enlightenment through the meaning of words. The text is, after all, a secondary element in most Kabuki performances. Parenthetically, it seems necessary to recall again the ideal of Artaud, a theater in which the text would be relegated to a relative position rather than dominating the other elements of production, and a theater that, like Kabuki, gives importance to sounds, cries, "the whole complex of gestures, signs, postures, and sonorities which constitute the language of stage performance." [11] Unlike much of the Western theater Artaud found so decadent, Kabuki speaks to deeper levels than consciousness because it speaks with other languages than words. In Kabuki we often forget the words and their meaning, and are suddenly aware that the voice, as an instrument, has an artistic function in the theater. Indeed, the actor's vocal range is so enormous, the emotional colorings so intense, that all reactions are heightened. The Kabuki audience is one of the most emotional in the world; as many tears are shed as by a Western audience "identifying itself" with a realistic performance.

The Kabuki character's way of talking tells us something about him. The young romantic lad speaks in a high voice, the rough warrior in a deep gruff voice, the princess in a fluty white falsetto, and the matron in a combination of falsetto and chest tones, breaking through with a kind of glottal stop that Michener compared with the grating of rusty hinges. Each of these voices, in addition to conveying the emotion that one has learned to associate with the tone, gives a distinct aesthetic pleasure, much as certain tones of an opera singer's voice may give us a kind of sensual thrill—a physical rather than an intellectual reaction, I believe. But no role is restricted to a single vocal register, and the Kabuki actor uses a striking variety in any given role. Unlike the Western actor, whose vocal range may cover three or four notes in a representational performance, the Kabuki actor sometimes covers two octaves or more, ranging from deep grunts to high falsetto tones. Such a range contains a vast variety of emotional expressiveness, again in a nonimitative manner. The hollow, drawn-out laughter of women, the whining stylization of weeping, the dark rasping sounds at the back of the throat which suggest intense anger, the deep earthquaking cough of a hero, the immense laugh rising from the entrails and continuing through howls and into a variety of gurgles—all are Kabuki transpositions of everyday reality into a theatrical key, a key that is aesthetically pleasing because we are aware of the artist as virtuoso, yet moving because the gigantic exaggeration is firmly rooted in reality.

Here precisely is the secret of Kabuki's stylization: it has not lost touch with reality, does not divorce itself utterly from its vital sources in life. Charles Dullin, who never saw true Kabuki, was aware of this secret from Tsutsui's performances which he saw in May, 1930. In that month's issue of his theater magazine, *Correspondances,* he made the following astute observation: "The Japanese actor takes his point of departure in the most meticulous realism and arrives at a synthesis through his need of truth. Among us, the word 'stylization' immediately evokes a kind of congealed aestheticism, set to a dull and docile rhythm; among them, stylization is direct, eloquent, more expressive than reality itself." [12]

Dullin was not alone in noting the vitality and authenticity of the Japanese popular theater's stylization. Georg Fuchs, after observing that "the Japanese theater reaches heights of intensity of which we have no idea and does so simply by stylistic means," goes on to explain this phenomenon: "The Japanese art of acting is indebted for this supremacy of style to its vital connection with fundamental principles, that is, with the elementary physical sources of mimic art. These principles are identical with those of the dance, of acrobatics, of

wrestling, and of fencing." [13] In other words, the basic movement of Japanese stylization is related to the same natural
movements we find in other activities that are extensions of
real activities.

The gorgeous, colorful costumes of Kabuki, and its symbolic
makeup, exhibit the same characteristics of high stylization
firmly rooted in reality which we have seen in the other elements of the production. There is little concern with the faithful representation of a historical period; the costumes sometimes are copies of and sometimes are theatricalized versions
of actual Japanese clothing. Particularly in the grotesque stylization of *aragoto* ("rough stuff"), which attempts to suggest
heroism through a broad and violent style of acting, we find
gigantic costumes and wigs that build the actor up and out to
almost monstrous proportions. The *kumadori* makeup that
characterizes *aragoto*—with the red and black lines standing
for strength, the purple and gray for wickedness, duplicity, or
demonic qualities—actually serves to stress the actor's
strength by accenting the musculature of his face and limbs.
The white makeup used in most other instances idealizes the
envied white complexion of the noble who can afford to keep
out of the sun, or derives from the necessity to be able to see
facial expressions for some distance in a theater that lacked
artificial lighting. In reality, such pallor finds its parallel, even
today, in the geisha and in the young lady who, when wearing
traditional Japanese costume, enhances her beauty by applying
a coat of white makeup to face and neck. The innumerable
emotional and artistic effects possible with such makeup and
costumes, rooted in reality but not limited by it, have already
been used in Western theatricalist productions independently
of Oriental influences. Effective use of makeup and costumes,
like masks and monsters, is a part of our theatrical heritage,
but a part we have too often neglected.

When one goes beyond imitative staging, one soon discovers
that seemingly minor production elements can—like the props
in certain "absurd" plays and like the clothing and looks of
Kabuki actors—make a major contribution to the theatrical

experience and its meaning. Since the reality to which Kabuki makeup and costumes correspond is not photographic, but interior, symbolic, and theatrical, makeup and costumes do not remain static, but change whenever the reality they represent changes. They may be altered between scenes, or onstage during the course of a scene, for purely theatrical reasons of color, surprise, stress, contrast; also, makeup and costume may be changed to show that the character is now appearing in his true identity. The eyebrows of a noble may be penciled on, or demon features may be drawn in, and suddenly revealed to the public at the same time that the actor, aided by an "invisible" stage assistant, steps out of one costume, appearing in a completely different one, and perhaps even lets his formal wig fall into a demonic mass (thanks to a system of strings). The tricks of rapid change onstage are dazzling, and serve to underscore the changing emotions of characters. Preparatory to fighting, an actor may simply remove one sleeve of his kimono, and show a brightly contrasting color underneath. Or he may wear several kimonos, basted at strategic points; the stage assistant holds the top kimono at the shoulders and, as the actor steps forward, pulls it off, revealing beneath a completely different and contrasting kimono. Such techniques are theatrical, but not arbitrary, for they are consonant with the aesthetics of Kabuki, and point to psychological and symbolic realities which representational costumes largely ignore.

In the total theater of Kabuki, music is not absent. Unlike the music of most Occidental theater, however, it does not exist for itself, but as an integrated part of the theatrical experience. Oriental music is rarely composed only for the listener; it generally exists as accompaniment to dance or song. Kabuki music grew out of earlier musical accompaniments, particularly from the Noh. Shortly before Kabuki began its long development, the samisen was introduced into Japan, and was quickly taken up as the Kabuki instrument par excellence. Today the Noh drums and flute still survive in Kabuki plays adapted from the Noh, but the samisen is most intimately identified with Kabuki drama. A long-necked instrument whose sounding board is covered with catskin, it has three strings and is plucked with a plectrum. Because its range is somewhat similar to that of the human voice, it is used to mimic and accompany the intonations of the actors. Along with a narrator, or a group of singers, the samisen may continue the actor's speech or emotions, or may accompany them. Or speech may pass, without break, from actor to narrator to instrument. Unlike Western theater music, Kabuki music gives no sense of interruption, or of one element dominating the other, for all three elements—acting, narration, music—are entirely integrated.

Needless to say, there are various kinds of music, and various degrees of integration. But Kabuki music never strikes the spectator as adornment, as the music in Western theater often does. It is part of the fabric of the production, and rarely calls attention to itself as music. There are some parallels between Kabuki music—and the other aural effects that are a part of the performance's attack upon our nerves—and concrete music. Neither calls attention to itself by romantic melody or rich harmonies. Both are characterized by a sparseness and austerity that are dramatically effective in underlining certain moments of the play.

Paul Claudel was particularly sensitive to the perfection achieved by Japanese theatrical music. He had long struggled with the problem of music in the theater; Kabuki was a revelation to him in this regard, as in many others: "I understood then what dramatic music was; I mean music as used by a dramatist and not by a musician, attempting not to create a sonorous tableau, but to jolt and move our emotions by purely rhythmic and sonorous means, more direct and more brutal than words." [14]

He goes on to speak, not only of the music as such, but also of the dramatic effects created by the smacks of the wooden clappers at heightened moments, and by the voice of the actor, or the narrator, "grunt, exclamation, doubt, surprise, all the human sentiments expressed by simple intonations." [15] This kind of music, Claudel points out, unlike the music used in

153

Western theater, does not form a sharp contrast to the spoken word; it belongs to the same order of experience. Thus, Kabuki music may support, strengthen, punctuate, comment upon the situations shown in the drama without drawing attention to itself. It seems to me that there are forms of Western music today, particularly since the development of so-called concrete music, which could be admirably adapted to the theater. Experiments in this direction might make possible a more perfectly integrated theater music.

Kabuki is a theater of feast from which no part of the spectator need go away hungry. There is food for thought, and for the emotions, as well as food that satisfies all the senses. It is no accident that the Kabuki audience usually eats in the theater. Several hundred years ago the Kabuki performance began before daybreak and ended at nightfall. The audience would retire to the adjacent teahouses for refreshment or would prepare their own food in their little cubicles. Even today the performance begins about 11 A.M. and lasts until 10 P.M., with the possibility of leaving halfway through. One may purchase a prepared lunch (*obentō*) in a little box and eat it in the theater while watching the performance. One day, from my front seat I turned around in order to see Shōroku, one of the most gifted of living actors, who was performing on the hanamichi. Sitting directly below was a little old lady calmly peeling an orange. The contrast between the calm of the woman in her homely activity, and the heroic proportions of the actor in his stylized and dynamic movements— accentuated by my realization that a two-way experience was taking place as the woman imbibed the thrill of the performance and Shōroku the odor of the orange—struck me as somehow the essence of Kabuki experience: intimate, heroic, stylized, realistic, appealing to the senses of sight, hearing, smell, and taste.

One Japanese critic has called Kabuki a "creation on earth of the nearest possible approach to Paradise." [16] If paradise means to live in intimacy with the gods and yet to be at home with an orange, then Kabuki is indeed an approximation of paradise. In the non-Christian Japanese paradise, no fruit is refused the inhabitants, not even the fruit from the tree of knowledge. But like all things Japanese, knowledge is approached in a roundabout way without destroying the flavors and perfumes of the other fruits and flowers. Another critic, claiming that Kabuki's basis is "an insatiable hunt for pleasure," describes it as "a complete mess of carnal appetites." [17] In Japan, or elsewhere for that matter, the satisfaction of carnal appetites and paradise need not be mutually exclusive; if Kabuki has both to offer, if seems foolish not to consider the possibility of appropriating such an amalgam for our own theater, if we can do so without simply tacking it on superficially. Imitation is not the way. We must adapt Kabuki forms to our own needs and to our own ways of feeling and thinking.

TRANSPOSITIONS

Kabuki can serve as a signpost only if we are sufficiently familiar with it as theater workers and as spectators. The few actors, directors, and scholars who have had the opportunity to study in Japan can make substantial contributions here, but in order to establish a broader base of familiarity, it is desirable that we have more opportunities to view Kabuki performances in this country. There are overwhelming practical problems which seem to prevent this at the present time. But at least today one can gain a kind of secondhand acquaintance with this exciting theatrical form through productions presented by American actors and students. Needless to say, such productions lack the polish and perfection of performances by actors who have grown up with the blood of Kabuki in their veins and have dedicated years of study to it. But since we are interested in what Kabuki has to offer us as Westerners, it seems to me that such experiments can be profitable. It is not so much a question of Americans or Europeans achieving a flawless imitation of Japanese theater, as it is the opening up of new perspectives to actors and audience alike, and doing so in the most finished and artistic manner possible, given the limitations of time, preparation, and money. No one would claim

155

that Joe Doakes could replace Baiko or Shōroku, but faithful imitation of acting is not the purpose of such exercises, for we in the West are simply students of the East in matters of theatrical stylization and total theater. At the present point in Western theatrical development, even a second-rate performance of such a theater could offer moments of revelation capable of changing the course of theater history.

There have been a number of interesting experiments with Kabuki in the United States, and I should like to discuss several of them here. The Institute for Advanced Studies in Theater Arts (IASTA), the University of Hawaii, Michigan State University, and Pomona College have produced Kabuki plays in one fashion or another. The productions range from an authentic restaging of a Kabuki performance in English, directed by a great Kabuki actor from Japan, through productions that have sought authenticity of mood and technique without imitating precisely the original production, to a free experiment using Kabuki techniques as an approach to a Western classic.

We have had occasion to speak of IASTA before. Its production of *Narukami* (*Thunder God*), one of the famous *Eighteen Plays* of the Ichikawa family, was the first Oriental production IASTA undertook. As such the institute posed— and solved—a number of problems, including that of the possibility of undertaking a work so highly stylized with American actors who were totally ignorant of the traditions of Asian theater. The director chosen for this undertaking was Onoe Baiko, one of the two most admired *onnagata* in Japan today. Baiko, more accessible than most of the other Kabuki actors, is known for his friendliness in helping foreigners interested in gaining a knowledge of Kabuki.

It was Baiko's inspired idea to spend several days teaching classical Japanese dance to the auditioning actors—since Kabuki is based on dance momement—before he chose the cast for *Narukami*. Only then did he listen to the reading of the parts. This method of cast selection has been used at IASTA

156

by other Asian directors, and also for less exotic forms of drama.

Before undertaking rehearsals proper, Baiko showed his actors a film of the Kabuki-za production of *Narukami,* played a tape of the same, and let them see slides. In this way, they gained a certain familiarity with the type of production they were aiming at. Assisted by Miss Miyoko Watanabe, who has attained great skill in Kabuki acting as well as in classical Japanese dance, Baiko coached each role in the play.

Baiko was constantly aware that he was working with professional American actors, and he respected their individuality. It is enlightening for the Westerner, who may believe that all forms of stylization must repress freedom and individuality, to know that Baiko wanted to avoid a strict copying of the Kabuki films and tapes, for fear that such an imitation might "destroy the inner truth of the play." [18] Using tapes and film as a point of departure, and under the close guidance of Baiko and Miss Watanabe, the actors worked extremely hard to find "a suitable and true evocation of the vocal style and delivery." Baiko pointed out the degree of freedom granted by the Kabuki tradition: "To learn and to master a tradition of acting and dance which 16 generations of performers have developed, does not lead to a loss of freedom; rather, that actor who applies himself to such mastery becomes truly free to express within a body of techniques what are uniquely his personality and insights as an artist." [19]

The freedom of the artist is reflected in the varying interpretations of the same roles by different actors, for the production was double-cast. One actor, in the role of the villainous priest who is the major character of *Narukami,* was classical in his portrayal, whereas the other (George Gitto) was romantic. The audience apparently felt a good deal of empathy for the latter. Rosamond Gilder, who had seen both casts, said, "One felt sad for the defeated priest Narukami when George Gitto played it. And it still seemed correct." Baiko agreed with this evaluation, Dr. Mitchell points out, and adds with a feeling for nuance: "So Kabuki's *kata* [patterns, techniques] are not at all rigid—just precise and distilled and refined."

There were various difficulties during rehearsals and performances. Several actors in small comic roles apparently felt that there was too much restraint and failed to use the requisite precision and discipline. Another actor, admirably adapted to naturalistic roles, had difficulties in learning the Kabuki style, but Baiko was loath to let him go, insisting that anyone who is prepared to work very hard may finally achieve what he sets out to do.

Even the actors who were able to forget their naturalistic training reached a point where they found it very difficult to accept the extreme presentationalism of Kabuki. The Kabuki actor does not pretend that he is anyone except an actor playing a role; consequently it is not uncommon for him to insert his own name into the text of the play, or to make some passing reference to a popular story of the day. This ability to adapt a play to current events, and to allow the actor's true identity to show, means breaking down the last bastion of naturalism. It was only upon the forceful insistence of Baiko that the American actors finally agreed to use their own, and therefore un-Japanese, names at the place where Narukami says, to please a lovely princess, "I'll change my name to ———— [the actor's name]." Such a technique is, by the way, more than a commentary upon Kabuki's blatant theatricalism; it is an indication of its youthfulness and ability to adapt—but always within clearly defined limits.

After the production, Baiko felt that the American actors who had had a strong desire to learn, had learned, while those who were unwilling to accept the constraints and disciplines of the form had, of course, not succeeded so well. He called Stephen Daley's grasp of Kabuki "amazing." One spectator commented that it was "an electrifying theatrical experience, something I can rarely say." [20] And Stella Adler stated that a single moment of *Narukami* had more style than a hundred years of naturalistic theater. [21]

University and college productions of Kabuki plays, without professional actors and often without assistance from a professional Kabuki actor, have succeeded in finding a style approximating that of the original. Audience and critical reaction to the three productions of which I am aware, was, to say the least, excited, and often even rapturous. Most Westerners viewing university Kabuki productions are astonished that a highly stylized theater is able to achieve strong emotional impact and to create an intimate relationship with the actors. Even those who had seen the Kabuki troupe in 1960 had probably not experienced the intimacy that is possible in a college or university theater, and above all they had not had the opportunity to follow a Kabuki play in a language they could understand.

The production of *The House of Sugawara* by the Theater Group at the University of Hawaii in 1951 was a historic occasion, marking the first production of a classical Kabuki play on a Western stage, in a Western language by Western actors, in a style approximating that of the original. Earle Ernst, with his rich background in Kabuki theater, directed the production, and was assisted in the choreography by Gertrude Tsutsumi. The same directors produced *Benten Kozō,* or *Five Thieves,* two years later and revived it for the opening of the John F. Kennedy Theater at the East-West Center in 1963. The magnificent new theater, with hanamichi and the latest stage machinery, permitted a lavish production rendered even more authentic by the presence of Onoe Kuroemon II as codirector and choreographer. This modern *sewamono,* by the most profound Japanese dramatist of the nineteenth century, Kawatake Mokuami, shows the decadence of Japanese society in the first half of the nineteenth century, and tells its melodramatic tale with pathos and humor. The English version of the play, by Yukuo Uyehara and Earle Ernst, is one of the liveliest and most playable of Kabuki translations; meaningful and amusing to a modern audience, it also allows for the stylization and colorful techniques of the original.

Professor Ernst's productions have been models of authenticity; when necessary, they even include a samisen player and narrators. Other university and college Kabuki productions have had to rely on recordings for the music. But the programs at Michigan State University and at Pomona College have striven for authenticity as much as possible.

In 1963 Professor James Brandon of Michigan State University directed two Kabuki plays, *Kanjinchō* and *The Zen Substitute*. The latter is a modern Kabuki work, but *Kanjinchō* is one of the enduring Kabuki classics, and a very difficult undertaking for actors not skilled in the techniques of Kabuki. Unlike the actors at the University of Hawaii, the student-actors at Michigan were not of Oriental heritage. The translation of *Kanjinchō* published in *Evergreen Review* (no. 14), was made by James Brandon and Tamako Niwa, and contains very complete stage directions. Costumes for the major characters were made in Japan. A hanamichi was constructed in the theater, and nine weeks were spent in rehearsal. The results were stunning and moving, as the review in the *Christian Science Monitor* [22] makes clear. Brandon's intimate knowledge of the form resulted in a production that faithfully represented the Kabuki movements, and he found a stylized parallel for voice patterns in a language so utterly unlike Japanese that an imitation would not be possible. Despite the nonrealistic presentation, the audience was deeply involved in the play, and, we are told, seemed to lean forward in anticipation of the actors' movements. Houses were sold out and a performance was added, proof of the success and popularity of the venture.

There was a similar reaction to the production of three scenes from *Benten* and a Kabuki dance play of Noh origin, *The Monstrous Spider*, at Pomona College in 1964. Again a hanamichi was constructed; costumes were borrowed or made and expenses kept within a modest budget; wigs were specially constructed. Six weeks were spent in rehearsal, about one third of each rehearsal being devoted to practice in walking, sitting, choreographed movement, and striking poses. The movement was taught by a skillful Japanese dancer who was generous enough to spend many hours a week with the neophyte actors.

Rather than attempting a move-for-move imitation of the Kabuki plays, the production aimed at reproducing the stylized, heroic spirit of Kabuki. *The Monstrous Spider,* since it is a *shosagoto,* was highly choreographed in its entirety; a dancer with professional experience was used in the difficult role of the spider-priest; featured, among the warriors who fight him, were two young students adept at the back flips that add so flamboyant a note to the fight scenes of Kabuki plays.

Once again, a Kabuki production played to full houses, and was enthusiastically received by the local audiences as well as by visiting Japanese, who enhanced the electric quality of the atmosphere by shouting suitable calls of approbation at climactic moments. Several Japanese spectators confided to a reviewer that, "given the enormous challenge such a production presents an unskilled Western cast, they were quite pleasantly surprised at the high quality of the evening." [23] A less inhibited student reviewer ended her article thus: "Wild leaps of colors, swooping, wailing music, lashing hair, heroic poses and faces, tongues of material, twisting hands, violent motion and noble stillness, MORE !" [24]

KABUKI AND ELIZABETHAN

The Kabuki production at Pomona College was followed the next year by an experimental production of Marlowe's *Jew of Malta,* using Kabuki techniques to heighten the theatricalism of that most flamboyant of Elizabethan plays. The juxtaposition of Kabuki with Elizabethan, which may at first seem surprising, is not only eminently theatrical, but also serves as a fruitful approach to the problem of style in the production of Elizabethan plays. Although a great deal has been written on the subject of acting styles in the Elizabethan and Jacobean eras, scholars must ultimately admit that little is known for certain. Kabuki offers a still-living theatrical tradition which exhibits astonishing similarities to much of what we are told took place on the English stage three or four hundred years ago.

Taking its cue from the theatricalism of Kabuki, the 1964

161

Jew of Malta may actually have achieved a more "authentic" Elizabethan style than many of the modern productions of the classics, which are more fundamentally naturalistic than we realize. We are so close to the representational style which dominates our theater that we often see even obviously presentational dramas only in the familiar, established terms.

The blending of the old and the new, the refined and the barbaric, which typified Elizabethan England and Tokugawa Japan, is seen in the theaters of both countries. Before reaching artistic maturity the Kabuki theater sometimes served as a front for prostitution, while in London the theaters were relegated to the south bank of the Thames near the infamous Stews. The famous actor, Edward Alleyn, seems to symbolize the era in England: the creator of Marlowe's major characters, he made much of his fortune by leasing land for bearbaiting, and invested his money in the founding of a college.

Prostitution, violence, bloodshed, vengeance, find an echo in many of the major Elizabethan and Kabuki plays. Refinement and barbarism, both occasionally beyond modern taste, shock us by their juxtaposition in Marlowe, Shakespeare, Ford, and Webster, as they do in the productions of works by Chikamatsu or Takeda Izumo. Both theaters raise the historical or legendary to the heroic, depict the encounter between natural and supernatural worlds, juxtapose scenes where insoluble problems end in death with scenes of the utmost gaiety.

The early Elizabethan actor was more versatile than his modern counterpart. Like the Kabuki actor, he was both a dancer and an acrobat. "In letters dealing with English players on the Continent in the 1580's," Beckerman tells us, "acting is always linked with dancing, vaulting and tumbling." [25] An Englishman visiting in Germany comments on how the Germans, "not understanding a word [the actors] said, both men and women, flocked wonderfully to see their gesture and action, rather than hear them, speaking English which they understood not." [26] Such an attitude suggests that there was something worth watching, beyond mere walking and the handling of objects. As late as 1592 a man writes from Nuremberg,

"The English comedians have wonderful music and are so skilled at tumbling and dancing that I have never heard nor seen the like." [27] I have found no indications that Alleyn or Burbage were tumblers or dancers. But it is interesting to note that they were part of a theater that did include dancing and tumbling, and that we may see just such a theater today, since Kabuki, unlike modern acting, has not entirely divorced itself from its early traditions.

Whether or not Alleyn and Burbage and the other major actors of their day tumbled and danced, they were at any rate masters of a formal acting style lost to us today. Beckerman characterizes their style as romantic, Harbage as formal, while Josephs feels quite certain that they employed the gestures common in contemporary rhetorical delivery, perhaps exaggerating them for the needs of the theater. A broad playing style must have been demanded by the poorly lighted theater, as well as by the public in the pit. Thorndike believes that "every means of facial expression and gesture should be employed in the depiction of emotion, making the action somewhat more intense than in the modern theater." [28] Nagler, quoting a report of a performance of *Othello* by the King's Men at Oxford in 1610, describes how one spectator was impressed by Desdemona's death, "especially when she lay in bed, moving the spectators to pity solely by her face." [29] Such an ability reminds one of the many occasions on which a Kabuki actor, for perhaps minutes on end, will register emotions by contraction of the facial muscles and movement of the eyes, achieving effects of great pathos. It was no doubt this gift that caused French audiences in 1900 to rhapsodize over Sada Yakko's performance of death scenes.

The Kabuki actor, using every facet of body and voice to portray character and emotion, presents himself quite frankly as a theatrical creation on a stage before an audience. The presentational aspect of the Elizabethan actor's performance was underlined by the three-sided stage, but in addition he might have used such techniques as symmetrical blocking, speaking directly to the audience, facing the public rather than his onstage interlocutor as he delivered his lines. Moreover, he tended to play not so much *in* a setting as *against* it. The same things might well be said of the Kabuki actor, who as we have seen still enjoys a stage structure and type of decor that thrust him toward the audience. The hanamichi might even be thought of as a hyperdevelopment of the Elizabethan three-sided platform which so resembles the Kabuki stage at its highest point of development.

Taking advantage of these parallels, the Pomona production of *The Jew of Malta* was able to use Kabuki as a living point of departure in its search for a viable style for an Elizabethan production. The actors studied their roles not only as speech, but as movement, and certain climactic scenes were precisely choreographed. While Kabuki works within a clearly defined tradition of gestures, Western dance has no highly developed vocabulary based on natural movement. One of the most difficult problems was to invent the necessary gestures; ideas came from modern dance, accepted symbolic gestures, and especially, following the suggestions of Bertram Josephs,[30] from the seventeenth-century books of rhetoric. Unfortunately, the Western actor, when speaking through nonrepresentational gestures, is working in an almost total vacuum, since his audience does not understand his gesture vocabulary. This was no doubt the least successful aspect of *The Jew of Malta* experiment. When the actors moved from gestures with a precise meaning into simply choreographed movement, they could speak more directly to the audience, since then their stance suggested a general emotion rather than a specific meaning. The fight-to-the-death between Lodowick and Mathias was one such movement. In a carefully controlled dance, containing several static poses, and using no direct contact between body and dagger, the actors thrusted and parried while the strokes were suggested by the sharp sound of wooden clappers. Another such scene was the death of Abigail in which the ebbing away of life was suggested by stance and a trembling hand.

The Elizabethan actor drew attention to climactic moments

by stamping. Since no one knows exactly how the Elizabethans stamped, the climactic stamps in *The Jew of Malta* were performed much like a mie, whose stylization renders it more aesthetic and more theatrical than a mere stamp of the foot. The experience with this kind of pose in a Western play suggests several things. It must not be used too often. It must be well prepared vocally and physically by the actor; a double climax must be achieved before he breaks into the mie pose, otherwise the spectator simply becomes aware of the pose as such. The mie of the low-life character, Pilia-Borsa, were particularly successful. The actor, who had never seen Japanese Kabuki but had had experience with the production a year earlier, played Pilia-Borsa from the start like an outsized *aragoto* character, with a booming, gruff voice, broad gestures, and fierce glances. His three or four mie seemed natural and completely in character.

In the Pomona production, the hanamichi brought a deep feeling of intimacy between actors and audience; many scenes were played at the point where the hanamichi intersects the stage. Particularly effective was the moment when Barabas the Jew, for the benefit of monks and nuns, is pretending to be angry with his daughter Abigail for having become a Christian, all the while whispering to her that he will meet with her that night and get the treasure she presumably will have dug up from the floor of his house-become-nunnery. Barabas' vigorous exit down the hanamichi, screaming, "Out, out, thou wretch!" was one of the most effective moments in *The Jew of Malta*. The hanamichi also permitted two spectacular processions, one for the arrival of the Turkish prince and his followers, the other for the entrance of the courtesan, Bellamira.

If the Elizabethan actor gave more importance than we do to the meaning of movement and gesture, it was not simply because he enjoyed picturesque movement, but because he believed that the inner man was manifested in a visible way. The hunchback was not to be pitied but feared, for his disfigured body was a sign of a disfigured soul. "Man carried the mark of his class and his nature, in his walk, talk, features and costume." [31] Kabuki still permits each man or woman a different manner of walking, a distinctive makeup, varying ways of using the voice, and diverse colors and forms of costume, in order to suggest differences in class, character, and feelings.

In an informative study of costume in Elizabethan drama, Linthicum describes in some detail the many symbolic uses of color on the Tudor stage. Not only was costume color indicative of character, but beards and hair reflected emotion and were altered to show changes in feeling.[32] We have already noted similar techniques in Kabuki.

Elaborate costumes immediately impress the foreigner viewing Kabuki. Accustomed to the relatively dull clothing worn on the realistic stage, he is unaware perhaps that the Western theater was once similarly prodigal in its use of costume. "No stage ever cared more for fine clothes than the Elizabethans," claims Thorndike, "or lavished on dress a larger portion of its expenses." [33] He goes on to point out that not authenticity, but rather display, was sought. The Elizabethans would indeed be shocked at some of our modern-dress performances of Shakespeare, for although they often wore contemporary clothing onstage, it was of a magnitude almost unknown to us; in fact, ruffs and farthingales became so large that finally their width had to be regulated by law.

Through the use of such Elizabethan and Kabuki customs as models for *The Jew of Malta* performance at Pomona College, symbolic value was assigned to each stance, gait, costume, wig, and color. Bellamira the courtesan is a good example. Sea green, considered by the Elizabethans to represent wantonness, seemed a natural choice for the color of her costume. Following Renaissance patterns, she was given bloomers and a long skirt opened at the center from hem to waist so that the audience could see her legs and her feet encased in gold chopines (thick-soled shoes). The upper-class courtesan in Kabuki, the *oiran*, wears excessively high clogs which give her an almost monstrous appearance and force her to lean upon the shoulders of two men in order to stay upright. Renaissance courtesans (and sometimes the "nice" women as well) would occasionally strut about on chopines, which added to their height if not to their grace. Since the chopines in Shakespeare's time ranged from 6 to 15 inches in height, when the Elizabethan woman put on the higher chopines she too had to be constantly accompanied by someone upon whose shoulder she could lean.

As Bellamira, wearing 6-inch chopines, advanced down the hanamichi, sea-green satin floating in a train behind her, she assumed a stance resembling a "debutante slouch," shoulders back and legs reaching out ahead of her. At either side her arms were spread out like huge wings, her hands limp and graceful as she stalked to the stage like some great bird of prey.

Like Kabuki women, the Elizabethan beauty desired nothing so much as a milk-white skin, and she often destroyed her complexion to achieve it. The standard cosmetic for this purpose was lead white, which soon marked the skin and required ever-thicker applications of white paint.[34] Bellamira, and the other women in the cast of the Pomona production, wore this masklike makeup, highlighted by vermillion lips and rouged cheeks and bosom. With her high shoes, immense dress, predatory pose, and ghostly but beautiful makeup, Bellamira resembled some of the forgotten theatrical monsters that Genet has resuscitated with such effect.

Although a college production inevitably suffers severe limitations (in rehearsal time, availability of actors, funds, etc.), the experiment with *The Jew of Malta* suggests that Kabuki is a rich storehouse for the director in search of a workable Elizabethan style. Similar performing techniques gave Kabuki and the Elizabethan theater many resemblances, but not all of them can be used in a single modern production. Because of the short rehearsal periods and the relatively stable acting companies in Elizabeth's time, a kind of repertoire of stage and scenic devices developed; these maneuvers were handled similarly from play to play, much like a *pas de deux* in ballet, for example, which has certain structural rules but permits a great deal of liberty within that framework. The manner of handling asides, monologues, disguises, observation scenes, and the like, was probably readily understood by the experienced actor so that only a minimum of time was needed for rehearsing the technical aspects of a play. Kabuki exhibits a similar repertoire of devices, including the beautifully choreographed murder scene which is both aesthetically satisfying and spine chilling, the stylized fight, the head inspection, the suicide, the recitation of offstage events accompanied by a pantomimed description of the action, the travel scene, the dance duets, and the pantomime lineup.

Because in both theaters performances were held in the daytime, night was evoked by means other than actual lighting, by dialogue in the Elizabethan theater and by the actors' movements in Kabuki. In the Pomona production of *The Jew of Malta,* both devices were used in an effort to achieve Eisenstein's concept of 100 percent acting.

The two different manners of dealing with this problem are symptomatic of a basic difference between Kabuki and Elizabethan drama: the former stresses movement, dance, gesture, color, music, largely discounting literary or poetic values of the text, while the latter gives more importance to the text than it does to the visual and musical values of the presentation. Or so we have been told. It is possible, however, that scholars largely concerned with literary values of the texts have tended to stress the words more than the Elizabethans did. As the contemporaries of Shakespeare and Marlowe were often lax in their preservation and handling of manuscripts (to say nothing of their revisions of them in performance), we are justified in wondering whether they attached to them the significance we do today. If the acting traditions of Burbage had come down to us in an unbroken line, as have the Kabuki techniques for two and a half centuries, perhaps we would be better able to determine whether we are putting undue emphasis on the text.

Precisely because of this fundamental difference between the literary (as we have been taught to believe) theater of the Elizabethans and the largely nonliterary Kabuki theater, it seems to me desirable that we attempt to find some way of harmonizing the two perspectives in one "total" theater. The many similarities we have noted suggest that such a wedding is possible. In combining the highly theatrical and sensual techniques of Kabuki with the more literary virtues offered by the classic Elizabethan texts (to say nothing of their own theatrical and sensual values) we hope to achieve a maximum of appeal to the senses, to the emotions, to the imagination, and to our atrophied sense of childlike wonder, at the same time arriving at a profound, and perhaps painful, perception of human truth.

VI Oriental Theater

Spirit and Form

In the human as well as the superhuman
the Orientals are more than a match for
us in matters of reality.

A. ARTAUD

In Yokohama, toward the end of the nineteenth century, the
Japanese had their first opportunity to see and hear an Italian
opera. The occasion, witnessed by one of the most perspicacious of Western observers in Meiji Japan, Basil Hall Chamberlain, professor of Japanese philology at the Imperial
University in Tokyo, is described in Chamberlain's *Things
Japanese,* an encyclopedic volume which has lost none of its
freshness and charm in the more than seventy years since it
first appeared:

> When once they [the Japanese spectators] had recovered from the
> first shock of surprise, [they] were seized with a wild fit of hilarity at
> the high notes of the *prima donna,* who really was not at all bad. The
> people laughed at the absurdities of European singing till their sides
> shook, and the tears rolled down their cheeks; and they stuffed their
> sleeves into their mouths, as we might our pocket-handkerchiefs, in the
> vain endeavor to contain themselves.[1]

More than half a century later the New York City Ballet,
performing in Los Angeles, presented a modern Western ballet inspired by the ancient court dances of Japan, and called,
like them, *Bugaku.* The music for this number was written by a
young Japanese composer and modeled upon the old court
music. In fact, it resembled it so much and sounded so strange
to an American audience in 1964 that they laughed much as
the Japanese audience had when confronted with classical

Western music in the late nineteenth century. As the orchestra began to play, a restrained giggle passed through the audience, punctuated here and there by guffaws.

In Tokyo today one can attend performances of Western opera several times during the year, and almost any day choose a program of Western symphonic music from among those offered by the three or four highly competent orchestras in the capital. Productions of Western ballet or modern dance are not difficult to find, and at any time one can choose among several playhouses offering Western-style drama either in translation or written by Japanese. And these offerings are in addition to the Japanese classical plays which are almost always available.

Confronted with the theatrical and musical richness of Tokyo, one turns with a sense of loss and shame to the great theatrical capitals of the Western world, which by comparison seem provincial. Paris, London, Prague, and even some of the smaller cities in Germany are well ahead of New York, for in the former group one can at least find a rich sampling of Western theater from many periods and countries. In New York it becomes increasingly difficult to find significant modern drama, to say nothing of the classics of the seventeenth and eighteenth centuries. Nowhere is there available a constant contact with the great theaters of other world traditions. The nearest approximation is the Théâtre des Nations in Paris, surely one of the most significant experiments of recent years. Here for three months of the year, troupes from all countries of the world perform, enriching the theatrical life of the capital, and fecundating the creative minds of dramatists, actors, and directors who have the good fortune to be in that city. But even this opportunity is far from ideal, for no real understanding can be achieved, no profound exchange of ideas can take place, in the short period of a week or two, which is the usual run of the visiting artists. Imperfect though such a plan may be, it is a step in the right direction, and one can only dream of the new perspectives that might be opened by the establishment of such institutions in many world capitals, and for six, eight, or even twelve months instead of the three that the Théâtre des Nations now enjoys.

If the expense of transporting the great stars or entire troupes for brief periods is too heavy, perhaps a theater could be established where representatives of the great foreign theatrical traditions could come to work and perform for long periods at a time. Classes offered by the actors might help defray expenses at the same time that they deepen our own actors' understanding. The teacher's shorter working day might also appeal to actors who habitually spend twelve or fifteen hours at the theater. If some of the competent younger actors could be wooed away for a year, it would give us the opportunity to study Kabuki and other great theatrical forms firsthand, and would at the same time allow the young Oriental actors the advantage of playing some of the important roles that they would not yet be allowed to play in major theaters in their own country.

At present, plans have been announced for both a Chinese opera house and a Kabuki theater in San Francisco. Whether a satisfactory equilibrium will be found between commercial viability and artistic integrity remains to be seen. But the venture is promising; well managed, it could contribute significantly to the growth of Western theater. If we are to grow and to profit from the great traditions of world theater, it will only be through such firsthand contact and experience. Books may make us aware of new areas to be explored, but only through disciplined study of techniques and styles will we be able to develop significant forms for our own theater.

Etiemble, the respected French professor, scholar, and writer, upon his return from Japan in 1964, wrote an article [2] describing the astounding knowledge and understanding that the Japanese exhibited for French literature and culture. He pointed out the discrepancy in French reciprocation, and asked, "When will we have our Meiji era?" His question might well be made on behalf of the entire Western world. When will we, like the Japanese—and perhaps to a lesser degree the rest of the Orient—wake up to the possibilities and perspectives waiting to be discovered on the other side of the world? The Japanese long ago lost their provinciality, and made an advance from the Middle Ages of the Tokugawa era in mid-nineteenth century to the modern Western era in which they are now living, within the startlingly short space of a few decades, known as the Meiji (1868–1912). With a kind of patronizing approval, Westerners continuously point to Japan's rapid integration of Western ways, seldom stopping to realize that, as far as the highly developed and refined arts of the East are concerned, most of us in the West are still living in the Middle Ages, and doing nothing to bring about a renaissance.

Faubion Bowers, who has surely done his share through the three or four books he has devoted to the East and particularly to the Oriental theater, describes what he calls "the cosmopolitan genius of Japan," and states that "Japan has one of the highest standards of modern theater in the world today." If this is so, it is because Japan has not only continued to develop her best traditional forms of theater, but has looked to the West in search of invigorating new traditions. She has not remained artistically isolated, geographically exclusive. No one would claim that the productions of Western plays, or Western-style plays, performed in Japan at the end of the nineteenth or in the early twentieth century, were models of Western dramatic art. But the Japanese artists and audiences had to spend many years of apprenticeship before they felt at home with what were essentially foreign forms of theater. Today the Japanese are comfortable with Western theater; one can witness remarkable performances of Shakespeare, Rostand, Anouilh, or O'Neill in Tokyo. If, as Faubion Bowers insists,[3] the performances of Western actors in traditional forms of Oriental theater cannot be taken seriously as art or appreciated in a broad aesthetic sense, it is not because drama must now and forever remain geographically exclusive, but because we are still babes learning to walk in the highly complex styles of Eastern theater. Granted, the theaters of the East, being more stylized, more "total" in their use of the actor, demand a longer, stricter, more complete training than Western styles of drama, which seem often to concentrate on psychological training to the exclusion of all other skills. However, we are not incapable of mastering a style that *now* may be foreign to us. Perhaps when we have taken as much time for, and shown as much interest in, their theater as the Japanese have exhibited in ours, we shall be able to produce as skillful a Kabuki or Chinese opera, say, as the *Cyrano* or *Hamlet* that the Japanese now produce.

But this should be only half the goal. We cannot go on playing *only* Kabuki any more than we could go on playing only Shakespeare or Beckett or Genet, for the theater is constantly growing and changing. It behooves us to take what is best, and what can fit into our own, from any tradition. If the Japanese performed only Anouilh or Rodgers and Hammerstein, their theater would have reached a dead end. We hope that classical works from the past, and from all traditions, might be a kind of ferment in the creation of new dramas, despite the fact that classics also have aesthetic and historical interest in themselves.

Bowers would apparently deny us this cross-fertilization and cosmopolitanism which he, paradoxically, admires in Japan:

> The point is now being reached in the world [he claims], where the geographical and artistic fact emerges, leave Kabuki to the Japanese, Shakespeare to the English, Chekhov to the Russians, and O'Neill to the Americans. In provincial areas where it is impossible for people to see these masterworks exchanged between nations, then yes, by all means, study and struggle to recapture as much authenticity and geographical verisimilitude as possible. But it is an exercise. Not art. Nothing to be taken seriously. One has only to think of Geraldine Page's ludicrously bad performance in *The Three Sisters* to realize how a great and competent actress can be defeated by a theatrical journey. (Of course, Kim Stanley crossed the border miraculously, but that was a special case, and a rare one.) [4]

One cannot help answering that all great theatrical performances are unfortunately special cases and, alas, all too rare. It does not require an exotic play to show up the weaknesses of a miscast actor. Neither is geography or race responsible for success; accomplishment in the theater depends largely upon sensitivity to and awareness of a certain tradition and style, and the willingness to spend the time and discipline required to attain that style.

If we measure "provincial areas" by the availability of "masterworks exchanged between nations," then every major capital in the world is a provincial town, for where can one find, even every other year, a first-class Russian troupe presenting Chekhov, Pushkin, Gorki, Ostrovski; a first-class English company playing Shakespeare and Congreve; the French producing Molière, Racine, Anouilh, the Germans Brecht and Kleist, the Japanese Chikamatsu and Zeami? This might indeed be an earthly theatrical paradise, but it does not exist. Instead, it seems wise to "struggle to recapture as much authenticity and geographical verisimilitude as possible" in productions that may sometimes strike us as exercises, but that will, given time, mature into valid artistic experiences, like the Théâtre National Populaire's production of *The Prince of Homburg* with Gérard Philipe, Strehler's productions of Brecht in Italy, numerous German productions of Shakespeare, Judith Anderson's portrayal of Medea and Laurence Olivier's performance of Oedipus, to say nothing of the Japanese productions of *Ivanov, Summer and Smoke,* and *Cherry Orchard,* which Bowers, in the same article, singles out for special praise.

The geographical and artistic fact that emerges is not, as Faubion Bowers would have it, that we must leave each theater to its nationals, but rather that we are hopelessly provincial and unskilled in our approaches to theaters whose traditions differ from ours. Institutions like IASTA and the Théâtre des Nations, in differing ways, are taking steps to broaden our understanding of traditions other than our own, and to increase the actor's skill by permitting him to work with men of stature in each of many theatrical traditions.

We examined the fruit of such experiments in earlier chapters. Recent productions like *Marat-Sade* and *Royal Hunt of the Sun* show that the Oriental theater is still contributing, directly or indirectly, to a vitalization of modern theater. Peter Weiss's play, set in a madhouse where the Marquis de Sade directs a production of a play showing the murder of Marat by Charlotte Corday, is quite clearly related to the efforts of Artaud. The effective use of costumes and makeup, musicians and singers, mime, a narrator, actors who convey several levels of reality, cries, screams, brutality, and lyricism—all point back to Artaud's theater of cruelty and the later impressive works of Brecht and Genet. Both the latter are mentioned in Peter Brook's preface to the American edition of *Marat-Sade,* and both are very much aware of Oriental theatrical techniques.

Peter Shaffer's *Royal Hunt of the Sun,* less cruel in its visual effects which tend to splendor rather than brutality, still reminds us, as Artaud would have it, that "the sky can fall on our heads." The story of Pizarro's conquest of Peru and the meaningless murder of the Inca king is a tale of disillusion and emptiness. Handled by an author with less verbal skill than Peter Shaffer, or by a director with less imagination than Peter Brook, *Royal Hunt* might very well have been another spectacular historical drama. Shaffer, however, has created, not a historical portrait, but a deeply moving theatrical experience based upon total theater and a ritual effect. In his notes he calls for "rites, mimes, masks and magics," and adds that the play belongs to the director, designer, musician, mime, and actor almost as much as to the author. Stylized movement, rich musical passages, hieratic costumes and makeup, symbolic decoration and staging, a use of a "special voice" for the Incas— all contribute to the experience of the play. As in the Chinese opera, the actor must use multiple resources, and can depend upon makeup and costume to aid him, but must not rely upon the decor, for the play is intended to be set on a bare stage with platforms.

Both *Marat-Sade* and *Royal Hunt* are, like Brechtian epic theater, constructed episodically, with each major episode bearing its own title. And, like Brecht's major works, they depend upon a stylized production for their fulfillment. These two plays, among the most successful of the past few London and New York seasons, indicate that Western audiences are ready to appreciate the kind of total theater characteristic of the East if it is well written and well produced. But we are only beginning. The Oriental theater, which we must at last begin to study in earnest on a professional level, offers us a number of invaluable lessons which can help us in our production of Eastern masterpieces, but which just as surely will be profitable in presenting Western works, and in preparing the terrain for a more vital theater in the future. For the lessons of the Orient, relating both to spirit and to form, are applicable on a universal as well as a particular level. In concluding, I should like to summarize precisely what I think the Oriental theater can contribute to the West. Always remembering that, in making generalizations about so vast a territory, exceptions and nuances exist, I think we may sum up the spirit of Oriental theater in three adjectives: participative, total, stylized.

A PARTICIPATIVE THEATER

The Oriental spectator, whether in China, Japan, or Bali, attends the theater as though it were a part of life, not a place set apart. In the same way that he relaxes at a picnic, becomes involved in it in a natural way, so he participates in his theater, where he feels at home. Unlike the Westerner who is usually compelled to sit in rapt attention in order to understand the dialogue, since the level aimed at is almost invariably that of the waking intelligence, the Oriental spectator may enjoy his theater as he would any other activity or pleasure. There is an atmosphere of joy and conviviality at theatrical performances in the East, for the theater is a place to live. The spectator rarely gives his undivided attention to what is happening on the stage. At the Kabuki he may get up and go out into the lobby to look at the goods in the many shops there, he may eat in one of a number of restaurants in the theater building, or he may purchase his box meal and return to the theater to dine while he watches the performance. Even while he is in the auditorium, he is not constantly involved in the performance. He may chat quietly with a neighbor, read his program, or have a short nap until a favorite scene is enacted. All these activities may take place at Western productions as well, but they are felt to be a kind of heresy, whereas in Japan they are not frowned upon. In earlier days the Kabuki audience sat in small cubicles, each accommodating five to seven people, often in family groups including the children; in the center was a hibachi on which a pot of tea or perhaps a meal was heated.

Chinese opera was formerly performed in teahouses where the audience drank and ate while watching the performance, or chatted and rested until favorite parts of the program were performed. In Bali, where the theater can be anywhere, the activities of everyday life are pursued around the performing area where the dance drama is taking place, actors and audience as undisturbed by dogs that happen to stray across the acting area as the Chinese or Japanese are by the stage assistants who skitter across the stage to help the actors or to place props at strategic points.

So relaxed an atmosphere makes possible a very long performance. In a Western theater, two-and-a-half-hour sessions can be very tiring. By eleven o'clock most are ready, and by eleven-thirty everyone is ready, to go home. The protracted effort of concentration, sitting in one's seat *listening* for two and a half hours, leaves one more numbed than moved, more fatigued than illuminated, more troubled than overjoyed. The extremely lengthy plays of Genet and Claudel take for granted, I believe, an attitude similar to that of the Oriental audience. The spectator is not expected to grasp, nor even to attempt to come to grips intellectually with every moment of the play. In passages that exist simply for their sensual values the spectator should relax, let himself (as Giraudoux suggested) be bathed by the style of the author. Such an approach to theatergoing renders possible the marathon productions of the Orient: Chinese opera (before Western influence was felt) went on for many hours; Kabuki ran from before sunrise to nightfall, and today one can still attend from late morning till late night without being overcome by fatigue or tedium. In Bali nightlong performances are frequent, and those who wish to may sleep and wake as often as they like during the night.

Obviously such lengthy performances are common not merely because of the kind of drama presented in these countries, or simply because of the relaxed attitude of the audience, who consider the theater a place to *live,* not a place to *sit.* Equally important is the fact that in the Orient people have not lost the ability to play at the theater; they have not lost their sense of joy in the theatrical performance. Asian countries are not devoted, as we are, to an ideal of rationalism; they have not allowed the rational faculties to destroy their ability to think, feel, and live with the other, equally important, parts of their being. Huizinga, in his study of play in culture, *Homo Ludens,*[5] considers that play began to disappear from Western culture sometime in the eighteenth century, the age of scientific rationalism. By the end of the nineteenth century it seemed dead for good. Certainly in the theater, the naturalists and their less talented disciples (still dominating the so-called serious theater today) taught us the importance of being earnest, and we have scarcely been able to smile at serious theater since. If we do, it is with the warmhearted sentimental smile that recognizes ourselves in the little man onstage. With dutiful concentration and knitted brows, we ponder the questions of the hour as they are presented to us by philosopher-sociologist-politician-psychologist-playwrights, and we consider frivolous and shallow every play that does not give us *food for thought.* Not food for the soul or the spirit, not a gigantic vision, but food for the intellectual mill to reduce to aphorisms, rules, laws, which kill the theatrical experience just as surely as the Oedipus myth is killed when reduced to "don't sleep with your mother."

We have lost our sense of joy; we are overwhelmed by our seriousness and by our commitment to the intellect. And yet the sense of joy is fundamental not only to play, but to those extensions of play, ritual and drama. We enjoy playing at least partly because we know we are playing and also because we like the sensation of creating within a restricted area an ideal world, conforming to certain laws or rules, and then entering into this created, artificial world as though it were real. We are aware and unaware at the same time, and this double experience is essential to the sense of profound joy that arises from theatrical experiences. When hypertrophied reason convinces the artist that he must, instead, make us believe that we are actually witnessing life behind an invisible fourth wall, then the experience in the theater takes on all the seriousness of a lived experience, denying us the sense of release and perfection (and perfection is possible in pessimism) which we feel in the presence of a more self-conscious art. Then, instead of achieving a double awareness, we lose sight of ourselves as we watch more objectively what is happening, behind the invisible fourth wall, within the confines of a picture frame that constantly rejects us, and denies us access to the artistic world onstage. We cannot "play with" the drama or the actors because we obviously do not form part of the play area. Such a rejection divides the theater into two distinct worlds where the mysteries of metamorphosis and identification can become meaningful to the spectator only in an intellectualized way.

The elevation, exaltation, and illumination arising from a profound and meaningful experience, whether in life, in ritual, or in the theater, might well be expressed if not by laughter at least by a smile of profound happiness and satisfaction at the perfection with which, say, a work of art reflects some aspect of life, some fragment of truth. And yet, how often have we sat in the theater during the performance of a deeply revealing play, watching a sober audience failing to respond, finding no *delight* in facets of the play which speak to our histrionic sensibility. Waiting perhaps to be *convinced,* the public is unprepared to respond on an unintellectualized level. Many plays and productions give them no opportunity for such response, even if they were prepared. Consequently, when they do attend a performance that permits play, they do not know how to respond. The works of Beckett are a case in point. Like many of the authors of the "theater of the absurd" Beckett provides a good deal of play, and expects his audience to experience his dramas on several levels. There are sensual and comic perspectives in a play like *Endgame* to which the larger part of most audiences is insensitive. Unable, or unwilling, to delight in the grotesque jokes played by life, and in the perfection of their theatrical transposition, the spectator is merely overwhelmed by the grim view he sees embodied there, or put off by what he considers pure foolishness, since he is unaccustomed to a metaphorical mode in the theater and therefore simply rejects garbage cans as a possible place of lodging.

It is difficult to understand how anyone attuned to the double awareness of the theater can fail to smile at the baroque heroics of Corneille's characters—not because they are absurd, but because they are so perfect—or the profound revelations of character in Racine and Shakespeare, moments in which reality and art meet in the perfected, theatricalized image, a metaphor for man's inner world. This sense of joy which is reflected in, and arises from, a feeling of participation, was expressed in the Elizabethan theater by a somewhat boisterous audience that had what Thorndike describes as an "attitude which we find oftenest in children listening to stories—a mixture of impatience and responsiveness, a willingness to let one's imagination go and an eagerness to have it spurred." [6] Apparently, the only way to enter into that "nearest approach to an earthly paradise," which the theater can be, is to become again as a little child.

The Oriental audiences have managed to keep this attitude toward their theater, partly, as I suggested before, because their cultures are not so reason centered as ours, and partly because the presentational form of drama and the structure of the theater itself contribute to such an attitude. The Kabuki audience today still shows its pleasure in the actor's performance by shouting his name or some suitable cry when he enters or when he strikes a pose or speaks a line in a particularly pleasing way. These electrifying cries help to draw audience and actors into the same field. A similar reaction was apparently widespread in the heyday of Noh drama, for Zeami mentions it in his treatises. Today the hushed atmosphere of the Noh theater is centuries removed from its earlier vigor and animation. The Noh, like the dance of Cambodia and of Thailand, lost much of its vitality when it was adopted by the courts, and refined through centuries of contact with aristocratic milieux. One has only to go from Thailand and Cambodia to Bali to see what an extraordinary sense of strength and life is imparted to dance and drama by direct contact with the people, for in Bali these forms are an integral part of everyday experience and are not set apart for a particular group. The most vigorous theater of past ages has always been a theater for the many, whether in Greece, Japan, England, China, France, India, Spain, or Bali.

It has also been a theater in which the audience was not rejected by, but integrated with, the acting area, usually from three, and sometimes from four, sides. Kabuki, Noh, and Chinese opera stages, surprisingly similar to that of the jutting Elizabethan platform, encouraged a presentational style. Only in recent years, under the influence of the West, have Kabuki and Chinese opera begun to use a proscenium-type stage; at the same time they have retained such essential appendages as the hanamichi or an onstage orchestra, and have continued, perhaps paradoxically, to play presentationally within the picture frame, thereby at least partly canceling out the ill effects of a structure so destructive to the double awareness that is a part of vital theater.

A TOTAL THEATER

If the Oriental theater encourages participation, it does so at various levels; it is, then, total theater in more than one sense. Among a number of ways of interpreting total theater, the most widespread is as an experience integrating all the resources offered by the theater. But Oriental theater, and any self-respecting total theater, should be total in two other ways as well: it should appeal to many levels in each spectator, and to all levels within a given society. Unlike the "théâtre populaire" of the French, which is designed to appeal to the workingman, and often takes advantage of his political leanings to win his attention and support, a total theater should not be aimed at a single segment of a society. It should be a true theater of the people, embracing the unlettered on the one hand, the intellectual on the other, and including the groups between these extremes. The forms of Oriental theater we have been studying represent precisely this kind of complete appeal. The Noh, at its beginning, before it was subverted for the sole pleasure of the aristocracy, was as popular a form as Kabuki. The latter, aimed at the merchant classes, and assiduously restricted to that class by the shogunate, was nonetheless a popular entertainment with the samurai and the nobility as well. Many stories tell of affairs between performers and members of the upper classes, who often attended the theater in disguise.

In Bali, where the theatrical experience is so integral a part of everyday experience, there can be no question of a coterie theater. In China, too, the opera belongs to everyone: the Empress Dowager was a protector of the Peking theater, whose music was familiar to ministers, scholars, and merchants and could also be sung by the meanest coolie. Apparently Chinese opera is so universally admired that the Communists have discovered they cannot eradicate it, but must be satisfied with discarding the medieval, "superstitious" stories, and substituting new ones in harmony with the party line, adapting them to the same old traditional techniques and music.

One reason Oriental theater holds a fascination for many levels of society is that it speaks to many levels of the human being. Since logical discourse has never dominated traditional forms of Oriental theater, the performance can address itself to the varied sensibilities of the members of an audience. An Asian audience at a traditional theater is no doubt more unified than the average Western audience, yet the Japanese public today resembles the Western public in its diversity and fragmentation. A Kabuki performance, however, can still exercise its appeal, for through its multiple resources Kabuki makes a significant contribution to the four primary appetites: emotional, physical, spiritual, and intellectual. Stress differs from play to play, but every play contains elements directed to each of the four needs. The emotional appeal—remembering that emotion means laughter, fear, admiration, and so forth, as well as sorrow—is an essential part of any Kabuki performance; it is grand and gigantic in an *aragoto* play, pathetic and human in a *sewamono*. The colors, poses, dances, musical accompaniments, costumes, and of course the food eaten in the theater, all satisfy the senses and are no doubt responsible for the definition of Kabuki, which we noted earlier, as "a mess of carnal appetites."

If we mean by spirit that which lies below the surface of the conscious, and which intuits a unity that the fragmented senses and reason itself would seem to deny, then Kabuki speaks a language of the spirit, addressing it through those very senses whose *correspondances* Baudelaire felt pointed toward the world of spirit. In a language that defies transcription and, like the Barong play in Bali, suggests the terrifying encounter between the immanent and the transcendent, *Dōjōji Maiden, The Monstrous Spider,* and similar plays point the way to a world beyond logical comprehension. But they do not avoid our own workaday world, for Kabuki is largely dedicated to a portrayal of the life of man, whether merchant, thief, or chivalrous commoner righting the wrongs perpetrated by the samurai upon the little man. Almost all Chikamatsu's plays performed today, not unlike drama in the West, deal with the quandaries of merchants, prostitutes, bankers, innkeepers, packhorse drivers, and similar individuals as they confront the problems of everyday living, colored by such real and human activities as drinking sake, smoking pipes, and counting money. Shattering decisions must be made, which sometimes imply criticism of society and reveal the workings of the human mind, the weaknesses of human nature. Even plays of a more exalted character are not devoid of these elements, which are almost the entire stock of serious theater in the West. Needless to say, in such plays the apparent realism is refined by the stylized performance; the actor can make

the drinking of alcohol a poetic moment of depth and significance undreamed of in the Western drawing-room drama. It is
as though Marcel Marceau, his talent for dialogue matching
that for movement, and accompanied by an entire troupe of
peers or near peers, were to perform even a relatively insignificant work—say, the first act of *The Cocktail Party*. One can
imagine the dazzling effects. How much more impressive it
would be were such a troupe to perform the masterpieces of
Western theater. Here too we might find a total theater.

At least we would come closer to a realization of total
theater as it is commonly conceived. Aided by costume,
makeup, music, decor, lights, the actor-dancer could create a
synthesis of the theatrical arts. A new Western total theater
would not be like musical comedy, whose separate elements are
glued together but never fused, or like ballet and opera in
which one element takes preponderance over the others, but it
would be a completely integrated production in which all facets
of the actor's art are used to create a moving, beautiful, and
meaningful production that would appeal to every facet of
men from all classes. In its inclusion of all elements of theater,
even those we consider peripheral, the Oriental theater is
faithful to its origins, for dance, music, acrobatics, song, and
story are typical of both its sacred and its profane dramatic
beginnings.

Debussy, like Artaud forty years later, was sensitive to the
expressiveness of nonliterary aspects of theater. Speaking of
the Javanese performers who had so impressed him at the
International Exposition of 1889 and were to mark his musical
style, he points out the variety of effects available through
pantomime and dance: "The seduction of the wordless language—pantomime—is irresistible because action and not formula is the medium of expression. The unfortunate thing
about our theater is that we have limited it to the more obviously intelligible elements. The other mode of expression
would be so beautiful that nothing else would satisfy us." [7]

The equilibrium achieved by a theater that is running on all
cyclinders, integrating every facet of the performance, not

allowing any one element to run away with the show, suggests that it may be impossible actually to *write* a play. What is written stands as a scenario, a score, or a partition, and from this beginning—as Gabriel Cousin suggests, following the lead of Artaud and no doubt of thousands of performers and writers in the Orient—the play is created in the theater. Aside from that creation it has no true being, and cannot be judged.

Some of the famous Kabuki plays illustrate the point: most of the celebrated *Jūhachiban,* or *Eighteen Plays* of the Ichikawa family, some of which still form the backbone of the *aragoto* repertory, are nothing more than vehicles for the actor's virtuosity. It would not occur to a Japanese to judge *Yanone* or *Kenuki* as text, since the interest is quite clearly not textual, but theatrical. A given performance might be judged, but not the text itself. It should be added that not all the plays of the Kabuki repertoire are devoid of literary value, but to read them is, in a certain sense, to betray the intentions of the author who visualized them in the theater. After all, it is unfair to judge a Rembrandt painting from a photograph, even if it *is* in color. How much more unfair it is to judge the masterpiece from a black-and-white photo, a mere skeleton, which denies us the sensuous appeal, depth, and emotional content given by color. Art, and surely the art of the theater, is a physical phenomenon that should produce a physical sensation in addition to the usual emotional or intellectual reactions we seem to consider normal. This harmony of impressions cannot be accomplished by words alone, but must arise from a combination of words and plastic, rhythmic values.

The Western theater has already recognized this theatrical truth, and some impressive experiments have been made. The works of Genet, Weiss, and Shaffer, when read, may strike us as puzzling, conventional, chaotic, or just plain dull. When *The Blacks, Marat-Sade,* and *Royal Hunt of the Sun* find their real existence in performance, however, they come alive, revealing facets not apparent in the reading; through color, visual symbol, choreography, music, vocal timbre, movement, and all the performing subtleties, they become deeply moving and meaningful, and are even capable of bringing about in us the essential change that Artaud considered necessary to theatrical experience. Despite the success of these plays, the West goes on performing as though the text were supreme, and color or movement distinctly subsidiary. The text may well be the skeleton upon which the rest of the performance hangs, but even a deformed skeleton can give fascinating and moving results—perhaps more theatrical than a well-molded skeleton. Zeami taught that the skeleton, while essential, is not enough, that muscle and skin are equally important. We stand to learn much about equality in theatrical values from the East.

The perfect flowers of the *Jūhachiban,* exhibiting such an equilibrium, combine the spectacular elements and the style of *aragoto* with a deeply moving human element, and contain—at least for us today—an implicit social commentary. Such plays are *Sukeroku* and particularly *Kanjinchō,* possibly the Kabuki play best known in the West. *Kanjinchō,* usually called *The Subscription List,* has become widely known through the Kurosawa film, *The Tiger's Tail,* based on it. The film, while preserving certain elements of the original, is an adaptation for a popular medium, and is in no way a Kabuki performance, lacking both the sense of transposed reality and the high style. The so-called Kabuki influence in Japanese films, so often mentioned by Western commentators, is usually derived not from Kabuki at all, but from common traditions in the Japanese past: the heroic samurai behavior, the ceremonial attitude toward living. Kabuki has stylized them by basing movements and characterizations on dance, whereas the films have tended to treat them in a realistic fashion. Considering the realism of our theater and films and our unceremonious behavior, it is not surprising that we see Japanese films as "stylized," but for the average Japanese stylization is nonexistent in such motion pictures.

A STYLIZED THEATER

It is precisely this stylization that characterizes traditional forms of Oriental theater; imported Western forms are more realistic and representational. Stylization does not mean divorced from reality, but simply approaching reality through a different perspective, choosing what is most significant, meaningful, pleasing, or dramatically effective. A vast spectrum of stylization can be seen throughout the Orient, from the subtly choreographed performances of recognizable everyday activities in the *sewamono* of Kabuki through the symbolic gestures of Chinese opera, to the rarefied and highly abstract movements of Noh or of certain Balinese dances. There is a point where reality is lost and stylization becomes pure dance. This zone is as dangerous for drama, which thrives on reality, as is its opposite, apparent in the Happenings, undisciplined, accidental, purposeless, which give no vision of reality because there is no forming vision behind them. Drama belongs in that vast territory between the two, tied to reality *and* to art, balanced dynamically between the two, and falling neither into the extreme of pure movement, which may be high art but is not drama since it is not connected to life, nor into the extreme of pure chance, which may be life itself but cannot be art since it is not purposed or controlled.

The artist is a man constrained and yet free; our varying kinds of art may be defined by the degree to which freedom or constraint dominates. In the West in recent years we have stressed freedom more than restraint, while the East has traditionally preferred restraint. Paradoxically, however, the Oriental actor has in one sense much more freedom than we: he can express himself in *more ways* and within a broader sphere. We are largely hampered by a convention of which we are unaware simply because it *is* a convention of our theater and therefore universally accepted: realism. The behavior of the actor must conform more or less to that of real people in real-life situations. We are not given the freedom to express our inner world, our obsessions and fears, in any way that might be bigger than life. The play, *Who's Afraid of Virginia Woolf?* may be violent, even inhuman, but violence and inhumanity are represented in a recognizable, believable human way, with gestures, voices, and facial expressions that could be used in everyday life as we live it. The Oriental actor, given such a play, might feel free within the traditions of Chinese opera, Kabuki, or Balinese dance play to develop moods, emotions, and character in a dozen different ways forbidden us. He has another freedom denied us: the freedom of the perfectly disciplined artist who is working within clearly defined traditions and who, within those limits, may develop his individuality. A connoisseur of Oriental forms of theater will be able to distinguish important differences in roles as they are performed by different artists. Actors are far from interchangeable.

The total actor, the stylized actor, is a disciplined actor. He has learned to use voice, body, face, in a special way, and to handle objects of significance in a particular manner. He is a virtuoso, in the sense that Marcel Marceau is a virtuoso, which does not deny his warmth, psychological insights, and ability to communicate emotion. He deals in human feelings, but he transposes them, for he is not a psychologist but an artist. He is also a priest in his dedication to his art; many years of study go into the making of an actor. Not just anyone in Asia can stand on the stage and thereby *be* an actor. Training methods in the East are as diverse as they are here. Students of Chinese opera begin study when they are tiny children and receive a disciplined training in schools where rules are imparted and adult actors are emulated. In Bali the teacher may be a dancer who no longer dances, but who moves with the young student as he or she exercises, manipulating the student's arms as though he or she were a puppet.

Kabuki training, similar yet different, might stand as a symbol, *mutatis mutandis,* of Oriental methods. As such, I should like to discuss it in a little more detail. The Kabuki actor must be a dedicated artist, willing to give up many of the pleasures of other mortals for the satisfaction and glory he will derive from the theater. For twenty-five days each month he must be at the theater from ten in the morning until after ten in the evening. And when he is not performing, there are studies (for the eminent Kabuki actors have been highly proficient in calligraphy, painting, and poetry), rehearsals, and the training of his disciples. Unlike the Western actor, who usually has a wide margin of freedom, the Kabuki actor must make of his profession a way of life. His training and discipline (roughly comparable to those of a ballet dancer in the West) start at an early age. When he is three or four he begins to spend much of his day in the theater watching the performances, studying classical Japanese dance, and even performing some of the many child roles in the Kabuki repertoire.

The Kabuki actor's training is what John D. Mitchell calls "non-verbal and non-directed." [8] That is to say, the young student simply watches for hours on end, is constantly exposed to the best of Kabuki acting, but is never given the kind of explicit training or explanation we expect in the West. This is the way of training in all the arts in Japan; it is felt that the art is transferred not through rules and precepts, but through a personal master-disciple relationship. Miss Miyoko Watanabe, who studied Kabuki for eight years at the Kabuki-za and now teaches Kabuki dance in New York, remembers watching a rehearsal at which a young Kabuki actor did not seem to be doing as well as he might. The master actor had not corrected him at all, and when Miss Watanabe questioned him regarding his silence, he answered, "The young person growing up to become a Kabuki actor must find his own way to the part; given time and opportunity for observation, the young actor will correct errors or deficiencies. We are sincere in our desire not to tamper with or to attempt to influence, or to interfere with the individual expression of the developing actor." [9]

This anecdote is of some interest to theater students in the West, since we tend to feel that any stylized acting, and surely the highly disciplined kinds we find in Oriental theater, represses individuality and forces the imitation of a purely exterior pattern. Perhaps we feel that highly disciplined acting lacks individuality because we in the West try to master the art of acting in a few years; to acquire a style would require a rejection of personal emotion in favor of almost slavishly following a model. In Japan, where the actor studies thirty years or more before he can be considered accomplished, a certain nonchalance is possible. Like Kabuki itself, which blends realism and stylization, the approach to acting mingles the discipline of a highly specialized technique and dance training with the freedom of the osmosis process.

Since the Kabuki actors are what we might call, paradoxically, natural actors, only rarely can they verbalize about their approach to acting, to training, and to the preparation of a role. Zoe Kincaid, in 1925, noted that they are "entirely unconscious of the laws that govern their art." [10] Perhaps the same may be said of some Western actors, but it is far from the general rule, particularly among those who have spent thirty or forty years in the theater. In fact, our actors are prone to verbalize at great length.

The "depth of emotion communicable through stylization," which Faubion Bowers reports as startling American actors when the Kabuki-za toured here in 1960, caused many queries regarding preparation. Bowers' comments deserve quoting at length:

> They [American actors] wanted to know how and by what means or tricks the Kabuki stars got inside their roles before going on stage and so instantly and unflaggingly carried their parts from beginning to end. The answers, while precise for Kabuki, were almost dismaying. Shōroku, the first time he was asked this, answered, "My world is my world; the stage is the stage. I step on the stage and I'm in *that* world." . . . Utaemon answered, "When you go to the theater early, you start putting on your make-up slowly and quietly, and by the time you are made up, there you are looking at the character in the mirror. You are 'prepared.'" [11]

Later Bowers tells how Shōroku, one of the most formidable actors performing anywhere today, said that his acting derived from the center of his conviction, and stressed his attempts to be a truthful actor at all times.

The Kabuki actor, like the Noh actors (and like Olivier), builds his character from without. Before his entrance at the back of the hanamichi, he sits in front of a mirror. As Utaemon suggests, a similar process takes place in the dressing room as the actor slowly becomes the character he is playing. It might be pointed out also that, unlike the Western actor, the Kabuki artist does not play one role each day. He may play as many as six or eight roles, or even more, in a single day, since the five-hour matinee is made up of four plays, and the five-hour evening performance of four more. At certain times an actor even plays two roles in the same drama.

While it may be dangerous to draw conclusions from this brief exposition, the differences between the Kabuki training and its results on the one hand, and Western representational training and its results on the other, suggest that the West has been selling stylization (nonrealistic acting) short on several scores. In the first place, it need not be shallow, superficial, exclusively exterior, and unrelated to a vital reality. Second, nonrealistic acting need not be cold and unemotional; its appeal is not exclusively to the aesthetic sensitivities of the audience, for it may be as moving as more psychologically oriented performances. Whether or not we can respond to a stylized performance depends upon our preparation and our own sensibilities. To condemn Gielgud, for example, as Charles Marowitz does in his study, *Stanislavski and the Method,* as "the ultimate triumph of artificiality; the triumph of the Conscious over the Unconscious; the Unreal over the Real; the Peripheral over the Essential," [12] is surely to lose sight of the fact that the theater *is* an art, *is* unreal, and that the actor must be conscious. Only a madman could believe otherwise.

The point of view represented by Marowitz, and that represented by the Oriental theater, are irreconcilable. The fusing of a split image (actor and role) into a single image gives rise to "satisfying and compelling" theater for Marowitz, whereas the Oriental theater is predicated upon the duality of the theatrical experience for both performers and spectators, for the Orient sees theater as art, not life. The difference is nicely summed up in a little incident related by Marowitz. While waiting in line to enter a movie theater he became aware of a girl across the street apparently waiting for her boyfriend. When the girl realized that she was being observed by him and other people in the line, she began to exteriorize her waiting, looking at her watch, gazing off into the distance, "her face becoming disfigured with a look of intense expectancy."[13] For Marowitz she then became a performer and therefore unconvincing, whereas when she was behaving naturally, unaware of her audience, she was a single image, pure subjectivity unaware of creating an impression. He considers the young woman "comfortably idling her time and watching for her [boyfriend's] arrival," superior, theatrically speaking, to the woman whose face and gesture underlined her emotions for the benefit of an audience. The former is surely a superior photographic image of life, but I think the latter must be deemed a superior transposition for the theater. The former is Mme Ranevsky sitting motionless on a sofa in her empty halls and regretting quietly that the cherry orchard must be sold, weeping real tears perhaps and surely suffering intensely within, whether this feeling is shared by the spectator or not. The latter is Medea, or some Oriental heroine, crying vengeance on her faithless lover, and, whether she actually suffers or not, causing the spectator's hair to stand on end.

Art in the Orient is neither life itself, nor a realm of fantasy utterly divorced from life. In the words of Japan's most distinguished dramatist, Chikamatsu, "Art is something that lies in the slender margin between the real and the unreal." By its very nature, it is a transposition, a re-creation, and not an imitation. After all, Chikamatsu argues, do we deny the actor makeup simply because the character he portrays would not wear makeup in everyday life? Chikamatsu, whose plays are probably the most "Western" of all Oriental plays written within the traditional forms, lived in an age that apparently shared the twentieth-century taste for realism. It was in reply to a representative of the realistic bias that he spoke the above oft-quoted words. In the same essay, set down after the dramatist's death by a friend who recalled his words, Chikamatsu gives a nice answer to Marowitz, or at least expresses clearly the contrary point of view:

In recent plays many things have been said by female characters which real women could not utter. Such things fall under the heading of art; it is because they say what could not come from a real woman's lips that their true emotions are disclosed. If in such cases the author were to model his character on the ways of a real woman and conceal her feelings, such realism, far from being admired, would permit no pleasure in the work.[14]

Art for Chikamatsu cannot resemble the real object, for such realism would soon begin to pall. He demands "some stylized parts in a work otherwise resembling the real form. . . . this is what makes it art, and is what delights men's minds." [15] Chikamatsu, we can see, was not a victim of hypertrophied rationalism and was able to find a more perfect blending than most modern theater men in the West.

Donald Keene concludes an illuminating article, "Realism and Unreality in Japanese Drama," by saying that "the great plays of the Japanese theater, have always combined realism and unreality in intimate conjunction." [16] We have seen this phenomenon in the Noh, in Kabuki, and in some forms of Balinese drama as well. One facet of this harmony of opposites of which we have not spoken, however, is the male actor of female roles, the *onnagata,* who is so important to the spirit and form of Kabuki. All the theaters of the East have, at one time or another, practiced this inverted relationship between performer and role. The most outstanding of all Peking opera artists, Mei-Lan-fang, was renowned for his female roles. In Bali boys may dance girls' dances and girls may dance as men. In a traditional performance of the Noh drama, women never appear. On the other hand, Japan possesses women's troupes in which men's roles are interpreted by actresses. "Asians delight in artistic interchanges," says Faubion Bowers.[17] Once again we note the element of play as an integral part of the theatrical experience, and the double awareness that is its corollary. Since the theater is art and not life, an Oriental might argue, there is no reason to require men in male and women in female roles. In fact, there is good reason to demand just the opposite.

Although this kind of reversal played a part in Kabuki almost from the start, it was only when it became a necessity that Kabuki developed as an art. Today Kabuki is inconceivable without the *onnagata* who, having developed techniques for several centuries, is able to incarnate the essence of femininity without actually imitating any woman ever seen. The *onnagata* are so successful that the spectator accustomed to their willowy beauty is utterly shocked at the "unfeminine" movements and behavior of women in modern Japanese plays. The stylization of Kabuki demands that a woman use a certain manner of walking; of moving the head, eyes, hands; of managing the kimono. Were a woman to attempt to play a Kabuki female role she would have to imitate the men who have so subtly and beautifully incarnated woman before her.

But it is unlikely that a woman has the necessary strength to play a Kabuki female part; the Japanese claim that only a man possesses the steel-like power hidden by softness which is requisite to a successful *onnagata* creation. Besides, with many layers of heavy kimonos, and a wig weighing as much as thirty pounds, a woman would probably not have the physical stamina to hold up such a weight for ten or twelve hours a day.

I do not think it likely that men will ever again play women's roles in the West, although as late as the Restoration they were doing so in England. Thorndike records Pepys's opinion that the actor Edward Kynaston in Fletcher's *Loyal Subject* "made the loveliest lady that ever I saw in my life." [18] And John Downes, Thorndike tells us, declared that "it has since been disputable among the judicious whether any woman that succeeded him so sensibly touched the audience as he." If a man like Kynaston could be lovely, feminine, and touching in a female part, it indicates not only his skill, but the fact that the audience was willing to accept this particular kind of stylization. While it would seem absurd to advocate the use of men to play women's parts today in the West, I think it important to bear in mind that a stylized performance, as required by this kind of impersonation, is not necessarily a cold, "alienated" performance which does not involve the audience. Just as the Kabuki actor can affect his audience, the Elizabethan boy could move his viewers to tears. The English critic Kenneth Tynan goes so far as to suggest that Lady Macbeth is "basically a man's role," and that "it is probably a mistake to cast a woman [in the part] at all." [19]

Whether we would go so far or not, we must agree that the Kabuki actor of female roles can teach us something about what it means to portray femininity on the stage. He stands also as a profound symbol of the mystery of metamorphosis, which is the mystery of the theater. He seems to join two totally different worlds, not only in his double identity as actor and character, but in his dual role of man-woman. The *onnagata* is a dynamic and gigantic archetypal figure possessing, beyond his theatrical dimension, a metaphysical dimension. Whether the spectator is aware of it or not, the *onnagata* stirs in his unconscious a dim memory of some perfection partaking of both feminine and masculine, the great Earth Mother who is creator and sustainer, the divine androgyn in whose bisexuality both dark and light are harmonized. To approach the *onnagata* is to draw near to the secrets of existence, embodied in human form through the art of the Kabuki actor. At the same time we draw near to a joyously theatrical creation which appeals to our histrionic sensibility. We delight in the perfection that the artist has imposed upon reality; in order to experience such joy, we must be at least slightly aware of the reality that the actor has dominated.

The *onnagata* who thus invites our participation, and does so as a total actor using a stylized technique, sums up the three aspects of Oriental theater: participation, totality, and stylization. Perhaps all three might fall under a single heading, "suggestive." Suggestion, as opposed to the representation that has largely dominated Western theater in the past sixty years, goes far beyond the reality that is its point of departure. Using a poetic mode, centuries ago the Oriental theater developed the allusive method that we find so modern today. When the Noh visited Paris in 1957, one critic claimed that it would not be surprising if an Occidental author would someday speak of the Noh as an ultramodern technique of theater.

A small group of writers in the West today embody some of

the characteristics we have found in Kabuki, Noh, Chinese opera, and Balinese dance drama. The plays of Beckett, Ionesco, and Genet use a metaphorical, allusive method not unlike that of the East. Drawing upon peripheral forms of theater, insisting upon the importance of participation, multiple resources, and occasionally of style, they present a particular view of man. Beckett, Ionesco, and Genet are widely accepted today because our theatrical horizons have broadened immensely since the end of the nineteenth century, when Aston could dismiss the Noh as "deficient in lucidity, method, coherence and good taste." Partly responsible for such a broadening have been the developments in the other arts, which since the nineteenth century have been working in the direction of fusion, suggestivity, ambiguity, abstraction, and stylization, and have thus prepared the terrain for the theater, which depends upon a more immediate comprehension than poetry or painting does. But equally responsible are the visions of such adventurous spirits as Copeau, Claudel, Artaud, Eisenstein, Brecht, and others, who have made the Western theater more aware of the treasures to be gleaned from the East.

But the Oriental theater has not yet "arrived." Rationalism dies hard; we still feel that an intellectual element is missing in the dramas of Japan, China, and the rest of Asia. We may reject realism, thesis plays, social commentary, but we still believe that the experimental plays we admire deal, no matter how obliquely, with human nature and man's condition. Can the Oriental theater be great, we wonder. Is it really a revelation of human nature and man's condition?

Indeed it is. The Oriental theater offers us a wide range of psychological and social commentary, from that merely suggested by the situations and movements of a dance to the more obvious moralizing in the tone adopted by the narrators in some *sewamono*. Whether we wish to learn about the problems of everyday living confronted by men of the past—and sometimes applicable to our own lives—or to study people's emotional reactions to the quandaries caused by society, the Oriental theaters offer rich ground. Chikamatsu, and other Kabuki

197

dramatists, like Mokuami, offer us crowded tableaux of eighteenth- and nineteenth-century Japanese society, and full-length portraits of merchants, thieves, prostitutes, and samurai in their nobility and in their weakness. And for those who prefer a play that teaches a lesson in the good old-fashioned way, there is the didactic theater of Chinese opera. But—and it is an important but—unlike the psychological, social, or didactic theater of the West, these plays are raised from the level of textbook, sermon, or treatise by the disciplined style imposed upon them. At the same time that the spectator may, if he so chooses, derive some lesson or make some profound discovery about human nature or about right and wrong from the performance, he may also enjoy the feast offered him.

But the Oriental theater is a revelation of the human condition in a much more profound way, a way that our rationalism may not allow us to accept. Perhaps we have lost our sense of mystery along with our sense of play, and are unable to experience as a totality, to think with body as well as mind. Our fragmented approach to reality denies us access to domains hidden beneath the surface. Plays like *Dōjōji Maiden* or the Rangda-Barong drama of Bali are meaningful in a general and sensual way that we are not accustomed to: they possess the same generality and depth of meaning as myth, enhanced by all the color and sensual appeal of a skillful presentation. Like a poem, which MacLeish says should not *mean* but should *be,* they reveal, at a further remove from rationality, the same basic insights we find in plays like *Everyman, Macbeth,* or *Endgame.* But, like myths, they reveal such insights without stressing a particular perspective. Francis Fergusson says that myths "are so suggestive, seem to say so much, yet so mysteriously, that the mind cannot rest content with any single form, but must add, or interpret, or simplify—reduce to terms which the reason can accept." [20] A similar problem arises for the Western spectator of Oriental theater. He rejects the Oriental vision of the terrifying struggle between good and evil, or of the fight between man and the invisible world, simply because the view is not rationalized for him and is not presented in the partial perspective to which he is accustomed. The Oriental theater of metaphysical dimensions, often a revelation of the absurd, the irrational—of the fact that "the sky can still fall on our heads"—takes us into areas beyond the grasp of the intellect. By creating these new areas of sensitivity, the Oriental theater invites us to enjoy the feast of total theater from which we have been excluded for too long.

Afterword

Since I wrote the opening pages of this book, interest in Oriental theater has become increasingly evident. Manifestations that have come to my attention may be divided into three groups: visiting artists from Asia, performances of Asian works by American groups, and publications that deal with Asian theater.

The visit of some *kyōgen* artists to the University of Washington several years ago aroused a good deal of interest. The Center for Asian Arts at the university will, it appears, continue its investigation of Oriental theatrical forms by giving a series of seminars for advanced students. Well-prepared Westerners are to study intensively, during the summer, some form of Oriental theater in the country of origin.

In 1965 the famed Bunraku puppet theater of Osaka visited the United States with tremendous success. Among the works presented was an unforgettable section of *Chūshingura,* in which the evil Lord Moronao laughs for many minutes, his voice covering the entire range of human sound and revealing every conceivable color of emotion from lighthearted mirth to towering rage. Here is an example of the theatricalization of a moment that, in our theater, would have been merely natural and quickly forgotten.

In 1966 the Hōshō troupe gave the United States its first view of the hieratic Noh form of art, and played to houses that were sold out. Hawaii had the opportunity to see actors from the Kabuki-za in 1967; the Expo 67 events in Montreal during the summer of 1967 offered a further chance to observe Kabuki artistry.

As mentioned earlier, Miyoko Watanabe, Baiko's assistant at the IASTA Kabuki presentation, teaches Kabuki dance and movement in New York. On the West Coast, one of the great teachers of classical Japanese dance, Fujima Kansuma, not only offers courses but occasionally presents her students in productions of Kabuki dance. In October, 1966, in a hall bulging at the seams with a standing-room-only crowd, she presented a four-and-a-half-hour program consisting either of scenes from Kabuki plays (the michiyuki from *Sembonzakura*), or of complete dance plays like *Yasuna, Renjishi,* or *Musume Dōjōji.* Those fortunate enough to be present undoubtedly witnessed the most dazzling and professional Kabuki production outside Japan, complete with magnificent costumes and wigs imported from Japan, colorful settings such as one finds on the professional Kabuki stage, and the techniques of costume changes, wooden clappers, hanamichi, and so forth, which make Kabuki so exciting a theatrical form. And all was performed with the utmost skill and refinement by students who have studied with Madame Fujima for many years; four of them have reached a peak of perfection, allowing them to take on the name of their teacher.

While unable to emulate the professional preparation of a group like Madame Fujima's, a number of colleges and universities have produced Asian works. The University of South Dakota in Vermillion presented a Festival of Asian Drama in May, 1965. Under the general direction of Wayne S. Knutson, chairman of the Department of Drama, six short plays were produced: one Chinese, two Sanskrit, and three Japanese. A year later the University of South Dakota Press published a volume of essays relating to the festival.

IASTA announced another Kabuki play for the 1967–68 season, this time the famous *Kanjinchō* with Matsumoto Kōshirō as director. Los Angeles' Immaculate Heart College in 1966 presented *Lady Precious Stream.* And Lubbock Christian College (Texas) which, in 1964 and 1965 produced a Kabuki-style *Mikado* and a puppet-style adaptation of Zeami's *Kagekiyo,* announced for 1966–67 a presentation of *The Damask Drum,* "freely adapting the Noh conventions and style to fit a small arena."

The University of Wisconsin's Far Eastern Festival of the Arts in April, 1967, included a production of a traditional Chinese play, directed by Professor A. C. Scott and Miss Hu-

Hung-yen. Pomona College staged another Kabuki play, *Miracle at Yaguchi Ferry*, adapted by Professor Stanleigh H. Jones, Jr., of the Claremont Graduate School from Hiraga Gennai's doll play. On Broadway, Peter Shaffer's new play, *Black Comedy*, successfully used the Chinese opera technique of suggesting darkness on a bright stage by the actor's movements.

The recently organized Council for Asian Theater Research, including representatives from Michigan State University, the University of Hawaii, the University of Washington, the Institute for Advanced Studies in Theater Arts, and the Japan Society, has set up a long-range program to coordinate visiting artists and their activities. From 1967 through 1973 the group plans to present the Chinese *Kun Chu* and *Ching Hsi*, the Korean Masked Dance, the Vietnamese *Cailung*, and Thai, Indonesian, and Indian productions.

The council, at its organizational meeting in February, 1966, discussed the need for new translations, but were encouraged when they found that they did not need to set up a special project for this purpose because all the participants were engaged in translating plays and planned to continue working in this field. Their optimism is well founded, if we may judge by recent publications. In 1966 New American Library published an inexpensive volume, *The Genius of the Oriental Theatre*, edited by Professor G. L. Anderson; it contains reprints of Sanskrit, Noh, and Kabuki (or puppet) plays; Tuttle brought out Frank Motofuji's translation of one of Mokuami's most famous *sewamono*, entitled *The Love of Izayoi and Seishin;* and the University of Wisconsin Press published two of A. C. Scott's translations of traditional Chinese plays.

In addition to the texts of plays, a number of important studies have been published recently. Most impressive are a monumental work on the Noh theater by Donald Keene and a thorough and beautiful book, *Kabuki Costume*, by Ruth Shaver. The Afro-Asian Theater Project of the American Educational Theater Association has published two volumes of the *Afro-Asian Theater Bulletin*, which has become an indispensable instrument of exchange for people working in the field of Oriental theater. *Modern Drama* devoted an entire issue in 1967 to the Oriental theater, while three new theater journals reflect the international character of today's theater: *Sangeet Natak* published in New Delhi by the Sangeet Natak Akademi, *Comparative Drama* published at Western Michigan University in Kalamazoo, and *Modern International Drama* published at Pennsylvania State University in University Park.

Notes

Introduction

[1] Antonin Artaud, *The Theater and Its Double,* trans. Mary Caroline Richards (New York: Grove, 1958), p. 41.

[2] Foreword to Faubion Bowers, *Japanese Theater* (New York: Hill and Wang, 1959), p. vii.

Chapter I

[1] Antonin Artaud, *The Theater and Its Double,* trans. Mary Caroline Richards (New York: Grove, 1958), p. 53.

[2] Jean Hort, *Antonin Artaud: Le suicidé de la société* (Geneva: Editions Connaitre, 1960), p. 28.

[3] Paule Thévenin, "1896–1948," *Cahiers de la Compagnie Madeleine Renaud Jean-Louis Barrault,* nos. 22–23 (May, 1958), p. 19.

[4] *Ibid.,* p. 21.

[5] Maurice Nadeau, *Histoire du surréalisme* (Paris: Editions du Seuil, 1945), p. 107.

[6] Thévenin, *op. cit.,* p. 23 n. 12.

[7] Antonin Artaud, *Œuvres complètes* (6 vols.; Paris: Gallimard, 1956–1966), I, 262.

[8] *Ibid.,* p. 287.

[9] Beryl de Zoete and Walter Spies, *Dance and Drama in Bali* (London: Faber and Faber, 1938), p. 45.

[10] Artaud, *The Theater and Its Double,* p. 65.

[11] *Ibid.,* p. 91.

[12] *Ibid.,* p. 46.

[13] *Ibid.,* p. 41.

[14] *Ibid.,* p. 64.

[15] *Ibid.,* p. 44.

[16] *Ibid.,* p. 65.

[17] De Zoete and Spies, *op. cit.,* pp. 17–18.

[18] I am deeply indebted to my friend Mr. Melvin Phillips for this detailed information, found in the programs he patiently tracked down for me while in Paris some years ago.

[19] Artaud, *The Theater and Its Double,* p. 39.

[20] De Zoete and Spies, *op. cit.,* p. 234.

[21] Artaud, *The Theater and Its Double,* pp. 55–56.

[22] *Ibid.,* p. 60.

Chapter II

[1] Quoted by Desflottes in his dedicatory epistle to Father de Prémare, *Tchao-chi-con-eulh, ou l'Orphelin de la Maison de Tchao* (Peking [Paris], 1755), from p. 177 of La Loubère, *Les Relations de la Chine.*

[2] François M. A. Voltaire, "Epître" to *L'Orphelin de la Chine* (La Haye: Jean Neaulme, 1755), p. v.

[3] M. Bazin Aîné, *Le Pi-pa-ki ou l'Histoire du Luth* (Paris: Imprimerie Royale, 1941), preface.

[4] Ferdinand Brunetière in *Revue Littéraire,* March 1, 1886.

[5] G. de Bourboulon, "Les Représentations dramatiques en Chine," *Correspondant* (May, 1862), p. 98.

[6] Quoted in an unidentified article in *Théâtre des Arts* (1910), dossier in the Bibliothèque de l'Arsenal, Paris.

[7] Camille Poupeye, *Le Théâtre chinois* (Paris and Brussels: Editions Labor, n.d.), p. 52.

[8] Tchou-kia-kian and A. Iacovleff, *Le Théâtre chinois* (Paris: Brunoff, 1922), is one of the first enlightened studies of Chinese theater.

[9] Kenneth Tynan, "Stars from the East," in *Tynan on Theater* (Harmondsworth, Middlesex: Penguin Books, 1964), pp. 238–239.

[10] Georges Lerminier in *Parisien libéré,* May 5, 1958.

[11] Robert Kanters in *Express,* May 5, 1958.

[12] In 1966, IASTA began to present productions for commercial audiences, with no little success. The first of these were Racine's *Phèdre* and *The Butterfly Dream.*

[13] Ananda Coomaraswamy, "Notes on Indian Dramatic Technique," *The Mask,* VI (Oct., 1913), 122.

[14] A. C. Scott, "The Butterfly Dream," *Drama Survey,* II (Fall, 1962), 170.

[15] *Ibid.,* p. 174.

[16] S. I. Hsiung, *Lady Precious Stream* (London: Methuen, 1935), p. xvii.

[17] *Ibid.,* p. 17.

[18] *Brecht on Theater,* trans. and ed. John Willett (New York: Hill and Wang, 1964), p. 94.

[19] *Ibid.,* p. 95.

[20] Martin Esslin, *Brecht: The Man and His Work* (Garden City, N.Y.: Anchor Books, 1961), pp. 128–139.

[21] *Ibid.,* p. 139.

[22] Tynan, *op. cit.,* pp. 238–240.

[23] Jean Genet, *Les Bonnes, précédées d'une lettre de l'auteur* (Sceaux: Chez Jean-Jacques Pauvert, 1954), p. 11.

[24] *Ibid.,* pp. 11–12.

[25] Jean Genet, *The Screens,* trans. Bernard Frechtman (New York: Grove, 1962), p. 17.

²⁶ *Ibid.,* p. 10.
²⁷ Jean Genet, *The Maids and Deathwatch,* trans. Bernard Frechtman (New York: Grove, 1954), pp. 103–104.
²⁸ Genet, *The Screens,* p. 10.

Chapter III

¹ W. G. Aston, *A History of Japanese Literature* (London: Heinemann, 1899), pp. 203, 205.
² See, for example, Zemmaro Toki, *Japanese Noh Plays* (Tokyo: Japan Travel Bureau, 1954), pp. 120, 125. Earle Ernst mentions this point also in his *Three Japanese Plays from the Traditional Theater* (New York: Grove, 1960), p. 15.
³ Michitaro Shidehara and Wilfred Whitehouse, trans., "Seami Jūroku Bushu (Kadensho), *Monumenta Nipponica,* V (Dec., 1942), 197.
⁴ P. G. O'Neill, *Early Noh Drama* (London: Lund Humphries, 1958), p. 98.
⁵ *Ibid.,* p. 100.
⁶ In an illuminating article, Jean Jacquot remarks that this young dancer, Michio Ito, knew very little about Noh drama and appreciated it hardly at all ("Craig, Yeats et le théâtre d'orient," in *Les Théâtres d'Asie* [Paris: CNRS, 1961], p. 275).
⁷ William L. Sharp, "W. B. Yeats: A Poet Not in the Theater," *Tulane Drama Review,* IV (Dec., 1959), 81.
⁸ In Ezra Pound and Ernest Fenollosa, *The Classic Noh Theater of Japan* (New York: New Directions, 1959), pp. 151–152.
⁹ Yasuko Stucki, "Yeats's Drama and the Noh," *Modern Drama,* IX (May, 1966), 106–107.
¹⁰ O'Neill, *op. cit.,* p. 9.
¹¹ René Sieffert, "Le Théâtre japonais," in *Les Théâtres d'Asie,* ed. Jean Jacquot (Paris: CNRS, 1961), p. 149.
¹² Camille Poupeye, "Le Théâtre japonais," *La Renaissance d'Occident* (Aug., 1923).
¹³ For example, see works in the Japanese theater and Noh bibliographies by Earle Ernst, Makoto Ueda, Arthur Waley, Zemmaro Toki, Pound and Fenollosa, Noël Péri, Toyoichiro Nogami.
¹⁴ Zeami's writings are discussed in some detail by both P. G. O'Neill and René Sieffert. There is no complete translation of Zeami's writings into a Western language. Two partial translations exist in German: Oscar Benl, *Seami Motokyo und der Geist des No-Schauspiels* (Wiesbaden, 1952), and Hermann Bohner, *Blumenspiegel* (Tokyo, 1953). The partial translation into English by Shidehara and Whitehouse is listed in my Noh bibliography, and I have quoted from it in the text where the translation is apropos. By far the best and most complete translation of

Zeami's treatises is that by Professor René Sieffert (Paris: Gallimard, 1960), and it is from this version that I have worked.

[15] René Sieffert, ed. and trans., *Zeami: La Tradition secrète du nô* (Paris: Gallimard, 1960), p. 10.

[16] Shidehara and Whitehouse, trans., in *Monumenta Nipponica*, IV (July, 1941), 210.

[17] Pointed out by Toyoichiro Nogami, *Zeami and His Theories on Noh,* trans. Ryoza Matsumoto (Tokyo: Hinoki Shoten, 1955), p. 82.

[18] Shidehara and Whitehouse, *op. cit.,* p. 217.

[19] *Ibid.,* p. 217.

[20] These are the interpretations given by Nogami, *op. cit.,* p. 60.

[21] See also O'Neill, *op. cit.,* pp. 77–78.

[22] *Ibid.,* p. 148.

[23] This notion is contradicted by what seems a more naturalistic approach in the *Mirror of the Flower* (1426) (see Sieffert, *op. cit.,* p. 117).

[24] See Sieffert, *op. cit.,* p. 326 n. 6.

[25] Shidehara and Whitehouse, *op. cit.,* V, 473.

[26] Sieffert, *op. cit.,* pp. 54–56.

[27] O'Neill, *op. cit.,* pp. 88–89; Sieffert, *op. cit.,* p. 41. For further discussion of this point see O'Neill's final chapter, particularly pp. 144–148.

[28] Jacques Copeau, *Souvenirs du Vieux-Colombier* (Paris: Les Nouvelles Editions Latines, 1931), p. 99.

[29] I am particularly grateful to M. André Veinstein and Mlle Christout of the Bibliothèque de l'Arsenal for allowing me to peruse the uncatalogued papers from the Copeau collection.

[30] Copeau, *op. cit.,* p. 100.

[31] Charles Dullin, *Souvenirs et Notes de travail d'un acteur* (Paris: Odette Lieutier, 1946), pp. 59–60.

[32] *Correspondances,* no. 26.

[33] Georges Lerminier in *Parisien libéré,* June 27, 1957.

[34] Jean-Louis Barrault, *Journal de bord* (Paris: René Julliard, 1961), p. 83. Claudel sheds a good deal of light on the Noh in his brilliant essay, "Nô," in *L'Oiseau Noir dans le soleil levant.* What he says about the fan may have helped Barrault in his interpretation.

[35] *Ibid.,* p. 87.

[36] Quoted by William Packard in "Experiment in International Theater: An Informal History of IASTA," *Drama Critique,* VIII (March, 1965), 69.

[37] From the program notes.

[38] Reported by *Caravello,* Oct. 10, 1964.

[39] *Ibid.*

[40] Quoted in a typescript in the files of IASTA, p. 5.

[41] William Packard, "An American Experiment in Noh," *First Stage*, IV (Summer, 1965), 61.

[42] Much of the information regarding the productions of IASTA has been relayed to me by Dr. John D. Mitchell. Without his generous cooperation my treatment of the IASTA productions, and an important segment of Oriental theater in the West, would have suffered.

[43] Documents regarding this change are to be found in Bertolt Brecht, *Théâtre Complet*, VIII (Paris: L'Arche, 1960), 231–234.

[44] Yukio Mishima, *Five Modern Noh Plays* (London: Secker and Warburg, 1957), p. xii.

[45] By the announcer during the BBC performance. *Curlew River* has been recorded commercially.

[46] In a note dated June 2, 1964, Paris.

[47] Marcel Ginglaris in *Paris-Presse*, June 28, 1957.

[48] Ruby Cohn, *Samuel Beckett: The Comic Gamut* (New Brunswick, N.J.: Rutgers University Press, 1962), p. 228.

[49] Arthur Waley, *The Noh Plays of Japan* (New York: Grove, 1957), p. 53.

[50] In Faubion Bowers, *Japanese Theater* (New York: Hill and Wang, 1959), p. 13.

[51] See Cohn, *op. cit.*, pp. 253–255.

Chapter IV

[1] Paul Green, *Dramatic Heritage* (New York: Samuel French, 1953), p. 169.

[2] *Moniteur*, July 22, Aug. 12, 1867.

[3] Ernest d'Hervilly, *La Belle Saïnara* (Paris: Lemerre, 1876).

[4] Georges Bousquet, "Le Théâtre au Japon," *Revue de Deux Mondes*, Aug. 15, 1874, p. 729.

[5] Motoyosi Saizu, "Le Théâtre au Japon," *Revue Brittanique* (1894), p. 396.

[6] Edwin Reischauer, *Japan Past and Present* (Tokyo: Tuttle, 1963), p. 99.

[7] Earle Ernst, *Kabuki Theater* (New York: Grove, 1956), p. ix.

[8] Bousquet, *op. cit.*, p. 728.

[9] *Le Théâtre* (Sept., 1900).

[10] *Lectures Pour Tous* (March, 1908).

[11] *Je Sais Tout* (n.d.).

[12] Arsene Alexandre in *Le Théâtre* (Sept., 1900).

[13] *Le Soir*, May 4, 1930.

[14] Adolphe Brisson, quoted in *L'Illustration théâtrale*, May 25, 1912, p. 37.

[15] J. Gautier in *ibid*.

[16] Sergei Eisenstein, *Film Form; The Film Sense,* ed. and trans. Jay Leyda (Cleveland and New York: Meridian Books, 1963), p. 20.

[17] See *ibid.,* pp. 21–22.

[18] *Ibid.,* p. 23.

[19] *Nation,* July 9, 1960, pp. 39–40.

[20] *New York Times,* June 10, 1966, p. 37.

[21] *Arts,* Oct. 27–Nov. 2, 1965.

[22] Gabriel Cousin, *Théâtre,* II (Paris: Gallimard, 1964), 273.

[23] *Ibid.,* p. 273.

[24] *Ibid.,* p. 275.

Chapter V

[1] Zoe Kincaid, *Kabuki: The Popular Stage of Japan* (London: Macmillan, 1925), p. 264.

[2] *Ibid.,* p. 375.

[3] Earle Ernst, *Three Japanese Plays* (New York: Grove, 1960), p. ix.

[4] Earle Ernst, *The Kabuki Theater* (New York: Grove, 1956).

[5] The reader is referred to the bibliography in this book, and to that in Ernst's *The Kabuki Theater.*

[6] Quoted in Vsévolod Meyerhold, *Le Théâtre théâtral,* ed. and trans. Nina Gourfinkel (Paris: Gallimard, 1963), p. 168.

[7] Antonin Artaud, *The Theater and Its Double* (New York: Grove, 1958), p. 96.

[8] *Ibid.,* p. 97.

[9] See Ernst, *The Kabuki Theater,* p. 65.

[10] *Ibid.,* p. 66.

[11] Artaud, *op. cit.,* p. 44.

[12] *Correspondances* (May, 1930), p. 60.

[13] Georg Fuchs, *Revolution in the Theater* (Ithaca: Cornell University Press, 1959), p. 60.

[14] Paul Claudel, *Le Livre de Christophe Colomb* (Paris: Gallimard, 1935), p. 21. The aesthetics of Kabuki music is, like other elements of the production, brilliantly discussed by Professor Ernst in his *Kabuki Theater,* pp. 114–119.

[15] Claudel, *op. cit.,* p. 24.

[16] In Yonezo Hamamura *et al., Kabuki,* trans. Fumi Takano (Tokyo: Kenkyusha, 1956), p. 54.

[17] Shoyo Tsubouchi and Jiro Yamamoto, *History and Characteristics of Kabuki,* trans. Tyozo Matsumoto (Yokohama: Heiji Yamagata, 1960), p. 145.

[18] This information on the rehearsal and production of *Narukami* has been supplied to me through the generosity of Dr. John D. Mitchell.

Much of the material here used is paraphrased from letters written by Dr. Mitchell.

[19] William Packard, "Experiment in International Theater: An Informal History of IASTA," *Drama Critique*, VIII (March, 1965), 64.

[20] Quoted in *ibid.*, p. 64.

[21] Quoted in a letter from Dr. Mitchell.

[22] April 16, 1963.

[23] *Claremont Courier*, March 3, 1965.

[24] *Student Life* (Feb., 1965).

[25] Bernard Beckerman, *Shakespeare at the Globe, 1599–1609* (New York: Macmillan, 1962), pp. 123–125.

[26] Alois Maria Nagler, *Shakespeare's Stage*, trans. Ralph Manheim (New Haven: Yale University Press, 1958), p. 37.

[27] *Ibid.*, p. 83.

[28] Ashley H. Thorndike, *Shakespeare's Theater* (New York: Macmillan, 1960), p. 403.

[29] Nagler, *op. cit.*, p. 82.

[30] See Bertram Joseph's *Acting Shakespeare* (New York: Theatre Arts Books, 1962), and *Elizabethan Acting* (London: Oxford University Press, 1964).

[31] Beckerman, *op. cit.*, p. 14.

[32] Marie Channing Linthicum, *Costume in the Drama of Shakespeare and His Contemporaries* (Oxford: Clarendon Press, 1936), p. 14.

[33] Thorndike, *op. cit.*, p. 394.

[34] See Elizabeth Burton, *The Pageant of Elizabethan England* (New York: Scribner's, 1958), pp. 235–242, and Carroll Camden, *The Elizabethan Woman* (Houston: Elsevier Press, 1952), pp. 178–186.

Chapter VI

[1] Basil Hall Chamberlain, *Things Japanese* (London: Kegan Paul, 1927), p. 466.

[2] Etiemble, "À quand notre Meiji?" in *Le Monde,* July 4, 1964.

[3] In *Afro-Asian Theater Bulletin,* I (Feb., 1966), 11–12.

[4] *Ibid.,* p. 12.

[5] Johan Huizinga, *Homo Ludens* (Boston: Beacon Press, 1955).

[6] Ashley H. Thorndike, *Shakespeare's Theater* (New York: Macmillan, 1960), p. 420.

[7] Quoted in Léon Vallas, *The Theories of Claude Debussy,* trans. Maire O'Brien (London: Oxford University Press, 1929), p. 173.

[8] John D. Mitchell, "The Actor's 'Method,'" *Players Magazine,* XXXVIII (April, 1962), 217.

[9] Quoted in *ibid.,* p. 216.

[10] Zoe Kincaid, *Kabuki: The Popular Stage of Japan* (London: Macmillan, 1925), p. 35.

[11] *Nation,* July 9, 1960, p. 40.

[12] Charles Marowitz, *Stanislavski and the Method* (New York: Citadel Press, 1964), p. 79.

[13] *Ibid.,* p. 99.

[14] "Chikamatsu on the Art of the Puppet Stage," in Donald Keene, ed., *Anthology of Japanese Literature* (Tokyo: Charles E. Tuttle Co., 1963), I, 388.

[15] *Ibid.,* p. 390.

[16] Donald Keene, "Realism and Unreality in Japanese Drama," *Drama Survey,* III (Winter, 1964), 351.

[17] Faubion Bowers, *Theater in the East* (New York: Grove, 1960), p. 230.

[18] Thorndike, *op. cit.,* p. 372.

[19] Kenneth Tynan, *Tynan on Theater* (Harmondsworth, Middlesex: Penguin Books, 1964), p. 108.

[20] Francis Fergusson, *The Idea of a Theater* (Garden City, N.Y.: Anchor Books, 1953), p. 28.

Selected Bibliography

ORIENTAL THEATER AND EUROPEAN WRITERS

Artaud, Antonin. *Œuvres complètes*. Paris: Gallimard, 1956–1966. 6 vols.

———. *The Theater and Its Double*. Trans. Mary Caroline Richards. New York: Grove, 1958.

Barrault, Jean-Louis. *Journal de bord*. Paris: René Julliard, 1961.

Beckerman, Bernard. *Shakespeare at the Globe, 1599–1609*. New York: Macmillan, 1962.

Bentley, Eric. *The Life of the Drama*. New York: Atheneum, 1964.

Bowers, Faubion. *Theater in the East: A Survey of Asian Dance and Drama*. New York: Grove, 1960.

Brecht, Bertolt. *Brecht on Theater: The Development of an Aesthetic*. Trans. and ed. John Willett. New York: Hill and Wang, 1964.

———. *Ecrits sur le théâtre*. Paris: L'Arche, 1963.

———. *Parables for the Theater: The Good Woman of Setzuan; The Caucasian Chalk Circle*. Trans. Eric Bentley and Maja Apelman. New York: Grove Press, 1963.

———. *Théâtre complet*. Vols. I, VIII. Paris: L'Arche, 1960.

Brozzi, Antonio P. *Teatri e spettacoli dei popoli orientali*. Milan: Fratelli Dumolard, 1887.

Claudel, Paul. *Le Livre de Christophe Colomb*. Paris: Gallimard, 1935.

———. *Œuvres complètes*. Vols. III, IV. Paris: Gallimard, 1952.

———. *Théâtre*. Vol. II. Paris: Pléiade, 1956.

Cogniat, Raymond. "Charles Dullin comme metteur en scène," *Comoedia*, Oct. 7, 1930.

Cohn, Ruby. *Samuel Beckett: The Comic Gamut*. New Brunswick, N.J.: Rutgers University Press, 1962.

Coomaraswamy, Ananda. "Notes on Indian Dramatic Techniques," *The Mask*, VI (Oct., 1913).

Copeau, Jacques. *Souvenirs du Vieux-Colombier*. Paris: Les Nouvelles Editions Latines, 1931.

Cousin, Gabriel. *Théâtre*. Vol. II. Paris: Gallimard, 1964.

Craig, Edward Gordon, ed. *The Mask*. 1913–1915, 1918–1929.

Dullin, Charles. *Souvenirs et Notes de travail d'un acteur*. Paris: Odette Lieutier, 1946.

Eisenstein, Sergei. *Film Form; The Film Sense*. Ed. and trans. Jay Leyda. Cleveland and New York: Meridian, 1957.

Esslin, Martin. *Brecht: The Man and His Work*. Garden City, N.Y.: Anchor Books, 1961.

Fergusson, Francis. *The Idea of a Theater*. Garden City, N.Y.: Anchor Books, 1953.

Fuchs, Georg. *Revolution in the Theater*. Ithaca: Cornell University Press, 1959.

Gassner, John. *Form and Idea in Modern Theater*. New York: Dryden, 1956.

Genet, Jean. *Les Bonnes, précédées d'une lettre de l'auteur*. Sceaux: Jean-Jacques Pauvert, 1954.

————. *The Maids and Deathwatch*. Trans. Bernard Frechtman. New York: Grove, 1954.

————. *The Screens*. Trans. Bernard Frechtman. New York: Grove, 1962.

Green, Paul. *Dramatic Heritage*. New York: Samuel French, 1953.

Hort, Jean. *Antonin Artaud: Le suicidé de la société*. Geneva: Editions Connaitre, 1960.

Huizinga, Johan. *Homo Ludens: A Study of the Play Element in Culture*. Boston: Beacon, 1955.

Jacquot, Jean, ed. *Les Théâtres d'Asie*. Paris: Editions du Centre National de la Recherche Scientifique, 1961.

Joseph, Bertram. *Acting Shakespeare*. New York: Theatre Arts Books, 1962.

————. *Elizabethan Acting*. London: Oxford University Press, 1964.

Linthicum, Marie Channing. *Costume in the Drama of Shakespeare and His Contemporaries*. Oxford: Clarendon Press, 1936.

Marowitz, Charles. *Stanislavski and the Method*. New York: Citadel, 1964.

Martino, Pierre. *L'Orient dans la littérature française au XVII et XVIII siècles*. Paris: Hachette, 1906.

Meyerhold, Vsévolod. *Le Théâtre théâtral*. Ed. and trans. Nina Fourfinkel. Paris: Gallimard, 1963.

Mignon, Paul-Louis. *Jean Dasté*. Paris: Presses Littéraires de France, 1953.

Nadeau, Maurice. *Histoire du surréalisme*. Paris: Editions du Seuil, 1954.

Nagler, Alois Maria. *Shakespeare's Stage*. Trans. Ralph Manheim. New Haven: Yale University Press, 1958.

Packard, William. "Experiment in International Theater: An Informal History of IASTA," *Drama Critique*, VIII (March, 1965).

Schwartz, William Leonard. *The Imaginative Interpretation of the Far East in Modern French Literature, 1800–1925*. Paris: Librairie Ancienne Honoré Champion, 1927.

Shaffer, Peter. *The Royal Hunt of the Sun*. London: Hamish Hamilton, 1964.

Thévenin, Paule. "1896–1948," *Cahiers de la Compagnie Madeleine Renaud Jean-Louis Barrault*, nos. 22–23 (May, 1958).

Thorndike, Ashley H. *Shakespeare's Theater*. New York: Macmillan, 1960.

Tillyard, E. M. W. *The Elizabethan World Picture*. New York: Vintage, n.d.

Tynan, Kenneth. *Tynan on Theater*. Harmondsworth, Middlesex: Penguin Books, 1964.

Vallas, Léon. *The Theories of Claude Debussy*. Trans. Maire O'Brien. London: Oxford University Press, 1929.

Voltaire, François M. A. *Œuvres complètes*. Vol. V. Paris: Garnier, 1877.

————. *L'Orphelin de la Chine*. La Haye: Jean Neaulme, 1755.

Weiss, Peter. *The Persecution and Assassination of Jean-Paul Marat as performed by the Inmates of the Asylum of Charenton under the Direction of the Marquis de Sade*. New York: Atheneum, 1965.

Yeats, W. B. *Collected Plays*. London: Macmillan, 1963.

BALI

Covarrubias, Miguel. *Island of Bali*. New York: Knopf, 1937.

De Zoete, Beryl, and Walter Spies. *Dance and Drama in Bali*. London: Faber and Faber, 1938.

CHINESE OPERA

Ainé, M. Bazin. *Le Pi-pa-ki ou l'Histoire du Luth*. Paris: Imprimerie Royale, 1841.

————. *Théâtre chinois*. Paris: Imprimerie Royale, 1838.

Alley, Rewi. *Introduction à l'Opera de Pékin*. Paris: Cercle d'Art, 1955.

Ampère, J. J. "Du théâtre chinois," *Revue des Deux Mondes* (1838).

Arlington, L. C. *Le Théâtre chinois*. Trans. G. Ohlmann. Peking: Henri Vetch, 1935.

Arlington, L. C., and Harold Acton. *Famous Chinese Plays*. New York: Russell and Russell, 1963.

Bourboulon, G. de "Les Représentations dramatiques en Chine," *Correspondant* (May, 1862).

Guy, Basil. *The French Image of China before and after Voltaire*. "Studies in Voltaire and the Eighteenth Century." Vol. XXI. Geneva: Institut et Musée Voltaire, 1963.

Hatchett, William. *The Chinese Orphan*. London: Charles Corbett, 1741.

Ho Ching Chi and Ting Yi. *La Fille aux cheveux blancs.* Paris: Editeurs Français Réunis, 1955.

Hsiung, S. I. *Lady Precious Stream.* London: Methuen, 1935.

———. *Lady Precious Stream.* Harmondsworth, Middlesex: Penguin Books, 1958.

———. *Lady Precious Stream.* Program for presentation in Los Angeles by Merle Armitage and Paul Posz, 1937.

Irwin, William, and Sidney Howard. *Lute Song,* in *The Best Plays of 1945–46.* Ed. Burns Mantle. New York: Dodd, Mead, 1946.

Julien, Stanislas. *Hoei-lan-ki ou l'Histoire du cercle de craie.* London: Oriental Translation Fund, 1832.

———. *Tchao-chi-kon-eul, L'Orphelin de la Chine.* Paris: Montardier, 1834.

Kalvodova-Sis-Vanis. *Chinese Theater.* Trans. Iris Irwin. London: Spring Books, n.d.

Li Tche-Houa. *Le Signe de patience et autres pièces du théâtre des Yuan.* Paris: Gallimard, 1963.

Poupeye, Camille. *Le Théâtre chinois.* Paris and Brussels: Editions Labor, n.d.

Prémare, Father de. "Tchao chi con ell ou le petit orphelin de la Maison de Tchao, tragédie chinoise." In J. B. du Halde, *Description de l'Empire de la Chine et de la Tartarie chinoise.* La Haye, 1736.

———. *Tchao-chi-con-eulh, ou l'Orphelin de la Maison de Tchao* (tragédie chinoise). Peking [Paris], 1755.

Roy, Claude, and Robert Ruhlmann. *L'Opéra de Pekin.* Paris: Cercle d'Art, 1955.

Scott, A. C. "The Butterfly Dream," *Drama Survey,* II (Fall, 1962).

———. *The Classical Theater of China.* London: Allen and Unwin, 1957.

———. *An Introduction to the Chinese Theater.* New York: Theater Arts Books, 1960.

———. *Mei Lan-fang, Leader of the Pear Garden.* Hong Kong: Hong Kong University Press, 1959.

Soulié de Morant, Georges. *Théâtre et musique modernes en Chine.* Paris: Librairie Orientaliste Paul Geuthner, 1926.

Tcheng-Ki-tong. *Le Théâtre des Chinois.* Paris: Calmann Lévy, 1886.

Tchou-Kia-kien, and A. Iacovleff. *Le Théâtre chinois.* Paris: Brunoff, 1922.

Vercors. *Les Divagations d'un Français en Chine.* Paris: Albin Michel, 1956.

———. *Les Pas dans le sable.* Paris: Albin Michel, 1954.

Zucker, A. E. *The Chinese Theater.* London: Jarrolds, 1925.

Zung, Cecilia. *Secrets of the Chinese Drama.* New York: Benjamin Blom, 1937. Reissued 1964.

JAPANESE THEATER

Arnold, Paul. *Le Théâtre japonais*. Paris: L'Arche, 1957.

Ashihara, Eiryo. *The Japanese Dance*. Tokyo: Japan Travel Bureau, 1964.

Aston, W. G. *A History of Japanese Literature*. London: Heinemann, 1899.

Bénazet, Alexandre. *Le Théâtre au Japon*. Paris: Ernest Leroux, 1901.

Bousquet, Georges. "Le Théâtre au Japon," *Revue de Deux Mondes,* Aug. 15, 1874.

Bowers, Faubion. *Japanese Theater*. New York: Hill and Wang, 1959.

Chamberlain, Basil Hall. *Things Japanese*. London: Kegan Paul, 1927.

Edwards, Osman. *Japanese Plays and Playfellows*. London: Heinemann, 1901.

Ernst, Earle. *Three Japanese Plays from the Traditional Theater*. New York: Grove, 1960.

Guimet, Emile, and Félix Régamey. "Le Théâtre au Japon," *Bulletin du Cercle Saint Simon,* no. 2 (1885).

Hervilly, Ernest d'. *La Belle Saïnara*. Paris: Lemerre, 1876.

Keene, Donald, ed. *Anthology of Japanese Literature*. Vols. I, II. Tokyo: Charles E. Tuttle Co., 1963.

——. "Realism and Unreality in Japanese Drama," *Drama Survey,* III (Winter, 1964).

Lequeux, A. *Le Théâtre japonais*. Paris: Ernest Leroux, 1889.

Magnino, Leo. *Teatro giapponese*. Milan: Nuova Accademia Editrice, 1956.

Matsuo, Kuni. *Histoire de la littérature japonaise des temps archaïques à 1935*. Paris: Société Française d'Editions Littéraires et Techniques, 1935.

Maybon, Albert. *Le Théâtre japonais*. Paris: Henri Laurens, 1925.

Miner, Earl. *The Japanese Tradition in British and American Literature*. Princeton: Princeton University Press, 1958.

Motoyosi-Saizu. "Le Théâtre au Japon," *Revue Brittanique* (1894).

Muccioli, Marcello. *Il Teatro giapponese*. Milan: Feltrinelli, 1962.

Poupeye, Camille. "Le Théâtre japonais," *La Renaissance d'Occident* (Aug., 1923).

——. *Les Théâtres d'Asie, Souvenirs de jeunesse*. Bruxelles: Les Cahiers du Journal des Poètes, 1937.

Reischauer, Edwin O. *Japan Past and Present*. Tokyo: Charles E. Tuttle Co., 1963.

Revon, Michel. *Anthologie de la littérature japonaise*. Paris: Delagrave, 1910.

Sadler, A. L., trans. *Japanese Plays*. Sydney: Angus and Robertson, 1934.

Séché, Alphonse, and Jules Betaut. "Le Théâtre au Japon," *Mercure de France* (Sept., 1904).

Sieffert, René. *La Littérature japonaise*. Paris: Armand Colin, 1961.

NOH

Arnold, Paul. *Neuf Nô japonais*. Paris: Librairie Théâtrale, 1957.

Challaye, Félicien. "Le Noh (Drame lyrique japonais)," *La Revue de Paris,* April 15, 1927.

Clark, David R. "Nishikigi and Yeats's *The Dreaming of the Bones,*" *Modern Drama,* VII (Sept., 1964).

Gérard, A. "Le Drame lyrique japonais," *Revue des Deux Mondes,* Sept. 1, 1917.

Jones, Stanleigh H., Jr. "The Noh Plays *Obasute* and *Kanehira,*" *Monumenta Nipponica,* XVIII, nos. 1–4 (1963).

Kaula, David. "On Noh Drama," *Tulane Drama Review,* V (Sept., 1960).

Mishima, Yukio. *Five Modern Noh Plays*. Trans. with an introduction by Donald Keene. London: Secker and Warburg, 1957.

Nogami, Toyoichiro. *Zeami and His Theories on Noh*. Trans. Ryozo Matsumoto. Tokyo: Hinoki Shoten, 1955.

Noh Drama, The. "UNESCO Collection of Representative Works: Japanese Series." Vols. I–III. Tokyo: Charles E. Tuttle Co., 1955–1960.

O'Neill, P. G. *Early Noh Drama: Its Background, Character and Development, 1300–1450*. London: Lund Humphries, 1958.

Packard, William. "An American Experiment in Noh," *First Stage,* IV (Summer, 1965).

Packard, William, trans. *Ikkaku Sennin*, in *Players Magazine,* XLI (March, 1965).

Péri, Noël. *Cinq Nô*. Paris: Edition Bossard, 1921.

Pound, Ezra, and Ernest Fenollosa. *The Classic Noh Theater of Japan*. New York: New Directions, 1959.

Sharp, William L. "W. B. Yeats: A Poet Not in the Theater," *Tulane Drama Review,* IV (Dec., 1959).

Shidehara, Michitaro, and Wilfrid Whitehouse, trans. "Seami Jūroku Bushu (Kadensho)," *Monumenta Nipponica,* IV (July, 1941); V (Dec., 1942).

Sieffert, René, ed. and trans. *Zéami: La Tradition secrète du nô, suivie d'une journée de nô*. "Collection UNESCO d'œuvres représentatives." Paris: Gallimard, 1960.

Stucki, Yasuko. "Yeats's Drama and the Noh: A Comparative Study in Dramatic Theories," *Modern Drama,* IX (May, 1966).

218

Toki, Zemmaro. *Japanese Noh Plays*. Tokyo: Japan Travel Bureau, 1954.
Ueda, Makoto, ed. and trans. *The Old Pine Tree and Other Noh Plays*. Lincoln: University of Nebraska Press, 1962.
Waley, Arthur. *The Noh Plays of Japan*. New York: Grove, 1957.

KABUKI

Anthelme, Paul. *L'Honneur japonais*, in *L'Illustration théâtrale*, May 25, 1912.
Banzement, A "Le Drame populaire au Japon," *La Revue*, Aug. 15, 1912.
Billès, André, trans. *"L'Ecole du Village"* (Terakoya), *La Nouvelle Revue*, Dec. 1, 1907.
Chikamatsu, Monzaémon. *Chefs-d'oeuvre de Tchikamatsou*. Trans. Asataro Miyamori and Charles Jacob. Paris: Ernest Leroux, 1929.
———. *Major Plays of Chikamatsu*. Trans. Donald Keene. New York: Columbia University Press, 1961.
Ernst, Earle. *The Kabuki Theater*. New York: Grove, 1956.
Florenz, Karl, trans. *Scènes du théâtre japonais, l'Ecole du Village* (*Terakoya*). Tokyo: Hasegawa, 1900.
Fukui, Yoshio, and Yasuo Ohashi. "Les Formes populaires du théâtre japonais," *Théâtre populaire* (May-June, 1954).
Halford, Aubrey S., and Giovanna M. Halford. *The Kabuki Handbook*. Tokyo: Charles E. Tuttle Co., 1961.
Hamamura, Yonezo, *et al. Kabuki*. Trans. Fumi Takano. Tokyo: Kenkyusha, 1956.
Iacovleff, A., and S. Elisséef. *Le Théâtre japonais*. Paris: Jules Meynial, 1933.
Inouye, Jukichi, trans. *Chūshingura*. Tokyo: Nakanishiya, 1910.
Izumo, Takeda. *The Pine Tree*. London: Risi Publishing Co., 1916.
Keene, Donald, trans. *The Battles of Coxinga*. London: Taylor's Foreign Press, 1951.
Kincaid, Zoe. *Kabuki: The Popular Stage of Japan*. London: Macmillan, 1925.
Komiya, Toyotaka. *Japanese Music and Drama in the Meiji Era*. Trans. and adapted by Edward G. Seidensticker and Donald Keene. Tokyo: Obunsha, 1956.
Lombard, Frank A. *Outline History of Japanese Drama*. London: Allen and Unwin, 1928.
Malm, William P. *Nagauta: The Heart of Kabuki Music*. Tokyo and Rutland, Vt.: Charles E. Tuttle Co., 1963.
Masefield, John. *The Faithful*. London: Heinemann, 1915.
Mitchell, John D. "The Actor's 'Method,'" *Players Magazine*, XXXVIII, (April, 1962).

Mitchell, John D., and E. K. Schwartz. "A Psychoanalytic Approach to Kabuki: A Study in Personality and Culture," *Journal of Psychology,* LII (1961).

Miyake, Shutaro. *Kabuki Drama.* Tokyo: Japan Travel Bureau, 1961.

Namiki, Gohei, III. *Kanjincho,* trans. James R. Brandon and Tamako Niwa, in *Evergreen Review,* IV (Sept.-Oct., 1960).

Pronko, Leonard C. *"Terakoya:* Kabuki and the Diminished Theatre of the West," *Modern Drama,* VIII (May, 1965).

Scott, A. C. *The Kabuki Theater of Japan.* London: Allen and Unwin, 1956.

Scott, A. C., trans. *Genyadana.* Tokyo: Hokuseido, 1953.

———. *Kanjincho.* Tokyo: Hokuseido, 1953.

Shigetoshi, Kawatake. *Kabuki: Japanese Drama.* Tokyo: Foreign Affairs Association of Japan, 1958.

Shioya, Sakae. *Chūshingura: An Exposition.* Tokyo: Hokuseido, 1956.

Tsubouchi, Shoyo, and Jiro Yamamoto. *History and Characteristics of Kabuki.* Trans. Ryozo Matsumoto. Yokohama: Heiji Yamagata, 1960.

Watanabe, Miyoko, and Donald Richie, trans. *Six Kabuki Plays.* Tokyo: Hokuseido, 1963.

Index

221